Shared Services in Local Government

Shared Services in Local Government

Improving Service Delivery

RAY TOMKINSON

GOWER

Published by
Gower Publishing Limited
Gower House
Croft Road
Aldershot
Hampshire
GU11 3HR
England

Gower Publishing Company
Suite 420
101 Cherry Street
Burlington
VT 05401-4405
USA

Ray Tomkinson has asserted his moral right under the Copyright, Designs and Patents Act, 1988, to be identified as the author of this work. Ray Tomkinson is the holder of a PSI Licence number C2006011155

British Library Cataloguing in Publication Data
Tomkinson, Ray
   Shared services in local government : improving service
   delivery
   1. Shared services (management) 2. Municipal services -
   England 3. County services - England
   I. Title
   352.1'5'0942

   ISBN-13: 9780566087233

Library of Congress Cataloging-in-Publication Data
Tomkinson, Ray.
   Shared services in local government : improving service delivery / by Ray Tomkinson.
     p. cm.
   Includes index.
   ISBN 978-0-566-08723-3
   1. Local government--England. 2. Shared services (Management)--England. I. Title.

   JS3111.T65 2007
   352.14--dc22

   2007002020

Printed and bound in Great Britain by TJ International Ltd, Padstow, Cornwall.

Contents

List of Figures

Glossary

4Ps The Public Private Partnerships Programme A body financed from top-sliced Revenue Support Grant funding to local government. Provides support and advice to local councils entering into partnerships.

Audit Commission An independent, national body responsible for promoting the best use of public money in local councils and the NHS, by ensuring proper stewardship of public funds and by helping those responsible for public services to achieve economy, efficiency and effectiveness. Established by the Local Government Finance Act 1982, the Audit Commission has responsibility for the external audit of all local councils and NHS bodies in England and Wales and for the inspection of a wide range of local government services.

Annual efficiency statements Submissions required annually from local councils, these are statements which outline activities intended to achieve efficiency.

Balanced scorecard A way of using meaningful measures and outcomes to drive performance improvement.

Beacon Council The government awards Beacon Council status to local councils in recognition of excellence in particular service areas.

Benchmarking-cost Comparing the direct and indirect costs of services – or elements of services – with other councils and other providers.

Benchmarking-processes Comparing methods of providing related or similar services in different sectors.

Best Value A legal duty on all councils to review all their services, to consult service users, to challenge whether they are the best organization to provide that service, to compare their performance with other similar service providers and to open up their services to competition.

Best Value Performance Indicator An indicator set by the government to measure the performance of local councils on a specific area of service.

Best Value Performance Plan A plan required annually from each Best Value Performance Plan authority showing its service aims, achieved service standards and improvement criteria.

BPR Business process re-engineering, which is the process of examining and amending the different tasks and processes used to perform an activity with the intention of improving the efficiency of that activity.

Cashable Savings Generated in response to the Gershon Report that reduces the net expenditure of a public sector body.

Centres of Excellence Organizations established following the National Procurement Strategy to assist improvement, disseminate learning and sponsor opportunities for improvement.

Comprehensive Performance Assessment A key element of government's performance framework for local government aimed at helping councils deliver better services to local communities. Carried out by the Audit Commission. The CPA assesses performance on two sectors – the quality of current services and the council's capacity to improve those services. Current and past performance, as well as future plans for targets, are combined to produce categorization of councils.

Community strategy Prepared by local councils in support of a local strategic partnership (comprised of local organizations and stakeholders), this is designed to reflect the direction for development of an area in accordance with the wishes of local people.

Continuous improvement Taken from the Japanese word kaizen ('change for the better' or 'improvement'), this is an approach to productivity improvement adapted by the Audit Commission to emphasize the improvement journey by councils through improvement on previous best results.

Corporate The organization as a whole entity, incorporating all its various parts.

Critical success factors Those aspects of a project, service delivery or the partnership relationship which are of prime importance and against which success will be measured and to which any contractual payment will be related.

CRM Customer relationship management system This is an IT-based system for logging and recording customer enquiries.

DCLG The Department of Communities and Local Government, which took on the local government responsibilities of the Office of the Deputy Prime Minister in spring 2006.

DETR (or DTLR) The Department of the Environment, Transport and the Regions or Department for Transport, Local Government and the Regions. This is a central government department which became the Office of the Deputy Prime Minister.

Governance The process by which the management of a partnership, an authority or other agency is governed.

Gershon Report This report was published in 2004, with Sir Peter Gershon as Chair, which set aspirations for greater efficiency in local councils (and the Civil Service).

Horizontal integration Merging or providing the same services with another service provider to gain efficiencies from the elimination of duplication.

ICT Information and communications technology

IDeA The Improvement and Development Agency Established by the Local Government Association to provide direct support to modernize local government. It develops and delivers innovative approaches for knowledge transfer along with practical solutions for performance improvement.

IEG Implementing e-government, generally used to describe the annual statement of intentions of an authority towards meeting the e-government targets.

Joined-up An approach to service provision across organizational and sector boundaries, focusing on the end user. An approach that is commended for the successful delivery of strategies for key areas, such as community safety, regeneration, integrated health and social care, and to improve the quality of life for people.

Joint committee This is an arrangement permitted by the Local Government Act 1972 where two or more local authorities may join together to arrange the joint provision of services. Such a committee is an unincorporated body and cannot enter into legal contracts, hold assets or employ staff.

Joint service delivery Where two or more public service bodies work collaboratively to deliver services or support the delivery of service outcomes across boundaries.

LAAs Local Area Agreements These are negotiated agreements between the government (through the Regional Government Office) and groups of local councils and their partners to deliver improved public services in return for defined freedoms and flexibilities.

Local councils A generic term to cover London boroughs, metropolitan councils, county councils and district councils across England. They were established under primary legislation to administer and provide a range of services in a defined area.

Local performance indicators Indicators selected by single councils or groups of councils of particular importance locally.

Lower quartile The bottom quartile of any table (bottom 25 per cent), when put in order of any selected scale of value, from highest to lowest; or the quarter of the population in any distribution with the lowest values of any selected attribute.

LPSAs Local Public Service Agreements
These agreements form a negotiated process between central and local government which incorporates targets for services that are relevant to the authority's residents. Greater freedoms and financial incentives are provided to reward achievement of those targets.

National Procurement Strategy A strategy published by the Office of the Deputy Prime Minister to ensure improvements in procurement activities by local councils.

Non-cashable savings generated in response to the Gershon Review. They improve the efficiency of a public sector body through allowing re-investment or increased outputs.

NPDO A non-profit distributing organization; for example, an industrial and provident society or a community interest company, a company limited by guarantees. There is provision under various Acts for its establishment. NPDOs can contract and own property.

OBC Outline business case, a combination of business analysis and investment appraisal to conclude on a way forward.

ODPM Office of the Deputy Prime Minister, now superseded following a ministerial reshuffle in Spring 2006. The ODPM was a central government department with a range of responsibilities; that is, regional and local government cross-cutting agendas.

Outcomes The end of the 'input, process, output, outcome' chain, or the effect (on services and their users) produced by outputs.

Outsourcing Delegation of a function usually via contract to an external entity that may specialize in that operation.

Partnering Behaviours and techniques aimed at promoting effective communication between local government and its partners to achieve openness and trust, better mutual understanding, earlier identification of problem areas in projects, and increased value for money in complex procurement projects.

Partnering arrangement This is a relationship which has adopted elements of the partnering ethos. A partnering arrangement is not generally in a legally binding form with remedies in the event of failure; instead, it is an expression of the intentions of the participants, possibly across a range of contracts. A partnering arrangement may be taken into account by a court as evidence of intended behaviour. In some circumstances, partnering behaviours and techniques may be underpinned by contractual provisions.

Partnering agreement Partnering agreements, like partnering arrangements, capture the partnering behaviours and techniques. Their distinguishing feature is that they legally bind the partners to collaborate to refine a requirement and/or to produce the solution of a requirement over the period of the agreement. Generally, partnering agreements are long-term contracts. So a partnering agreement both defines the work to be done and governs the behaviours of the parties in a legally binding contract, which provides remedies in the event of breach by either partner. The agreement also sets out the roles of the partners in pursuing the objectives of the contract. It must reflect the agreed objectives of both parties.

Performance indicators These are defined measurements that enable the level or cost of a service to be quantified. They may be any numerical data or ratios collected and used for the purpose of making initial comparisons (preferably subject to further research before firm conclusions are drawn) of the performance of groups of similar bodies.

PFI The Private Finance Initiative PFI was introduced to improve the quality of services and facilitate the acquisition of new tangible assets that enhance delivery of services. It was designed to secure value for money in the public sector, most notably by the transfer of more project risks to the private sector, where the private sector is considered better at managing those risks well.

Pooled budget The pooling of budgets between public sector bodies where there is express statutory authority so to do.

Private sector The private sector is made up of entities not controlled by the state, such as private firms and public companies and organizations.

Project owner The project owner, sometimes called the project sponsor, is the person accountable, in governance terms, for the successful outcome of the project. The project owner may be formed of a group of 'project sponsors' who collectively 'own' the project.

Procurement The process of obtaining goods and/or services.

Public sector consortium This is an entity formed by a joint arrangement between a number of public bodies. It can manifest itself as an administrative legal structure (such as a joint committee), a contract between the public councils or a private corporate entity between the public bodies.

Risk analysis A review of all risks in a project, partnership or contract with an appraisal of cost, impact and probability, leading to a risk management assessment and risk limiting in an accountable framework. Risk analysis can be at a high level for a strategic outline case but at a more detailed level for an outline business case.

RSG Rate Support Grant This is a form of government financial support paid annually to local councils against a formula to support the provision of services.

Scrutiny/overview A feature of each of the four forms of new constitution which councils were required to introduce by June 2002. There are key roles for overview and scrutiny and for holding the executive (or policy committees) to account.

Secondment Arrangement whereby staff work for another organization on a temporary basis whilst retaining their employment with their employer – the Retained Employment Model.

Service plans Plans utilized by a head of service to effectively and efficiently manage their services.

Single Regeneration Budget Government funds for regeneration provided for all activities in a particular area of a local council's activities without regard to particular funding stream requirements.

SOC Strategic outline case This is a planning and scoping document that contains the results of a business review.

SPV Special purpose vehicle, a legal entity created specifically for a project, normally having a corporate framework and defined equity structure with shareholders.

SSP Strategic service delivery partnership This is a collaborative way of working with a strong relationship focus. It can be between public, private and/or voluntary/social enterprise sector partners.

Strategic partnering This an umbrella term that covers those partnering behaviours, techniques, arrangement and agreements which incorporate the partnering ethos. These can take any partnering form that has strategic importance and are designed to secure a step-change in performance.

Strategic Partnering Taskforce This taskforce was set up in the Office of the Deputy Prime Minister to support the development of strategic partnerships in local government in a research and development programme.

Stakeholders All those with a particular interest in the authority and the services delivered; for example, staff, elected members, service users and so on.

Support services Internal council services that 'support' the front-line services by providing an infrastructure to ensure that the council has the means and ability to do its job.

Target Something that quantifies a performance measure, or determines the success criteria or level of performance that the body setting the target aims to achieve.

TUPE Transfer of Undertakings (Protection of Employment) Regulations

Upper quartile The top quartile of any table (top 25 per cent), when put in order of any selected scale of value, from highest to lowest; or the quarter of the population in any distribution with the highest values of any selected attribute.

Value for money The optimum combination of whole-life cost and quality (or fitness for purpose) to meet the user's requirement (HM Treasury, Value for Money Assessment Guidance, August 2004).

Vertical integration The bringing together, in a single supply chain operation, of processes that might be carried out by different organizations. In the case of local government in England vertical integration is the process of bringing together functions that are carried out by different tiers of councils such as refuse collection by district councils and refuse disposal by county councils.

Vires The statutory powers under which all actions of a local authority are taken. *Ultra vires* actions are beyond the powers and a matter for which the authority has no legal locus and as such would fail a judicial review test. *Intra vires* actions are within the legally constituted powers of the authority.

Workforce issues Issues relating to the terms and conditions of a workforce, for example remuneration and pension issues.

About the Author and Acknowledgements

Ray Tomkinson M.Sc. (Public Sector Management, Aston) has spent the whole of his working career working in councils, particularly in Birmingham City Council, where in 34 years he rose from a junior clerk to an assistant director. His last substantive post was as Head of Strategic Policy for the Environmental and Consumer Services Department. During his time with the council he was involved in committee and civic administration, recreation and community services, management of procurement and client-side functions and strategy and policy development and management effectiveness.

Innovations he was involved in included implementation of Birmingham's first 'dual use' policy for school leisure facilities, a 'customer first' programme for catering and markets, a unique partnership for catering and domestic management in social services premises, the creation of a green purchasing policy and the innovative 'local involvement, local action' programme.

After leaving Birmingham he was a part of the government's improvement agenda as a Best Value inspector with the Audit Commission, undertaking 21 Service Inspections in a variety of areas including leisure and outdoor services, planning, local taxation and transportation and specializing in strategic partnerships for support services. Additionally, he was a member of the working party that produced the Audit Commission's *Learning from Inspection* report on procurement, which was published in February 2002.

After the commission, as a freelance consultant Ray's first major assignment was to act as the project manager on behalf of the five councils that comprise the Welland Partnership, developing a roadmap for the implementation of a series of shared services between them. Sponsored by the ODPM, this capacity-building fund project tested the potential for the creation of a shared service with councils remote from the Welland Partners. The ODPM hoped this model would become a blueprint for shared services in other councils and groups of councils. Working directly to the partners' chief executives group, the project challenged existing thinking and developed new ways of achieving the practical implementation plan. As the project came to a close the partners accepted the business case for the creation of four shared services.

Subsequently, Ray has worked with a number of councils on a variety of projects including a critical evaluation of three councils' proposals for creating shared services for procurement and internal audit services, a 'mock' Direction of Travel Statement for all the services in a district council prior to its submission to the Audit Commission as evidence for an inspection, and the development of a new community strategy and corporate plan for the same council. Ray has also worked on the creation of a Performance Framework for a large Support Services Strategic Partnership.

Ray would like to acknowledge all those who have contributed to this book by taking the initiative to explore or develop shared services and allowing their experiences to form the backdrop to this book. Ray would especially like to thank Colin Rockall for his pertinent and informative comments on early drafts of this text; Steve Knights for his encouragement to the project and Nicola Yates and John O'Halloran for their support during the writing. He would also like to thank those who read and commented on the case studies.

Thanks also to Moira Tomkinson for her encouragement at all times.

Foreword

In July 2004, the Government launched a debate on a new vision for local government. A series of papers have flowed from this that seek to identify some of the new ways local councils might manage their role in the future.

On 26 October 2006 the White Paper 'Strong and Prosperous Communities' was published. Introducing the White Paper, the Secretary of State for Communities and Local Government, Ruth Kelly said 'We are also proposing a new framework for local councils to work with other public service providers, with new duties for them to work together to meet local needs and drive up service standards. And we endorse the way in which some of our best local councils are coming together across wider areas to drive up the economic prosperity of our towns, cities, city-regions and rural areas. Our vision is of revitalized local councils, working with their partners, to reshape public services around the citizens and communities that use them.'

Chapter 7 of the White Paper acknowledges that councils are likely to meet the Government's local authority 2007–8 efficiency target of £3.0 billion, a year ahead of schedule. But people's expectations of public services are rising and the financial climate is changing, putting pressure on councils to deliver highly tailored services, without massive investment from central government, or excessive council tax increases. The best local councils are already doing this. But we need to increase the pace of change. This will mean local councils and other public bodies working together to overcome administrative boundaries that sometimes act as a barrier to service transformation. It will mean sharing assets, systems, data, skills and knowledge more effectively, and keeping all council activity under review to drive out waste.

This book then comes at an opportune time. Not only does it survey the history (such as it is) of shared services in local government but it also provides a wealth of practical detail for practiners at all levels in councils to use to plan their own approach to sharing. The descriptions of existing shared services in the case studies should provide the solid evidence Members and Senior officers need to support their vision of more efficient, effective and economic services that can deliver the improvements needed to meet the rising aspirations of local people.

1 *Introduction*

Why shared services?

As it entered the twenty-first century, local government in England was facing a huge range of challenges. The new Labour Government of 1997 approached the task of renewing public services with considerable energy. The resultant plethora of initiatives (described in this book as 'waves') demonstrated a determination to re-invent local government, giving the needs of local people the highest priority and seeking to make services as effective and efficient as possible. The prime mechanisms for doing this were partnership and 'Best Value', both emphasizing quality in delivery rather than purely economic measures of good performance. Also there was a desire to modernize the organization of delivery.

This book focuses on local councils in England. The structure of councils is different in Scotland, Wales and Northern Ireland though the issues there are very similar. They have their own agendas for improving services and shared services is a part of this. This book, however, concentrates on the story in England since it is here that progress has been best catalogued.

Written from the standpoint of an expert observer, this book is intended to lay out for those in local government who want to be in the forefront of improvement in service delivery the means and methods they can use to achieve improvement. This is essentially a practical guide to creating shared services. Analysis of the philosophy of sharing is of secondary importance to the learning of 'how to go about it' contained in these pages.

There are 388 local councils in England, each having broadly similar structures, legal statuses and reporting requirements. As a result many similar activities are carried on in each council. Under pressure to be as efficient as possible, local councils have shared activities over a long period but, as this book outlines, the potential that sharing gives to restrain expenditure and improve service delivery has become more and more important since 1997.

Despite the extensive public scrutiny of councils it is not easy to get a clear picture of the extent of shared services in councils. As such the material for this book and the case studies is drawn from a wide variety of sources that are not readily comparable. Consequently, the learning from the material suffers from a lack of objective comparison, but this is compensated by the richness of the possibilities covered in the material. What is more, sharing arrangements are described in a wide variety of ways by councils, which means that it is not always easy to see the scope and design of sharings in publicly available publications in order to draw out comparisons. A reading of this book will reveal the different terms used to describe shared services, thus confirming the impossibility of being definitive. Moreover the focus of this book is on those sharings that are most recent and have stretched the capacity of councils through their own determination to improve rather than continue to focus on traditional areas of collaboration. Much earlier sharing may have gone unnoticed.

In order to capture as much learning as possible this book will look at the range of possible arrangements as widely as possible. However, there must be some limitations. The first of these is that there must have been some form of agreement, tacit or explicit, between more than one autonomous council to share. Secondly, the result of this agreement must have been the delivery of a service for which the public were the end customer – that definition has been drawn as widely as possible so that the end customer benefit can be taken either through enhanced service or a benefit such as reduced council tax charges. My definition of a shared service is therefore:

the shared provision by more than one local council of a specified service in which service aims and objectives are mutually shared and for which local people are the end customers.

The adoption of this definition clearly implies more than just centralization (where services are funnelled into an existing department as an added-on responsibility) within a single council. It does not rule out sharing without a separate and distinct organization but stresses that there should be an agreement that delivery of a specified function is the main focus and so is treated as of primary importance. Moreover, the sharers have, through the agreement, put a critical emphasis on 'shared' responsibility for end results and/or on 'service'.

In addition this definition implies that the shared services organization is typically responsible for providing services to an agreed service level and reporting on service effectiveness, which has positive implications both for benchmarking and for determining the value for money of the services.

Additionally, while cost cutting may be the initial rationale for implementing shared services, this definition specifically permits a more value-oriented approach, seeking to leverage the full potential of shared services as an opportunity to improve public sector value and transform service delivery.

The definition is independent of whether a private sector firm, a voluntary organization or other public sector bodies are involved. The definition is independent of the type of governance arrangement used to control the service provision.

So what will this book look at?

In this book Chapter 2 will take an in-depth look at the background to shared services.

Chapter 3 will examine the impetus to share; the structural background to sharing and the 'waves' towards sharing services in local councils. The chapter will discuss the different routes to sharing.

Chapter 4 will survey the extent of shared services in existence and use a series of case studies to identify how and why the sharing was developed and the practical issues resulting from this.

Chapter 5 will review the experience of Breckland District Council and Forest Heath District Council in creating a shared service, the Anglia Revenues Partnership, for revenues and benefits administration.

Chapter 6 will discuss a large project to create several shared services amongst a number of councils who form the Welland Partnership.

Chapter 7 will explore the case studies and attempt to evaluate the potential for improvement they display and, by identifying some of the learning, point to the issues that need to be resolved for the successful development of shared services.

Chapter 8 will look at the development of shared services currently under way in local councils and at proposals for the future.

Chapter 9 will outline some of the trends for the future including the wider picture of government developments in the public sector.

Chapter 10 develops some thoughts on the future of shared services particularly focusing on the impact of the government's White Paper on the future of local government.

2 *The Background to Shared Services*

Why is shared services so important now?

Most local councils have traditionally based their organization on a series of vertically integrated, technically orientated departments to deliver services. In the main, even now, the service will be headed by a manager who is professionally qualified in the service area; for example, the leisure department is managed by a member of the Institute of Leisure Management, the environmental health department by a qualified environmental health officer. Legal departments are headed by a qualified solicitor and finance department by a member of the Chartered Institute of Public Finance Accountancy.

Despite the attempts initially outlined in the Mallaby Report of 1972 to promote the concept of generic managers, the culture of technical professionalism is still strong. The result of this has been that, whereas most large organizations already share services internally – where people undertaking functions such as finance, human resources or information technology are grouped together in order to allow the specialist activities to be carried out more effectively – this is not universal practice in local councils. Whilst there may be a finance department there are often accountants, human resources or IT specialists in 'service' departments.

Even less common is the sharing of services between local councils. As this book will demonstrate this position is beginning to change but progress is sporadic and, as yet, fraught with uncertainty and difficulties. Because of this pressure has had to be exerted by external sources to get local councils to consider the opportunities.

All governments emphasize the need to ensure that minimum standards are achieved in all councils but the Labour Government has sought, since it was elected in 1997, to raise standards across local government in order to avoid what has become colloquially known as a 'postcode lottery' (where the provision of services differs depending on where the recipient lives) in part to respond to rising expectations, such as service access being available when 'customers' want it rather than when it is offered. This government's policies have also sought to combat social exclusion by safeguarding the interests of vulnerable communities, groups and individuals, and in addition there is been a strong emphasis on the importance of 'technical efficiency', in other words a link between inputs in terms of money and the outcomes, primarily to respond to a desire to secure investment in health and education by reducing expenditure on bureaucracy.

It is difficult to put a starting date on the beginning of 'shared' services in local councils. There have been instances of councils sharing an element of service for several years. There have also been instances of services being shared. And there have been statutory requirements for shared bodies such as the six English Passenger Transport Authorities and their executives (PTAs/PTEs) (that is, Greater Manchester, Merseyside, South Yorkshire, Tyne and Wear, West Midlands and West Yorkshire) and Strathclyde in Scotland. They are responsible for securing public transport services for some 14 million people and were first established by the Transport Act 1968. The PTAs are now responsible for subsidizing bus services which are not profitable to run but are considered socially necessary, and for providing bus shelters and stations. The PTAs are made up of councillors representing the areas served and are not 'precepting councils' so they have to negotiate a 'levy' every year on the local councils of the area they serve.

Despite this and other examples, councils still favour self-sufficiency rather than joint working in terms of their form of organization. In his paper 'Crossing Boundaries' written for the New Local Government Network, Ian Roxburgh (a former chief executive of Coventry Metropolitan District Council) says there are 'deeply ingrained attitudes and cultures' and 'invisible barriers' to joint working. However, he also writes 'there are encouraging signs of the potential benefits' and he reports that a survey of senior councillors and chief executives by the Local Government Association at its 2002 annual conference showed that two-thirds of those questioned were considering selling services to other councils once trading rules are relaxed, while 82 per cent said their council would consider buying services from another authority.

In spite of this openness, and the pressure created by the government, the capacity of many councils to respond is inadequate. As we will see some councils are too small and do not have the volume of resources to respond to the government's improvement and efficiency requirements at the same time as responding to the rising expectations from local people. Sharing has not generally been the first thing a local council has considered.

Elected with a clear desire to improve public services, the Labour Government has set about the task by a dual approach of investment combined with reform. However, rather than take the traditional route of reforming the structure of local government, the government has taken the approach of emphasizing partnership as a means of getting local councils to engage fully with the remainder of the public sector and the voluntary sector.

'Best Value' is perhaps the most important mechanism for doing this. Based on the four 'Cs' – challenge, consultation, comparison and competition – local councils were to engage in a process of continuous improvement that emphasizes local council's community leadership role and downgrades the importance of direct service delivery. The critical emphasis was placed on service delivery improving, irrespective of who delivered the service described by Tony Blair, Prime Minister, as the importance of 'what works'.

In this Mr Blair was reflecting a worldwide trend. The US Office of Management and Budget (OMB) has defined five 'lines of business' for which they are advocating cross-agency consolidation, integration and possibly shared services. The lines of business include financial, human resources, grants, health and case management. The goal of the effort is to identify opportunities to reduce the cost of government and improve services to citizens through business performance improvements.

In Singapore, the government has targeted a 3 per cent manpower reduction each year. As part of the ongoing drive, the government has identified 12 services that will be market tested: a process known as 'best sourcing' (including shared services) that will help the government deliver services more cheaply and efficiently.

In Ontario the province consolidated payments, payroll and strategic procurement functions from 21 different ministries into a shared services bureau, which operates under a separate management structure and claims savings of CAN$240 million.

Other examples include the Commonwealth of Massachusetts human resources shared services, which reduced staff head count by approximately 100, significantly reducing hiring times (which increased client satisfaction), reducing duplication of training curricula and automating processes, reducing the need for staff intervention. The United States Postal Service has reduced the cost of its finance function by 16 to 18 per cent thanks to shared services.

Within a year of starting operations, the Queensland (Australia) whole-of-government shared services saved AU$10 million, despite the fact that no savings were even expected for the first year. In Ireland, the Eastern Health Shared Services took 15 per cent out of operating costs between 2002 and 2003.

And a trend is beginning in central government in the UK. By 2004 the Department for Work and Pensions (DWP) had announced the closure of an initial 37 sites through 'rationalization of processing work' and the Public and Commercial Services Union (PCS) says it understands that the DWP will eventually cut the number of 'back office' sites from the current 650 to a maximum of 100 'big processing factories', as the PCS calls them.

As an example from local government, five district councils in and around Sydney, Australia (Lake Macquarie, Hornsby, Wyong, Parramatta and Randwick), have collaboratively sourced a 'state-of-the-art' IT system which integrates technologies from ten vendors with a total cost of £54 million over ten years. The system went live in May 2004 and the councils estimate savings of £120 to £140 million over the next ten years. This is represents a saving of about 4 per cent of gross expenditure with payback of five years. The councils had found they faced a common set of challenges namely:

- the need to deliver public services electronically to customers;
- the need for increasing integration with back-end systems across the council;
- the need to produce extensive management information from the system.

Figure 2.1 describes the IT system supporting the shared services of the five councils, demonstrating how local people access the services (the portal) and via a customer relationship management system get services delivered.

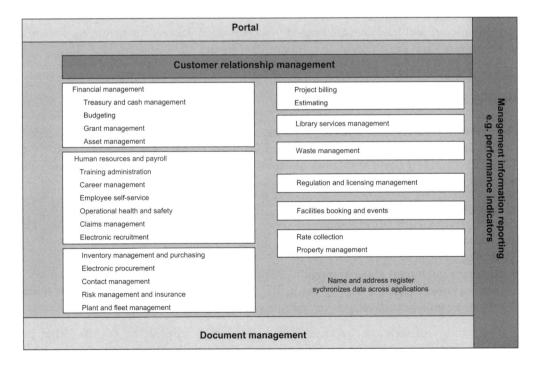

Figure 2.1   **Model of customer interface created by five local councils in Sydney, Australia**

The councils estimate the potential benefits from the system as:

- 20 per cent efficiency improvement in financial management and reporting;
- significant improvement in the visibility and management of service requests;
- 20 per cent improvement in the efficiency of HR administration;
- 10 per cent savings in the 'smarter' procurement of goods and services;
- 30 per cent improvement in the efficiency of purchasing processes;
- 40 per cent reduction in customer calls, which is due to new systems and proactive management of assets;
- significant efficiency gains from system produced letters and documents;
- a more than 40 per cent reduction in time and effort to process development applications (from over 90 to 39 days);
- improvements in customer attitudes because of their easier access to order the service they require.

The councils highlight the following benefits from partnership working:

- introduction of self-service technology for staff and customer benefits;
- applications and infrastructure management processes are outsourced;
- hardware and software costs are contracted at less than 50 per cent of the price than if the projects had been commissioned separately;
- implementation staff costs are reduced by 60–72 per cent;
- council staff effort involved in implementation are reduced by 40–60 per cent due to sharing in-house efforts across the councils;
- estimated savings of 50–57 per cent on infrastructure management and applications management services;
- infrastructure and hardware are housed in a centralized data centre, saving each council the costs of supporting a separate corporate data centre.

What services could be shared?

Expenditure by local councils is large. According to the consultation paper and interim report of the Lyons Inquiry into local government, expenditure in 2003–4 was a total of £101,492 million. Even broken down into areas of activity the figures are still large. The figures for 2003–4 are:

- education – £33,247 million;
- social services – £18,792 million;
- transport – £9,087 million;
- housing £17,012 million;
- culture, environment and planning £13,031 million;
- other services (financial management, democratic controls, registration, council tax collection, economic development and internal management) – £10,323 million.

The number of different 'services' is also large. It is difficult to describe what an individual 'service' is, but for the purposes of statutory returns the Office of the Deputy Prime Minister (ODPM) provides a classification of council services. Supplementing this with some cross-cutting activities such as paying employees (payroll) we get the extensive list shown in Figure 2.2

Education
Primary education
Secondary education
Special education
Pre-school education
Adult education
Youth services
Other continuing education and community services

Transportation
Parking
Transport planning, policy and strategy – transport
Expenditure on bus services
Payments on local rail services
Concessionary fares

Revenues and benefits
Housing benefit administration
Council tax benefit administration
Cost of domestic/non-domestic rate collection
Council tax collection

Leisure and Libraries
Libraries
Museums and galleries
Archives and records
Art activities and facilities
Conservation of historic environment – planning
Conservation of historic environment – other
Sports facilities
Sports development services and community recreation
Tourism

Environmental and consumer protection
Waste collection
Waste disposal functions
Public conveniences and rural sewerage schemes
Street sweeping and cleaning
Food safety
Consumer protection
Community safety
Cemeteries and crematoria
National parks
Parks and open spaces (including country parks)
Core planning services
Building control
Economic development
Community development

Highways
Traffic management and road safety
Structural maintenance
Routine maintenance
Roads – public lighting
Winter maintenance
Bridges – structural maintenance and strengthening
Transport planning, policy and strategy – highways
School crossing patrols

Personal social services
Central strategic (SSR)
Children and family services
Older peoples services
Adults with physical or sensory disabilities
Adults with learning difficulties
Adults with mental health needs
Asylum seekers

Agricultural services
Flood defence
Coast protection
Other agriculture and fisheries

Housing (general fund)
Bed and breakfast accommodation
Private sector leasing
Other homelessness
Administration (homelessness)
Home renovation grants
Other housing renewal functions
Housing support to individuals

Cross-cutting
Human resources
Payroll
Pensions
Recruitment
Finance
Audit
Accountancy
Contracts
Procurement
Property
ICT
Customer contact
Legal
Facilities management
Press and PR
Building maintenance
Vehicle maintenance

Figure 2.2   Breakdown of local council services

Although not all local councils operate all of these services, this listing displays the range of services which can be shared either individually or in groups. Most councils will group these individual services according to the professional specialism they most closely fit. As such the individual titles shown above will not always be evident. This is because councils tend to look at their structures hierarchically rather than as a set of horizontal layers of activities. Furthermore, few councils will be organized in exactly the same way. Different combinations of functions in different departments tend to make it difficult to generalize what is a 'service' in any particular council. This makes it difficult to make sweeping assertions about the opportunities for councils to share services.

Another factor is the statutory responsibilities of councils and the legal requirement that a council is exclusively responsible for defining and carrying through that responsibility. Nothing, however, prevents the council organizing someone else to provide the service on its behalf – the council performing the 'enabling' role – but in so doing there is an additional risk of potential loss of control. Accordingly, historically, councils have been very conservative in their organization, preferring to ensure they have the identified resources to perform specific legal responsibilities. This concentration of responsibility for a particular service has restricted the willingness of the various 'professionals' to subject departmental interests to the 'corporate' centre and as a result even today within councils there is a marked reluctance to 'share' services that are common to all services.

Shared services in the private sector

The private sector has not been restricted by this organizational thinking and has tended to look at their organizations differently, tending to see them as a series of separate processes that interlink at key points in the organization rather than be an integrated whole. Bangemann (2005) shows how this process orientation makes the organization customer focused and goes on to describe how this form of organization makes it easier to form alliances.

In the private sector this type of analysis can free up thinking and has allowed the development of purchaser/provider relationships internal (and external) to the company. For the service purchaser this can stimulate greater accountability than having multiple points of responsibility and varied management practices. Purchasers can specify what services they need and can expect the provider to take responsibility for meeting those requirements; service providers can expect to have their performance evaluated objectively because measurable criteria have been established in areas such as:

- *Service*: individual customers and their requirements are known, performance is measured and problems are promptly resolved. Providers know what their purchasers expect for each service and are capable and motivated in meeting these expectations.
- *Price*: services to be performed are agreed upon with purchasers and priced based on services consumed.
- *Accountability*: accountability and responsibility are clearly delineated and compensation is linked to satisfactory delivery of service.
- *Delivery*: purchasers and providers co-define their respective roles and agree upon how work is performed across organizational boundaries to meet service requirements and expectations. Providers anticipate new service needs. Purchasers see service providers as direct contributors to profitability.

This creates new relationships between the customer and the provider as described in the model shown by Figure 2.3.

Because of this the private sector has made much greater progress in sharing services. In part this is a factor of the size of the operations but there are other reasons. The first is the more acute need to restrain all areas of cost in areas of secondary importance to the company, the primary cost concern being customer service. Secondly, there is a focus on volume-based services – transactional, processing and administrative – that are delivered to most employees or to external customers and can be maximized by aligning economies of scale. Thirdly, this model requires a more flexible approach to organizational structures to which local government in England has not traditionally been open.

A report produced by the USA-based management consultancy, the Aberdeen Group, in 2004 sought to prioritize these separate factors and said the major influences for sharing services were lower ongoing costs, improving end-user service and allowing focus on core business objectives, followed by avoiding capital investment, gaining better access to data and improving compliance.

Initially a private company may have established a shared service centre (SSC) to streamline, consolidate and improve processes but also to reduce headcount. The centralization of a core administrative function will tend to lead to a more customer-focused approach to the service provided, bringing about changes in management and delivery. By setting up an SSC in one centralized location, companies that operate across international borders ensure that they are using standard processes for all of their operations rather than employing different methods and processes in several different countries. This enables them to not only keep costs under control but also ensure that they offer the same standards of service to all of their internal customers. This is no different to a local council who can create (and in many cases has done so) internal shared services.

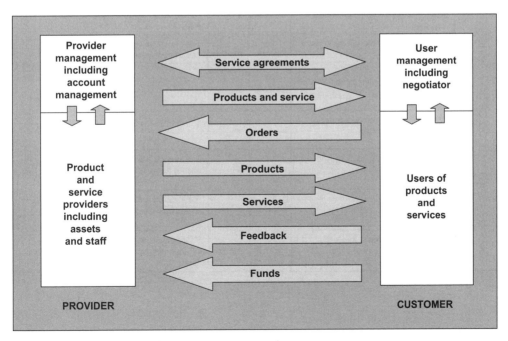

Figure 2.3   The relationship between provider and customer in shared services

The evidence is though that private companies are much freer in their thinking and are not afraid to 'share' an ever-increasing proportion of their activity with others even though they continue to be an autonomous body. Once a private sector company establishes the success of this business model there are two possible routes they can take to further improve cost and performance. The private sector is focused on its main money-making activities and therefore the business seeks to emphasize these activities – protection of the 'brand' being at the centre of this – and does not see 'routine' activities as 'core'. As such these sorts of services are not critical to the business and can be regarded as suitable for operation at arm's length through outsourcing. The thinking that leads to this sort of conclusion can be demonstrated through the decision-making process to determine whether to share a service shown in Figure 2.4. Though not conclusive, the more the service is described by the attributes on the right the more it might benefit from a 'sharing'.

What we can see from the private sector experience is that certain services are more likely to be shared than others. Thus the more a service is based on standardized, identifiable outputs (as in customer call handling), transactional (accounts payable), non-strategic (payroll), standardized (IT support) and low risk (HR administration), the more likely it is that these sorts of services can be shared.

The evidence of the private sector is that success in these areas leads companies to search for other services where similar operational efficiencies and cost reductions can be achieved.

SHARING IS NOT A GOOD OPTION OPTION GOOD AS IT GETS	Description of the service under consideration			Description of the service under consideration	SHARING IS A GOOD OPTION
	The service is strategic to the business.	→	←	The service is an administrative overhead rather than strategic.	
	The service is a critical activity to the good governance of the business.	→	←	The service is not 'core' and the activity could be done by someone else.	
	The service is carried out throughout the business.	→	←	The service is concentrated in one department or section.	
	An alternative supplier for this service does not exist.	→	←	There are alternative suppliers.	
	The service is currently producing 'best in class' service.	→	←	The service is under-performing.	
	The service has the capacity and capability to meet foreseeable challenges.	→	←	The service has limited capacity to absorb future business needs.	
	Loss of direct control will have limited impact on the risk profile of the business.	→	←	Provision by a third party will have limited increased risk to the business.	
	The service is complicated with numerous decision points and referral requirements.	→	←	Service is standardised with infrequent need to change service detail.	

STATUS QUO

Figure 2.4   **A forcefield analysis of the creation of shared services**

The logical choices for this second stage are knowledge-based services – specialized expertise, consultative and integrated solutions – targeted to supervisors, department managers and teams. Facilities management, security, building and project management are frequently undertaken by a third party. Linked by common technology and operating systems the provider is able to minimize overheads and expand service hours. The end customer will not notice but should enjoy a level of service that could not be provided by the individual companies alone.

The results of this process are surprisingly common in the United Kingdom. For example, electricity or gas meters will be read by someone employed by a company that provides a service to all the utility companies. Ring a credit card company to activate a new card or call a tour company to book a holiday and you will be calling a call centre which services several companies. A housing association will have arranged to have the maintenance of their housing stock managed by a specialist company. Motorway service stations may be branded by one of the major High Street names but they are operated on a day-to-day basis by a company specializing in facilities management.

In all these sorts of situations the service purchaser, though still retaining control through service specifications and regular monitoring, allows service providers to use their expertise in the particular area of activity and achieve greater value through risk-taking and entrepreneurism. Providers can become specialized and concentrate on value-added services. This process is described in Figure 2.5, which shows how a shared service organization refines the service it delivers.

Companies also outsource to shared service providers to gain access to new skills and technology, because providers often have much more awareness of and access to new products as these are their areas of speciality. Outsourcing can reduce the start-up time for new initiatives as they become the main focus for the provider whereas the the purchaser's primary concern is their main business. Also the purchaser company gets reduced complexity – the outsourcing of non-core activities means that companies can focus on their core business and adding value to

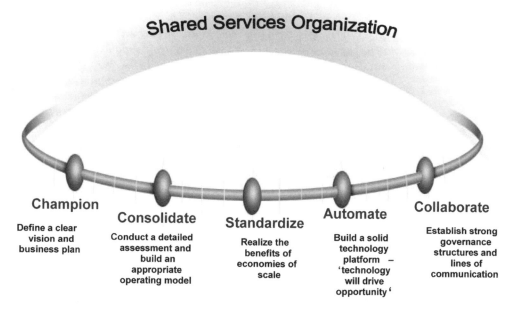

Figure 2.5   The stages of development of a shared services organization

this. Furthermore, the purchasing company will achieve lowering of costs, advantages of scale for purchasing and market insight, and flexible costs – outsourcing usually gets rid of fixed costs and changes them to variable costs. There is a downside – the outsourcing company will have to find new skills to manage their outsourcing arrangements. This can be a new cost for the management of the service provider and this can require the development of new skills by the purchasing company.

The trend to sharing is still developing. Whereas in the 1980s there was a concentration in private companies of the use of business process re-engineering to achieve improvements, and in the 1990s there was a growth of creation of shared services, in the last ten years sharing has focused on achieving cost reductions by offshoring. If that is the standard pattern and timescale then it suggests local councils are 20 years behind the private sector and that it could be ten or more years before sharing is truly universal.

Shared services in local government

One of the reasons councils are so far behind the private sector is that, whilst most councils will have departments (often grouped together and called the 'corporate centre') undertaking activities such as finance, human resources and information technology, they have not tended to manage the relationships with service delivery departments (such as Highways or Planning) in the above terms (that is, purchaser/provider) and the active use of service level agreements is rare. This relationship has changed and is still changing under the pressures being experienced by all councils.

An example of this was contained in the Audit Commission's study *The Efficiency Challenge: The Administration Costs of Revenues and Benefits* (2005a). This said that:

> *Internal recharges are a significant factor in determining the overall cost of a service to a council. We identified a large variation in these costs with the councils we sampled. For example, two councils with very similar levels of activity had a difference of over £2.3 million in recharges for revenues and benefits. While one of them (the more expensive one) was able to provide us with a breakdown of these costs, the other could not. We found many variations in recharges; for example, two district councils with similar levels of activity had IT recharges varying by over £350,000 per annum. However, service managers were unable to ascertain whether this was because of the level of the IT cost or activity. Therefore, there remains a risk in examining (and comparing) the costs of service in isolation from the rest of the council. Most councils have service level agreements (SLAs) to provide internal services with a basis on which to charge support costs. While we recognize that in the past the monitoring of these agreements was disproportionately time consuming, there is now very little evidence that they are consistently monitored. While this is not the case in all councils, for many there is no robust forum for services to challenge the internal recharges. (p.22)*

The major change that started a focus on this issue results from the compulsory competitive tendering (CCT) legislation of the late 1980s when it was made compulsory for many services (usually called 'blue collar'), such as refuse collection and grounds maintenance, to be offered to the private sector through tendering. Many council services found it difficult to win the tender unless the council took a marginal cost view of their overheads such as finance, human resources and information technology, arguing that these costs had to remain intact to support the remainder of the council.

The impact of this decision was that the fixed cost of the 'corporate centre' as a proportion of the total cost of the council's services was increased. In addition, the impact of losing services through the winning of the tendering process by the private sector meant that the costs of other services not exposed to tendering legislation and the services in the corporate centre were increased because of the need to absorb the overheads they could not recover from the services lost to the private sector.

The reaction of many service heads has been to secure the HR, finance and administration resources within their vertical structure as this allows them to closely manage these costs rather than expose them to higher overheads they cannot control. This is exacerbated by the tension felt when budget reviews take place. A view common among many service managers is that, because they control the 'purse-strings', corporate officers protect the corporate centre at the expense of service costs.

Efforts to resolve this were to have been tackled under CCT for 'white collar' services but this was not pursued due to the change of government in 1997, the Best Value regime replacing the tendering legislation. Since then, many councils have sought to reduce the costs of their corporate centre by traditional methods such as budget restrictions and cuts and by undertaking Best Value reviews, without significant success. Often, because these services tended to be a mix of functions (some statutory such as employment legislation, some reflecting 'corporate vision' such as 'environmental policy management', some required for regulatory reporting such as financial reporting, some for internal support such as IT networking and some for customer services such as 'one-stop shops'), councils have found it difficult to isolate and rationalize these services and little progress has been made in reducing the costs.

Many councils will have mitigated some of the diseconomies of small scale through 'internal joint working' – that is to say they have organized themselves in such as way as to avoid too high a management overhead. At a simple level this can mean combining two related activities (for example council tax collection and benefits administration) which are separate units in some larger councils. This may also explain, in part, the widely differing organizational structures in place in councils and some of the relatively unusual directorates that appear in some councils (for example, Housing and Consumer Protection; Regulation and Resources).

However, because of the advent of Best Value and the public reporting that supported it, costs and performance are now more apparent. With the reduced range of services provided directly by councils, poor performance in service delivery and the level of costs, particularly that generated by the corporate centre, are more unsustainable. As a consequence, many councils conducting service reviews under Best Value find that the cost of overheads is a disproportionate percentage of service costs and there is growing pressure to reduce those costs. Rationalization of the service required directly by services responding to this then reduces the volume of service required and, as councils have less services to spread the costs, the costs of central services are now a problem for many councils.

There has undoubtedly been a reluctance to develop internal trading between service departments which has prevented the sorts of purchaser/provider relationships common in the private sector. This is because of the natural resistance to entrepreneurial activities in a 'public service ethos' organization and the reluctance to allow true internal accountability where services and fees are specified and charged based on services rendered, as many councils have not wanted to expose such costs, since to do so would create systems that involve 'playing shops' – particularly if this raises costs overall and increases organizational tension.

The result of this has been that shared services is not an organizational feature of local councils to anything like the degree it is in the private sector. The pressure to change however is increasing and, as we will see in Chapter 3, has now reached the point that means that sharing has become imperative for many councils.

3 *The Impetus to Share*

The structural background to sharing

Elected county councils were established in England and Wales for the first time in 1888, covering areas known as administrative counties. The county areas were two tier, with many municipal boroughs, urban districts and rural districts within them, each with its own council. Some large towns, known as county boroughs, were independent from the counties in which they were physically situated.

Apart from the creation of new county boroughs and the establishment in 1965 of Greater London and its 32 London boroughs, covering a much larger area than the previous county, there was little change in the structure until the 1970s by which time many areas of activity undertaken by councils, such as the provision of utilities, bus services and health services, had been taken away.

Despite mergers, there was still a proliferation of small rural district and urban district councils in more rural areas, and in the major conurbations the borders had been set before the pattern of urban development had become clear. For example, in the area that was to become the seven boroughs of the metropolitan county of West Midlands, local government was split between four administrative counties and eight county boroughs.

As a result it was generally agreed that there were significant problems with the structure of local government and the Redcliffe-Maud commission was set up in 1968. In 1969 it recommended a system of single-tier unitary councils for the whole of England, apart from three metropolitan areas of Merseyside, Selnec (Greater Manchester) and West Midlands (Birmingham and the Black Country), which were to have both a metropolitan county council and district councils.

This report was accepted by the Labour government of the time, but the Conservative Party won the 1970 general election, on a manifesto that committed them to 'two-tiers everywhere'. The Local Government Act 1972 abolished previous existing local government structures, and created a two-tier system of counties and districts everywhere. Although called two tier, the system was really three tier, as it retained parish councils.

In England there were 46 counties and 296 districts, in Wales there were 8 and 37. Six of the English counties were designated as metropolitan counties (Greater Manchester, Merseyside, Tyne Tees, Wearside, West Midlands, West Yorkshire). The new English counties were based clearly on the traditional ones, albeit with several substantial changes.

The new metropolitan counties contained metropolitan district councils. The allocation of functions differed between the metropolitan and the non-metropolitan areas (the so-called 'shire counties'); for example, education and social services were the responsibility of the shire counties, but in metropolitan areas were given to the districts. The distribution of powers was slightly different in Wales than in England, with libraries being a county responsibility in England.

The system established, however, was not to last. In England, the county councils of the metropolitan counties (and the Greater London Council) were abolished in 1986, effectively re-establishing county borough status for the metropolitan boroughs. A further local government reform in the 1990s led to the creation of many new unitary councils, and the complete abolition of Avon, Cleveland, Hereford and Worcester and Humberside. There was also a requirement for councils to consider creating mayoral posts, elected directly by local people, the most prominent of which was London (supported by a new Greater London Authority), and to adopt new streamlined methods of organization (particularly the creation of executive and scrutiny roles).

The 'waves' towards sharing services

The impetus to share has come in four 'waves'. Though the 'waves' are overlapping it is possible to separate them and show the differing sources. Together they have provided a 'tidal wave' that has engulfed the local government scene.

The first of these waves came in the aftermath of the 1974 re-organization (resulting from the Local Government Act of 1972) and the second was created by the 1997 Labour government's determination to 'squeeze value' from public services.

The third was created by councils themselves – a number of high-profile private sector partnerships changed the landscape and convinced many of the need for a fundamental change in the way services were delivered. Though the results of this wave have not been universally successful there is little doubt that they gave rise to the fourth wave.

The fourth wave was based on a desire of the Labour government to secure improvements in local authority services by incentivizing co-operation backed up by the imposition of targets through a combination of the National Procurement Strategy and the Gershon Report.

THE FIRST WAVE

The first wave was two pieces of legislation in the early 1970s.

Section 1 of the Local Government (Goods and Services) Act 1970 permitted local councils to trade with other 'public bodies' designated on an ad hoc basis following application to the Secretary of State and the consequential grant of an Order. This enabled local councils to arrange, for example, to share the procurement of goods and services. Examples of this working were the creation of purchasing consortia such as the Yorkshire Purchasing Organization (YPO) which is established constitutionally as a joint committee of local councils and was formed in 1974 to provide a purchasing and supply service to customers in constituent and other councils. The largest formally constituted local authority purchasing consortium in the UK, YPO is governed by a management committee of elected representatives from constituent councils.

Of more fundamental importance, however, was the Local Government Act 1972 which, apart from creating the new structure of councils, created in Section 101 the ability for local councils to provide services through an agency arrangement. Under this sort of arrangement, one local council (usually a district) could act as an agent for another council. For example, since road maintenance was split depending upon the type of road, both types of council might have had to retain engineering departments. A county council could delegate its road maintenance to the district council if it was confident that the district was competent. Some powers were specifically excluded from agency, such as education.

This enabling power was supported by Section 111. This allows local councils to do anything, including incurring expenditure, borrowing or lending money or acquiring or disposing of any property or rights, which facilitates or is conducive or incidental to the discharge of their functions.

However, the operation of this provision has been riddled with difficulty, especially as a result of the restrictive interpretation of this provision adopted by the courts. Fears arose during the 1980s that Sections 111 and 137 (a power to use a specified proportion of the rates to fund anything the council wished) were being used by local councils to establish companies that undertook activities not expressly permitted to be carried out by local councils under statute. In order to restrain such activity, the then Conservative government sought to introduce a regulatory regime to control the use of companies by local councils. The regulatory regime was designed to recognize that local councils could use companies to perform certain functions, but they did not have a 'carte blanche'. The framework for this regime was contained in Part V of the Local Government and Housing Act 1989. Councils must initially ascertain whether the Local Government and Housing Act 1989 regulatory regime applies to the type of company in question.

The impact of the above regime was softened to a large extent by the Local Councils (Companies) Order 1995, which signalled a shift away from detailed controls for local councils companies towards the adoption of private sector company tests of control. The Order distinguished between private sector influenced companies (effectively controlled by the private sector and therefore not subject to the regulatory regime) and public sector influenced companies (which are subject to the regime). Local councils can hold up to 50 per cent of the voting rights in a local authority influenced company, provided the authority does not have 'effective control' (in other words, it does not take an active part in management and operations of the company) and, theoretically at least, the company would not be subject to the regime.

THE SECOND WAVE

The new Labour government of 1997 produced the second wave of the impetus to share services. Elected on a clear desire to sweep away the Conservative government's compulsory competitive tendering legislation yet constrained by their political commitments to hold back public sector spending, they introduced the twin concepts of partnerships by all public sector bodies and by the philosophy of 'Best Value'.

They used a 'carrot and stick' approach.

On the one hand local councils were encouraged to bring forward innovative ideas and the government introduced specific funding through the Invest to Save Budget, for which the guidance to councils included: 'Bids will be particularly welcomed from imaginative new partnerships which bring together local councils (perhaps including different tiers of local government) to procure and deliver services jointly.'

The former Department of Transport, Local Government and the Regions (DTLR) established the Strategic Partnering Taskforce (SPT) in September 2001 to support local councils that wished to implement strategic service partnerships (SSPs). The SPT invited applications for pathfinder status and in early 2002 received 117 applications, many covering more than one authority. Twenty-four pathfinder projects received support.

Rethinking Service Delivery Vol. 1: An Introduction to Strategic Service Delivery Partnerships (Office of the Deputy Prime Minister 2003a), published by the SPT, explained in more detail what strategic partnering was and when it might be considered. The distinctive nature of SSPs was that an SSP is output- or outcome-driven and where a public–private sector SSP is concerned there will be an output or outcome specification. In a public–public SSP the equivalent of the output or outcome specification often takes the form of a partnership agreement which sets out the expected deliverables from the partnership. The characteristics of a SSP are shown in Figure 3.1.

The paper confirmed that delivery of services in an SSP can be provided by any party to the SSP or jointly. For example, where local councils are working jointly for waste-related services, crews made up of employees from differing councils can form the refuse collection teams.

The Local Government Act 2000 contained a 'well-being' power that introduced 'a power of first resort' to 'do anything' to promote the economic, social and environmental well-being of an area subject to any prohibitions, limitations or restrictions contained in any enactment (including the 2000 Act, which amongst other things contains a restriction on raising money whether by precepts, borrowing or otherwise, for well-being). Supporting guidance states that local councils are able to form or invest in companies, in the pursuit of well-being, and the receipt of dividends on shares or interest on debentures does not constitute 'raising money' within the meaning of the prohibition in the Act. The guidance further states that the duty of Best Value is central to the exercise of well-being powers in that a local authority will be able to set up and participate in companies in pursuit of well-being if, and only if, such action represents Best Value. An Order issued pursuant to Section 16 of the Act removed any remaining anomalies in respect of powers to undertake functions in partnership with others.

The stick of this 'carrot-and-stick' arrangement was provided not just by legislative requirements and imposing new duties on working in partnership but also by creating new responsibilities and supervisory arrangements.

The Crime and Disorder Act 1998 was introduced to bring the joint working arrangements developed between the police and local councils in the context of the 'safer cities' projects conducted in the 1990s onto a statutory basis. The Act places joint responsibility on the police and local councils to work together, as well as with other relevant agencies including the probation service, fire services and primary care trusts (PCTs), to formulate joint strategies to reduce crime, social disorder and the misuse of drugs within their localities.

❑   Brings about a step-change and a cultural change within the organization.

❑   Scope includes a large range of services, allowing partners to maximize synergies.

❑   Generates external investment assisting step-change or cultural change.

❑   Provides a major contribution to meeting strategic and service objectives.

❑   Adopts a partnering ethos rather than a confrontational approach, helping the council to meet its goals and to develop strategy.

❑   Output-/outcome-based with incentives for the provider to secure continuous improvement.

❑   A medium-term to long-term commitment to the partnership.

Figure 3.1   Characteristics of a typical SSP

Source: Office of the Deputy Prime Minister (2003a)

Sections 27 to 32 of the Health Act 1999 contain powers enabling local councils to work in partnership with National Health Service (NHS) bodies in relation to the discharge by both parties of their respective health and welfare related functions. Effectively the Act enables a NHS body to undertake a local authority's health-related functions or vice versa (as prescribed in the Regulations) or for them to work together and exercise such functions jointly. Under such partnership arrangements, NHS bodies and local councils may maintain a 'pooled fund,' established through contributions by each partner, delegate functions to each other and integrate provision so that partners amalgamate their staff, resources and management structures.

A 1998 White Paper set initial government targets for public contacts and transactions to be performed electronically. Subsequently, targets were set for local government to achieve 100 per cent of electronic transactions by 2005. According to early estimates the investment required to meet the target would be around £2.5 billion for local councils alone. In recognition of the need for investment, the Spending Review 2000 made available £350m earmarked for the Local Government Online programme. To promote this programme, the DTLR, in collaboration with central and local partners, issued guidance on local targets, on implementing e-government and set out a 'route map' to guide councils. The guidance emphasized the need to take a corporate and collaborative approach, and to see e-government as an opportunity to transform customer access, service standards and cost-effectiveness. To pursue this challenge most local councils came together in partnerships designed to rationalize the work needed to be done to achieve the targets. A total of 75 partnerships were identified by the ODPM in 2002, based on councils' IEG statements. Of those 33 were based on all councils in a particular county.

The Local Government Act 1999 (Best Value) gave local councils a duty to make arrangements to secure continuous improvement in the exercise of their functions, having regard to the principles of economy, efficiency and effectiveness, and empowered the Secretary of State (by way of a Statutory Instrument) to modify or exclude enactments, to remove obstacles to compliance with Best Value and to do anything which is designed to facilitate Best Value, including the contracting out of functions, where this would achieve Best Value.

Circular 10/99 which provided guidance on how to undertake Best Value reviews made reference to councils 'making decisions on the best value option for service delivery'. Councils must show that they have applied the 4Cs of best value:

*   **challenging** why and how a service is being provided;
*   **comparing** their performance with others' (including organizations in the private and voluntary sectors);
*   embracing fair **competition** as a means of securing efficient and effective services; and
*   **consulting** local taxpayers, customers and the wider business community.

The Circular lists seven main options, which includes 'the joint working or delivery of the service'. Thus, in theory, all Best Value reviews undertaken by councils should have considered joint working as an option.

The Act that set up the Best Value regime also allows the Audit Commission to carry out inspection activity to ensure that a Best Value authority (all local councils and some other bodies) is complying with this duty, and may issue a report as to its findings. In practice in the majority of cases where an inspection was carried out between 2000 and 2003, the Audit Commission published the Best Value inspection service's report. This built up a body of evidence on the relative performance of councils that paved the way for the Comprehensive

Performance Assessment (CPA) of councils that began in 2002 and completed its first round of all councils in 2005. These assessments were published and are (for upper- and single-tier councils) updated annually.

The Health and Social Care Act 2001 facilitates funding for the health service by way of partnerships with third parties. The Act also provides for care trusts to be established to commission and provide integrated services covering health, social services and other 'health-related' local authority functions.

The *Waste Strategy 2000 England and Wales* presented the government's vision for managing waste and resources by sustainable development. A key objective of this strategy and the European Landfill Directive is to reduce the use of landfill as a means of the long-term disposal of waste, in order to reduce emissions of the greenhouse gas, methane, and to protect water supplies from contamination. The government set targets collectively for local councils to recover value through materials (by recycling, composting or energy), and reduce landfill of biodegradable waste (the element of municipal waste which may break down to produce methane).

Under the Waste Emissions and Trading Act 2003 each waste disposal agency (WDA) was given allocations of biodegradable waste that might be landfilled for each year from 2005–6 to 2019–20, consistent with the United Kingdom meeting its obligations under the Directive. WDAs may trade these allocations with one another. They face a penalty of £150 per tonne of waste landfilled in excess of their allocation (augmented by any allocation they have purchased from another WDA). Faced with this requirement many local councils were forced to consider partnerships as a way of meeting the challenge, since WDAs could not work alone and needed other councils who were waste collection agencies (WCAs) to act upstream and reduce the amount of waste entering the waste stream. In addition, the Household Waste Recycling Act 2003 requires all local councils to provide a kerbside collection service for at least two recyclables to all domestic properties by 2010, and the government has set individual recycling standards for each local authority.

As an indication of how successful this process has been Figure 3.2 demonstrates the change in the relative amounts of municipal waste recycled and sent to landfill in the last five years. Overall the amount of waste has reduced by only 2.2 per cent during the five years but, whereas in 2001–2 the percentage of the total amount recycled was only 17.48 per cent, by 2005–6 the percentage was 30.3 per cent.

'Supporting People' is the government's long-term policy to enable local councils to plan, commission and provide housing-related support services, which help vulnerable people live independently. The Supporting People programme brings together significant funding streams including transitional housing benefit, the Housing Corporation's supported housing management grant and the probation accommodation grant scheme into a single pot to be administered by 150 councils. Unitary and metropolitan councils and counties are designated as administering authorities, with the county taking the lead in most cases for the districts in their area.

Administering councils work in partnership, with districts where this is relevant, to agree Supporting People strategies and delivery mechanisms for housing-related support services with housing, social services, health and the probation service providers. Negotiation and consultation is also required with service users, all housing and support service providers, other statutory service providers, the private sector and voluntary organizations to plan and commission support services to meet identified needs. The ODPM has published a number of consultation papers on the developing programme and a workplan setting out what

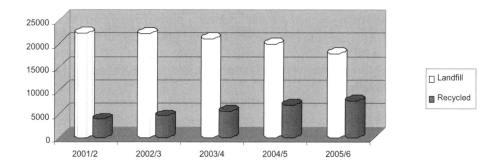

Figure 3.2   Amount of municipal waste sent to landfill and recycled (thousands of tons)

Source: Defra (November 2006)

local councils and their partners will need to achieve in order to deliver the programme effectively.

The Local Government Act 2003 allowed local councils to charge for providing a service that it had the power ordinarily to charge for. The power to charge contemplates charging for the cost of the services and not making a profit per se. The Act also contains a new power for local councils to trade in function-related activities through a company (as defined in Part V of the Local Government and Housing Act 1989 and being regulated by such capital expenditure rules). These provisions have now been implemented via regulations and enable Best Value councils to do for a commercial purpose anything which they are authorized to do for the purpose of carrying on any of their ordinary functions.

This trading power is supplementary to existing local authority powers, and it is envisaged that the rules on local authority public–public trading (Local Government (Goods and Services) Act 1970) will remain, thereby enabling local councils to trade with other prescribed public sector bodies in relation to certain defined services. The Secretary of State is able to specify which local councils may benefit from this new trading power, which is only to be exercisable by local councils classified within the top three categories, following completion of their CPA.

THE THIRD WAVE

The third wave in the development of shared services among local councils consisted of individual local councils creating a number of large 'strategic' partnerships. High value, high risk and high profile, these partnerships created huge interest in the concept of shared services and ultimately led the way, in part at least, to the Gershon Report.

The reasons for this wave is not clear, but some councils, convinced of the cost savings that could be achieved through larger-scale working, accessed these through individual arrangements with private sector providers rather than through joint working. These providers, encouraged by the Best Value regime, had a strong incentive to expand in order to achieve economies of scale, and were clearly prepared to spend significant sums to gain this business and make significant future commitments. Those councils who went down this road saw this approach as offering significant and more easily implementable benefits than joint working arrangements with other councils.

The extent of this should not be underestimated. Whereas the second wave has to be seen as the government creating the framework for a different approach to the delivery of services by councils and exerting pressure on councils, the success of some very large third-party partnerships were a significant influence on many councils. The effects of this were exacerbated by a number of them being brought to fruition in a short period of time. The most notable are outlined below.

In April 2000, Hyder Business Services (HBS) began to provide a series of support services for Lincolnshire County Council under a ten-year partnership agreement. These services had been provided by the council's finance and resources directorate and consisted of finance, human resources, information technology, property, other administration services and catering (on a two-year agreement).

The partnering agreement was unusual and attracted national attention. The headline features were its size – over £20m of annual revenue expenditure and the substantial benefits it would bring. These included:

- £5m savings in revenue costs per year;
- major investment in information technology;
- the creation of a Regional Business Centre in Lincoln – with 500 new jobs – and service improvements so that – under HBS – service would be 'best in class'.

In early 2001 Middlesbrough concluded an agreement with HBS for a ten-year partnership called 'Service Middlesbrough' including public access services, housing benefits administration, council tax collection and awards and benefits and financial transactions (including accounts, pensions administration, insurance, payroll); asset management (including financial and information technology services and property management); human resources services (including health and safety, strategy and standards and training and development together with departmental personnel services) and business services, service administrative support, services to internal customers and the council's communications unit. The gross cost of these services in 2000–1 was estimated at £21.6 million.

The expectation was that this would mean that HBS would provide the agreed services at a cost of approximately £2 million less per year than they cost the council to provide in 2000–1 and that HBS would work with the council to transfer more activities to HBS in the future and, through efficiencies to be identified, to save the council as much as a further £22.9 million over the life of the contract through systems renewal avoidance and purchasing savings. HBS would make an investment in the services of £20.2 million; create a regional business centre at a total cost of approximately £20 million; create 750 new jobs in the centre by the end of the contract with a guaranteed minimum of 487 new jobs and create customer contact services that would eventually totally reconfigure the way council services are delivered and citizens access those services.

Liverpool City Council set up Liverpool Direct (LDL) and signed a ten-year, £300m joint venture with BT whose aims were to rationalize and radically improve back office functions in the areas of ICT infrastructure, customer contact centres, revenues and benefits, and payroll and HR in 2001. The contract cost represented a reduction in the council's cost base, largely by re-engineering its administrative processes. Almost 800 council staff have been seconded to LDL, which now provides the council's call-centre, ICT, HR and payroll, and revenues and benefits services. It is now providing services which were previously provided by several council departments.

By streamlining services and using the latest technology, LDL is saving council taxpayers £5m a year and providing a better, more efficient service for the people of the city. The city council's call centre is now the largest council-run call centre in the UK, open 24 hours a day, seven days a week, allowing people to get in touch with the council at any time of day or night. The call centre receives more than 45,000 calls a week and nine out of every ten enquiries are resolved first time without the call having to be passed to another department.

Through LDL, the city council has also set up nine one-stop shops, bringing council services to the heart of communities, and allowing people to get information and advice about the council on their own doorstep. Between April 2002 and March 2003, the one-stop shops dealt with 450,000 requests for service, resolving eight out of ten enquiries straightaway. In April 2004 the Audit Commission judged Liverpool's customer contact as 'good' with 'excellent' prospects for improvement.

In late 2001 Bedfordshire County Council selected HBS to operate a range of support services that would reduce the annual cost of the transferred services by £10.8 million (based on 2001 prices) over ten years. The agreement included 2 per cent efficiency savings, an investment of £7.8 million in new information technology (primarily by the introduction of a SAP resource management system), an investment in improving accommodation, the development of a customer contact centre and the creation of a regional business centre.

The fact that the Bedfordshire agreement was terminated in late 2005 should not disguise the groundbreaking nature of its formation and the powerful message it, together with the other partnerships, sent out.

THE FOURTH WAVE

The National Procurement Strategy for Local Government (Office of the Deputy Prime Minister 2003b) makes reference to local authority collaboration as a theme running through it. It includes the target that 'by 2005 Councils should identify opportunities for collaboration with neighbouring councils for shared commissioning and/or delivery of services'. It also says that collaboration amongst local councils will be promoted through new regional centres of excellence (RCEs) in procurement and project management, and that local councils will be expected to join these centres of excellence. Its definition of collaboration is: 'the various ways in which councils and other public bodies come together to combine their buying power, to procure or commission goods, works or services jointly or to create shared services. Collaboration is a form of public–public partnership. Its major benefits are economies of scale and accelerated learning.'

The RCEs are owned and managed by local government and have been established with support from the government (ODPM) and the Local Government Association (LGA). Governance structures and delivery plans enable councils from across the region to play an active part. The RCEs are hosted by councils and have management boards and member forums that have representatives from a cross-section of councils in their region. The main roles for the RCEs include:

- acting as the first point of contact for local councils in relation to the efficiency agenda;
- co-ordinating and analysing data relating to local authority performance across the four workstreams to enable decision-makers in councils to understand the options for improved performance;

- providing support, including identifying and bringing to bear available resources, to local authority-led projects designed to achieve efficiencies;
- developing opportunities for shared working across local councils and the wider public sector, involving, where appropriate, the private and the voluntary and community sectors; and
- coordinating the support for local councils to ensure that the efforts of individual organizations support the needs of the region.

Since their creation the RCEs have 'pump primed' a significant number of collaborations/sharings.

Perhaps the biggest impetus, however, was the Gershon Report which was the result of a public services efficiency review announced by the Chancellor of the Exchequer in April 2003. Published in June 2004, the report is a comprehensive attempt to recast thinking about the way government does business. Though it covers both central and local government, important elements are related to local councils. It aims to:

- make annual savings of up to £20bn by 2007, around £13bn of which could be recycled into other priorities;
- reduce the running costs of central government by 16 per cent (£5.5bn);
- identify substantial savings in the £15bn costs of 'bureaucracy and red tape' for both public and private sectors;
- drive forward the government's reform agenda by:
  - reshaping and simplifying the relationships between government and the front line
  - aggressively realizing the benefits of current investments
  - significantly cutting operating costs of local government, housing associations and construction by better management of the market
  - increasing e-government transaction take-up by a factor of ten
  - relocating functions out of the affluent south east
  - developing better back office functions to support top managers and the front line, with more professional senior staff and coherent systems.

In support of these aims, six workstreams were singled out as having the greatest potential for efficiency improvements, namely procurement; the back office; transactional services; public sector policy, funding and regulation (PFR); private sector PFR; and productive time. Some of these are clearly interlinked but references to sharing were evident in most of the streams, as shown in Figure 3.3.

The different routes to sharing

ROUTES

Before sharing is contemplated by any council they are likely to engage in a debate about whether they need to share. This debate is likely to result from pressure to improve economy, effectiveness or efficiency. Traditionally a council tends to seek to achieve its objectives 'in-house' before it resorts to sharing. Figure 3.4 describes the possibilities the council may have before it needs to consider sharing. The relative complexity of the different routes will vary from council to council.

• Procurement – Procurement will account for £120 billion by 2005–6 and comprises nearly half of all local government spending. Despite these huge totals, however, the public sector is paradoxically a weak and fragmented customer, capable neither of squeezing value from the supply chain nor of shaping the market to its advantage in the long term. Demand is shared among no less than 34,000 purchasing organizations operating independently, there is little sharing of experience and knowledge across organisations and professionalism is in short supply. By increasing professionalism, better management of the market and consolidating procurement in focused clusters, the review aimed at the interim stage to produce savings of £7.15 billion in 2007–08.

• Back office functions – Effective administrative functions such as ICT, finance, HR, and estate management are essential to support service delivery by front-line staff. They currently consume around 25 per cent of resources (£8.6 billion) in central government and 10 per cent (£20 billion) in the public sector overall. There is enormous disparity and duplication across the public sector, with potential for equally large savings through economies of scale gained by sharing policies, processes and transaction support services across 'clusters' of organizationally or geographically related organisations. By such means the government wants to see continuous improvement yielding a 30 per cent cost reduction in the back offices of central government by 2008 and a 6 per cent reduction in those for other public sector organizations by 2007 – efficiency savings of £2 billion in all.

• Transactional services – Government currently spends £11.5 billion a year and employs 250,000 people in administering taxes and benefits of various kinds, mostly in self-contained vertical 'silos'. For example, 300 local councils collect council tax, 400 process housing benefit. Limited data sharing means applicants are asked the same questions on many occasions, government presents multiple interfaces to each customer segment, citizen/customer data cannot be looked at as a coherent whole, and outsourcing takes place piecemeal. By switching customers to cheaper e-channels, reducing duplication and joining up the front end around customer groups (for example, a unified retail network for working age claimants), the review reckons savings of 20 per cent should be possible by 2010.

• Sharing services and functions – Examples of services that can be shared:

– procurement
– front line customer contact
– call centre/Internet customer contact
– payroll and human resources
– recruitment and training
– processing payments, financial management and treasury
– electronic records and case management
– ICT
– housing management
– building management
– estate management
– legal services
– command and control centres for emergency services
– fraud inspectorates
– bailiff services
– physical security
– disaster recovery.

Joining up is therefore critical at all levels. The interim review says that over the public sector as a whole there are no less than 30,000 back offices employing 4m staff at a cost of £200 billion, but only 1000 are full-scale operations. Data for functions such as IT, HR and finance show wide performance variations within government and between government and the wider public sector. This yields a large potential for sharing and consolidation – just 5 per cent of central government bodies and 2 per cent of wider public sector bodies are large enough to justify their own back-office transactional support services, according to the review. Just bringing standards up to public sector best levels would save £2 billion by April 2007.

Figure 3.3   Workstreams resulting from the Gershon Report

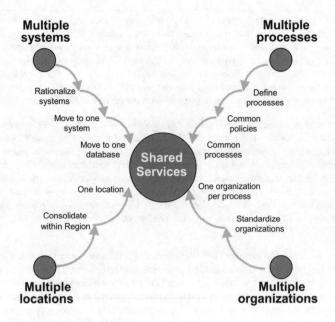

Figure 3.4   Routes towards shared services

The process of undertaking this type of analysis may also lead to cost efficiencies and improved service delivery but, most importantly, it is likely the council through this process will have comprehensively reviewed the service under consideration and formed a high level view of the strengths and weaknesses of that service. Such an analysis may also have created the opportunity for the 'sharing' of service internally.

Another advantage of taking on this analysis before reaching the conclusion that sharing is required is that the council will have 'sweated the asset' of its service and should have refined the service and maximized the efficiency and effectiveness of the service. Potentially this makes for easier sharing since the service will be the 'best' possible.

It also makes the sharing process easier as the details of the service under consideration are better understood and the specification of the service required has been tested and clarified.

Investigating these possibilities are the traditional ways in which councils have achieved efficiencies. However, as we have seen before, the potential opportunities are becoming less and less as the volume of council spend is reduced. As a result looking at sharing is more and more common.

Once a council decides it has maximized the value it obtains from a service then the council needs to conduct a high-level review of the potential for sharing. This must include an analysis of the likely benefits and risks that might be obtained.

MODELS

To decide which model is 'best' depends heavily on what the aims of the council are. Up until now, because of the strong traditional hierarchical structures of councils, sharings have tended to focus on sharing identifiable services/functions.

Therefore for the purposes of the analysis of sharings to date (as demonstrated through the case studies in Chapters 4, 5 and 6) the 'models' of sharing are based on the organization of councils through individual services.

The four models are:

1. 'Intra-service' to describe a sharing where the sharing relates to only part of a service;
2. 'Service' where there is a sharing of a complete service but the organization is not changed to meet the challenge of the sharing;
3. 'Corporate' where there is a change of the local councils organization (such as the setting up of a management group);
4. 'Supra-corporate' where there is a new or different organization created to provide or support the shared service.

It must be emphasized that this type of analysis is somewhat artificial and many existing examples of shared services display evidence from more than one category. However, as a working categorization it does allow the identification of models of possible service delivery (see Figure 3.5).

The models explained

INTRA-SERVICE MODEL – COLLABORATION ON SPECIFIC AND/OR SPECIALIST SERVICES

This model could allow a single or several services or councils to share aspects of a service. This could, at its most basic level, provide for services to gain goods and services from a central agency such as a purchasing consortium.

The model is useful where one or more local councils combine operations with a view to generating synergies and economies of scale. The powers to use this arrangement come from the Local Government (Goods and Services) Act 1970. Regional procurement models already widely operate where local councils can become subscribed members of a regional purchasing consortia (for example ESPO and YPO), who are able to provide procurement and purchasing services to members (credit assessment, bulk purchase supplies, e-catalogues and other services).

All of the risk of service delivery stays with the local council providing the service.

SERVICE MODEL – SHARED SERVICE WHERE ONE 'SHARER' TRANSFERS RESPONSIBILITY TO ANOTHER

Generally (as in agency arrangements) one council allows another to provide the service with a transfer of control and responsibility. A degree of formality would be required as such a shared service implies that some responsibility has transferred between two or more councils. Because management responsibility will have been transferred it is likely the 'lead' council would control all the budget belonging to the 'shared' service, the service specification and possibly the responsibility for fulfilling statutory responsibilities. This would probably involve the adoption of the host authority's systems and procedures of operation. The transfer of staff could be undertaken either by secondment (where the subsidiary authority could 'take back' its staff) or by transfer/TUPE (where the lead authority could agree to maintain the other authority's employee terms and conditions).

This would involve the development of service-level agreements and contracts for the outsourced services and would run on a longer-term basis, which would allow for more robust financial and service delivery planning for all concerned parties. Contract management

Characteristics	'Intra-service' Model	'Service' Model	'Corporate' Model	'Supra-corporate' Model
Degree of informality of arrangement	Informal/formal	Informal/formal	Formal	Formal
Type of agreement	None/agreement	Service level agreement/ agreement	Agreement/contract	Agreement/contract
Legal basis	Local Government (Goods and Services) Act 1970	Local Government (Goods and Services) Act 1970/ Section 101 Local Government Act 1972	Section 101 Local Government Act 1972/ Joint Boards (Section 20 LGA 2000)/Public Sector Consortiums, Pooled Budget and Joint Commissioning (Section 16 LGA 1999).	Joint Venture Companies / Local Authority Company (Section 2 LGA 2000).
Risk transference	None	Limited	Limited/moderate	Substantial
Management arrangement	Normal management	Normal management	Supervisory joint committee	Special purpose vehicle
Example	Yorkshire Purchasing Organization	Wellingborough and Northampton councils. National Non-Domestic Rates Collection Service	Anglia Revenues Partnership	ConsortiumAudit (Northampton, Kettering, Corby and Wellingborough district councils); Trading company – NPS Property Consultants Ltd, wholly owned by Norfolk County Council.

Figure 3.5   The four models characteristics

systems would need to be established and the cost and difficulties involved in this should not be underestimated.

CORPORATE MODEL – TWO OR MORE COUNCILS JOIN TOGETHER TO 'SHARE' A SERVICE

In this 'model' (see Figure 3.6) the partners join together and form an arrangement to deliver services. The implication is that there would be an agreement on the standard of service to be delivered. This would have to be negotiated and agreed. Because the application of this model implies that there is a 'sharing' of not just benefits but also costs of the shared service there is likely to be the need for the creation of a joint governing body to sit between the 'sharing' councils and the delivery body.

This does not imply that the delivery body has to be a separate organization. One of the partners could assume the lead in delivering a service for the whole of the shared service. Staff could transfer to this council but would work flexibly across the service within various specialisms as appropriate. This might involve the adoption of the lead authority's systems and procedures of operation, terms and conditions of employment, and the pooling of all budgets under the host authority.

Alternatively, whilst management control would be transferred to one council, the shared service could operate with pooled budgets, separate policies and processes and staff employed by the two individual sharers. Any changes would have to be negotiated between the sharers. This would allow for more robust financial and service delivery planning for all concerned parties.

SUPRA-CORPORATE MODEL – SHARING BASED ON CREATION OF SPECIAL PURPOSE VEHICLE TO DELIVER THE SERVICE OUTCOMES

In this model (see Figure 3.7) the partners join together and form an arrangement to deliver services. All of the partners join together and form a special purpose vehicle to deliver services on behalf of all the partners. The councils will specify the service they wish to have delivered and the anticipated outcomes. Because all of the risk is transferred the delivery vehicle would control all of the assets and the means of delivery.

The sharing councils may choose one of a number of differently structured delivery vehicles. The choice will depend primarily on the amount of risk to be transferred, but it is possible that the sharers would choose to retain the staff and second them to the delivery

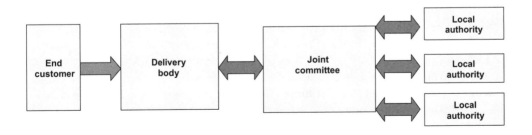

Figure 3.6   Model of a corporate shared service

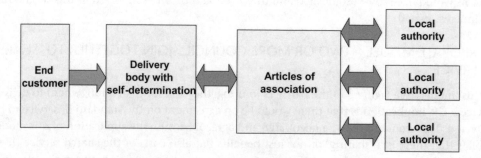

Figure 3.7   Model of supra-corporate shared service

vehicle, thus retaining a substantial part of the risk. At the other end of the scale, all staff would transfer to this new entity and the councils would thereby minimize the risk to them as in the event of failure the special purpose vehicle would have to meet the costs.

A variety of different structures are possible. The choice will depend on the wishes of the sharing councils, this depending in turn upon the number of partners and the form of engagement the partners would wish to undertake, how much liability the respective partners wish to retain and what levels of control the respective partners would wish to have.

Local Authority Company (LACos) is a collective term for all companies in which local councils have interests. A regulated LACo is one that is either controlled or influenced by a local authority. Arm's-length LACos have all directors appointed for fixed terms of at least two years. Local authority members and officers make up less than 20 per cent of the directors. Directors have to act in the interests of the company rather than the councils that appointed them. The company agrees to use its best endeavours to achieve a return on assets. Secondment and TUPE staff transfer arrangements apply to all types of LACos.

There are several types of LACos including:

- *Joint ventures companies* formed for defined purposes such as provision of services, investment, development, to which two or more partners contribute, and in which they share risks and rewards. Flexible financing arrangements are secured on the assets and activities of the JVCo.
- *Companies limited by shares* are corporate bodies, owned, and operated exclusively in the interests of their shareholders. They are subject to the Companies Act, and are registered by the Companies Registrar. The functions of councils can only be delegated with specific statutory authority, but they do have access to partnering funding with price and dividend policy determined at the discretion of the board of the company. They are normally subject to the Local Authority Capital Control/Prudential Code if regulated by a local authority.
- *Companies limited by guarantee* are corporate bodies with members, not shareholders. Members guarantee to pay a fixed sum of one pound, to cover any debts of the company. They are subject to the Companies Act, and are registered by the Companies Registrar and with the Financial Standards Authority. Local authority functions can only be delegated with specific statutory authority and the company is normally subject to Local Authority Capital Control/Prudential Code if regulated by a local authority.

- *Not-for-profit organizations (NPOs)* such as industrial and provident societies, co-operatives, trusts, friendly societies and so on are subject to specific legislation, with most being for the benefit of the community. They are corporate bodies able to borrow, contract, employ staff and take legal proceedings. In general terms their members hold at least a defined minimum number of shares in the NPO and their liability for debts will be limited to their shareholding. Surpluses are re-invested in the organization and they can attract European Community and National Lottery funding. Often used to promote or improve economic, social or environmental well-being of the whole or any part of their areas.
- *Limited liability partnerships* represent a relationship between two or more people carrying out a business in common with a view to profit, but partners' liability for debts is limited to a pre-determined threshold. Local authority functions can only be delegated with specific statutory authority. The LLP has access to partnering and European Community structural funding. Local councils can make grants or loans available to LLPs.

Each option has its own regulatory control, but in general companies controlled by a local authority will need to have regard to Part V of the Local Government and Housing Act 1989, Local Councils Companies Order 1999, the Limited Liability Partnership Act 2000 and the 1985 Companies Act.

Irrespective of the vehicle chosen for joint procurement, local councils (as creatures of statute) must ensure that the arrangements they propose fall within their existing statutory powers. These may be (depending upon the circumstances) general powers such as the 'well-being' powers contained in Part 1 of the Local Government Act 2000, Section 1 of the Local Government (Contracts) Act 1997, Section 111 of the Local Government Act 1972 or any specific subordinate legislation made under Section 16 of the Local Government Act 1999 to facilitate the attainment of Best Value.

These differing vehicles are particularly useful for the introduction of a third-party involvement such as the private sector. Such vehicles have the advantage of being able to import investment and use this to redesign cost structures.

Advantages and disadvantages of the models

All of the models have some advantages and disadvantages for a local council contemplating a sharing. There are a number of matters that each model shares; others are specific. The following can only be indicative as specific circumstances are likely to give rise to many other advantages and disadvantages.

GENERAL ADVANTAGES

Sharing is designed at its most basic to produce economies of scale or removal of duplication of effort, giving the potential for greater organizational resilience and capacity. Due to the specialism provided by sharing, greater focus will lead to better systems for supporting services.

The sharing approach retains the individuality of councils and will be familiar to many councils being well supported in local government law and regulation and relatively simple in structure. Similarly, it could provide a visible and accountable delivery arrangement familiar to councils and enabling 'open book' reporting.

It does hold out the potential for step-change improvement since it allows 'good' practice to be shared and developed and standards applied by different local councils can be identified and resources pooled for the development of solutions. Such an arrangement holds out the prospect of improved consistency in service delivery with an opportunity to re-engineer service and therefore generate a step-change in efficiency, effectiveness and economy.

Sharing also allows a more focused approach to the management of risk. Potentially there will be greater organizational resilience, particularly in staff retention/recruitment, and 'sharing' can have positive impacts for transferred staff with greater options for training for the future, greater variation of work type, increased opportunities to develop and utilize skills and harmonization of salaries and terms and conditions.

Sharing between two councils is easier because of the shared understanding of the 'public sector ethos'; also it will retain the traditional relationships into the remaining parts of each sharer even though these links will have to be subject to greater formality. Sharing too, will free up resources to be transferred to other services and allows council to concentrate on services of greater strategic importance. Finally, sharing will have a positive impact on improvement judgement of external inspectorates being seen as an innovative response to the challenge of Best Value.

GENERAL DISADVANTAGES

Many councils find the concept of sharing difficult because of the implied release of control over resources, policies and practices. To an extent this is true.

Also true is that good sharing arrangements take time to establish and deliver improvement and many councils feel that it is better for them to achieve efficiencies and improvements themselves and give direct benefit to their taxpayers.

The shared service may, unless clearly tackled, have to deal with the uncertain effect of the variable political control of the two councils with a potential 'conflict of interest' and 'clashes of culture' between officers and members of the sharers (particularly if one 'sharer' seems to be in the majority and a 'client' and 'contractor' role is established) because of the loss of the governance role of one sharer which may be of concern to some members. This could lead to loss of public accountability and audit regulation unless clear reporting is maintained. There would be a need also to overcome the service standards applied and investment profiles of different councils.

Steps would have be taken to deal with the statutory reporting issues (who 'owns' relevant Best Value performance indicators) and this could lead to a lack of independence to develop 'new delivery methods'.

There will be staff concerns and perceived threat to middle management in the council 'giving up' the service. Staff displacement is particularly sensitive – redundancies in one authority and the creation of new jobs in a neighbouring authority will be difficult politically. In addition, centralization of the service may require staff relocation and staff may be unwilling or unable to relocate and TUPE and secondment may result in staff on different terms and conditions working in the new entity. If long-term secondment is used, it may complicate who is the employer, and could present problems at the end of the contract when staff return to the authority and may limit the scope for savings on staff costs. Finally, transfer of staff may signal a reduced commitment to staff, which may impact on other services. There is also an issue about 'branding' – each council will have to take a view on whether it is acceptable to have the service identified as belonging to an unfamiliar name whilst it carries out part of the council's service.

PARTICULAR ADVANTAGES OF THE INTRA-SERVICE MODEL

A sharing of only one aspect of a service (even though it is across the whole council) will have little or no impact on the 'whole' council thus being easier to 'contain' the risk and participation costs can be controlled as much as individual councils wish it to be. Because the sharing is limited, the participants retain flexibility in their use of the sharing and can minimize changes for customers/service users. It is likely that this arrangement will allow councils maximum flexibility to react to changes. This arrangement retains within a council the skills and capacity it needs to manage services.

PARTICULAR DISADVANTAGES OF THE INTRA-SERVICE MODEL

Because the sharing is relatively limited its impact on service delivery is uncertain in the mid to long term as the policies of participating councils need not be synchronized to improve service delivery. Furthermore, the outcomes are vulnerable if and when personnel change or priorities are altered in individual sharers, since there is likely to be little organizational change and impact on overall cost structures (indeed they may be worse if staff have to travel to service or support work in other councils). This general air of uncertainty may lead to a lack of clarity about achievements since there may be limited commitment shown by one partner which will produce uncertainty amongst other partners.

In addition this arrangement will not significantly enhance capacity to improve and it is not likely to create opportunities to meet rising customer expectations. Because the arrangement is generally informal there will be no transfer of risk and generally this will not be suitable for the introduction of third parties. Finally, this limited approach will have little impact on the improvement judgement of external inspectorates.

PARTICULAR ADVANTAGES OF THE SERVICE MODEL

Sharing of only one service will restrict the impact on the 'whole' council thus being easier to 'contain' the risk and the change on the remainder of the council. It restricts the need for widespread assimilation of objectives, procedures and systems between different partners but allows a more focused approach to the management of risk in the service being shared. This arrangement may retain within a council the skills and capacity it needs to manage services.

PARTICULAR DISADVANTAGES OF THE SERVICE MODEL

The sharing is likely initially not to have significant impact on costs and would not attract external investment initially since generally this is likely to be a sharing based initially on the bringing together of two or more existing functioning units. This arrangement is not likely to enhance the skills and capacity a council needs to manage services.

PARTICULAR ADVANTAGES OF THE CORPORATE MODEL

This demonstrates significant commitment by both councils to the concept of sharing that will have a cultural impact beyond the boundaries of the shared service. It also enriches the governance capability of the council and provides the opportunity for a levelling up of standards and policies.

PARTICULAR DISADVANTAGES OF THE CORPORATE MODEL

The joint committee is vulnerable if and when priorities are altered and there could be a lack of clarity about achievements. As a result there is a risk that relationships between the joint committee and the 'home' councils could become strained and staff in the 'middle' of this may find themselves having their loyalties divided between their 'home' council and the 'shared' service. If the joint committee pursues staff reduction, the redundancy costs and the pension implications must be settled.

The joint committee is not a separate corporate entity and, therefore, cannot contract in its own right which means the shared service is still constrained by the risk and financial policies of the sharing councils. As a result the shared service could be constrained for future ongoing investment.

There will also be a potential impact on the support services of the 'home' councils and the cost of managing the relationship with the shared service may be prohibitive. Also the flexibility of one council to respond to change is restricted.

PARTICULAR ADVANTAGES OF THE SUPRA-CORPORATE MODEL

Creating a special purpose vehicle allows partner councils to avoid a disagreement over who should take the major risk and avoids any difficulties caused by historical difficulties and rivalries. The decision to adopt this model demonstrates significant commitment by both councils to the concept of sharing that will have a cultural impact beyond the boundaries of the shared service.

Giving clarity of governance, as an independent legal entity it provides a visible and accountable delivery arrangement familiar to councils and enabling 'open book' reporting. However, the partners do not take on additional not-for-profit distributing organization (NPDO)/company law responsibilities.

Potentially there can be positive impacts for transferred staff as there may be greater options for career development in potentially a wider 'industry'. This model does also give more flexible operating costs, for example in the hiring and firing of staff. It allows a more focused approach to the management of risk which is held by the special purpose vehicle and risks are allocated and managed by the party best positioned to manage them. It also frees up trading opportunities for the special purpose vehicle to work with other councils. If bidding for external work and income generation are strategic aims, there may be no job losses and even job creation in the areas of the partner councils. The model also makes it easier to determine and manage payment and liability issues and can create an opportunity for income generation through profit sharing. It can also provide for a limit on risk. Such an arrangement will be a useful vehicle to attract investment and can widen the availability of business skills to the partner councils. Finally, this will have a positive impact on the improvement judgement of external inspectorates, being seen as an innovative response to the challenge of Best Value.

PARTICULAR DISADVANTAGES OF THE SUPRA-CORPORATE MODEL

There is potentially a high set-up cost to the supra-corporate model which cannot be undertaken in a fully equalized way as a lead partner will be required (to lead on the procurement of the service provider if nothing else) and financial start-up costs may be difficult to fund (particularly of procurement costs).

Partnering in the public sector of this type is comparatively new, without an established 'track record'. The shared service will have to deal with the uncertain effect of the variable political control of the two councils and may have to deal with the conflict between any members who are part of the management of the special purpose vehicle and those outside it; loss of the governance role in the area being shared may be of concern to some members. This could lead to loss of public accountability and audit regulation unless clear reporting is maintained as there may be a reduction of transparency of transactions due to commercial confidentiality. This could cause complications as functions cannot be delegated. There is the danger of conflict with a council's regulatory role unless council retains decision-making in relevant services. Such a move could conflict with the public service ethos unless carefully managed.

The service standards applied and the investment profiles of different councils are further obstacles to be overcome. Without assimilation of objectives, procedures and systems between different parties the potential for conflict remains. Introducing a third party into the setting of objectives, procedures and systems between the partners is a further complication. The partners may need to ensure important values, for example in terms of equality, equity and environment, are maintained by the special purpose vehicle. A council's flexibility to respond to change, whilst not necessarily restricted, can only be achieved through the special purpose vehicle and this is likely to require contractual change to achieve.

The special purpose vehicle may be vulnerable if and when priorities are altered and there could be a lack of clarity about achievements.

There will also be potential impact on the support services of the 'home' councils and the cost of managing the relationship with the shared service may be prohibitive with two sets of relationships having to be managed (that is, between the partners and between the partnership and the service provider). There are also NPDO/company filing requirements and potential exposure to taxation.

Also, having the service undertaken by a third party reduces the flexibility of councils in that the vehicle will 'control' an element of service and resources. Furthermore, should the third party 'fail', the council will have to create a new structure to deliver the service.

The choice of a model

Which model is selected depends to a large extent on the results of the potential partners' high-level view. This analysis will indicate what the sharers wish to achieve from their sharing. The analysis of advantages and disadvantages above demonstrate the often fine balances between these and the difficulty of making definitive conclusions without knowing the detail of any particular situation.

In a sharing the services being brought together need to be carefully analysed for their cost, performance and quality and compared in detail before the most appropriate model can be assessed as best meeting the desired outcomes. The case studies outlined in the next chapter demonstrate the range of outcomes from sharings and the wide spread of possibilities.

A definitive analysis is difficult as how the best model for any sharing of services in local government is best chosen has never been proven in quantifiable terms, and there is little empirical evidence. The headlines that are publicly available and positively promoted as in the Gershon Report all suggest that the more ambitious the sharing (or transfer to a third party) the more benefit is likely to be obtained. However, as there is no central register of joint working nor is there comprehensive unit cost data on which to base conclusions, firm evidence is not prominently available. Furthermore there has been little evaluation of the success or otherwise of sharing. Where there are longstanding sharings such as in procurement consortia there is a presumption they continue to exist because of the financial advantage they offer councils. But there are councils that restrict their participation and must therefore achieve the same or better benefit from making their own arrangements preferring to carry their own risks because of the certainty it brings.

We will return to this issue in later chapters as the evidence of the case studies captured in the next three chapters will give some clarity to it. Whatever that indicates, the case for exploration of sharing now seems almost unarguable in that the reasons for not sharing have been swamped by the four waves outlined above and councils, particularly smaller councils, have limited room for manoeuvre. Whether it be because of limited availability of resources, the need to make significant improvement, or aspirations for self-induced change or delivery of the government's agenda, the tide seems unstoppable.

The only issue that has to be resolved for many councils is what to share and how. The following chapter describes the available evidence of what has been happening through a review of some of the many existing sharings and will give a basis for councils to choose the service and model they can use to achieve their aims.

4 Shared Services Case Studies

Introduction

Despite the extensive public scrutiny of councils it is not easy to get a clear picture of the extent of shared services in councils. There is no specific requirement to report them except as part of normal reporting by individual councils to their public or through bilateral relationships with the government, the Audit Commission, the Local Government Association or bodies such as the Improvement and Development Agency (IDeA).

It is, however, possible to get some clues from the annual efficiency statements (AESs) now required from each council. Because these are directed at demonstrating how each council will achieve the targets set out in the Gershon agenda these are not exclusively about shared services. A degree of interpretation is therefore required. As a result the picture is incomplete. Many 'shared services' listed are not mentioned by the council with which another council claims to be sharing services and many councils use the term 'partnership' to describe their arrangement.

In addition some councils will consider such arrangements as now so commonplace that they are not of high enough importance to feature in these statements. A reading of the analysis also demonstrates the different terms used to describe the shared services thus confirming the impossibility of being definitive.

CASE STUDIES

As said above, collecting case studies on shared services is not easy and this makes analysis difficult. Moreover the focus of this book is on those sharings that are most recent and have stretched the capacity of councils through their own determination to improve rather than continue to focus on traditional areas of collaboration. Therefore this chapter is split into three. The first section illustrates examples of the five most common types of shared service in local government: highways, procurement, waste, e-government and supporting people. Though these are important sharings that have driven improvement in delivery of service they are the result (with the exception of procurement) of direct government intervention or, as in the case of highways, the result of a shared statutory function responsibility.

The second section of the chapter is extracted from the annual efficiency statements for 2005–6 and shows the range of services currently being shared and the variety of ways they are described. This does not list the many references to the five areas of highways, procurement, waste, e-government and supporting people, except where there is reference to a sharing outside the types of sharings described in the earlier part of the chapter.

The third section gives detail on those examples of sharing where it has been possible to source additional information. Those mentioned are not necessarily those that are most advanced, most extensive or most innovative. They do, however, display many of the features outlined in the previous chapter thus providing a good illustration of the current range and nature of shared services. In the third section the case studies have been categorized into the structure outlined in Chapter 3. This section does not generally seek to outline the benefits from the sharing – these are shown in Chapter 7 where conclusions are outlined as to whether the evidence of improved outcomes and benefits from the sharing is evident.

The five most common areas for sharing

The five most common types of shared service in local government are highways, procurement, waste, e-government and supporting people. Examples of each type of sharing follow. The examples chosen are indicative and are not included (and others excluded) because of a judgement as to whether these are the 'best' or most prominent examples.

HIGHWAYS: STAFFORDSHIRE HIGHWAYS PARTNERSHIP

The county council carries out all highway maintenance functions in the county and manages over 3000 miles of roads. This covers road maintenance and co-ordinating the work of other services which may involve the need to disrupt the road, such as water and gas. It operates computerized urban traffic control systems that help maintain the flow of traffic in busy towns. Roads signs and road safety programmes are other responsibilities, and currently around £150 million is being invested in new street lighting. Also it maintains road bridges and cycle paths. A dedicated fleet of gritters and snow-ploughs keep the traffic moving in winter. There is a single call centre for all residents to use for all highways-related matters.

The Staffordshire Highways partnership approach claims to be delivering a wide range of benefits:

- major economies of scale in purchasing
- long-term investment in quality
- a committed, stable and highly skilled workforce
- greater accountability
- commitment to innovation and value for money
- close co-operation and monitoring delivering for the long term
- planning and programming improvements.

Recently Staffordshire Highways formed a public/private partnership which is delivering the county's highway maintenance and construction projects. Over the next ten years £300 million will be invested, with two private sector partners, Accord and Wrekin Construction.

PROCUREMENT: EASTERN SHIRES PURCHASING ORGANIZATION

Eastern Shires Purchasing Organization (ESPO) is a local authority purchasing and distribution consortium, formed in early 1981 by the county councils of Leicestershire and Lincolnshire. Cambridgeshire County Council joined later in the same year, and Norfolk, Warwickshire, Leicester City Council and Peterborough City Council joined later.

ESPO as a joint committee of local councils operates within the Local Government (Goods and Services) Act 1970. It acts as a purchasing agent for its member councils and other customers and provides a professional cost-effective procurement and supply service. The annual turnover exceeds £400 million and the procurement services provided can be grouped into four categories as follows:

- A strategic role offering best practice relating to the procurement function as a whole. ESPO offers leading-edge advice on major complex procurement and contracting issues, competition and services, Best-Value-driven reviews of service provision and one-off project-based procurements. This aspect of procurement activity and expertise has grown significantly.
- A procurement role for goods and services commonly used by a number of customers throughout the consortium area. This type of activity includes framework call-off contracts and some local contracting where local issues are of key consideration.
- A catalogue-based provision where ESPO is able to purchase products in volume (usually low-value, high-volume type products) from manufacturers in the main, and the resultant economies of scale means that it operates a central warehouse and delivers to customers using a combination of its own and contracted transport. An online ordering facility is available for those who want to use it.
- A procurement service for ad hoc goods and services required by customers where advice, guidance and good practice are required. Often customers need commercial solutions to meet a need or specific requirement in this field.

As a self-financing organization utilizing the aggregate buying volumes of member councils and other customers, ESPO seeks to maximize the potential savings for all customers in every area of procurement activity. ESPO has developed a number of key performance indicators (KPIs) against which performance is assessed. Many of these KPIs are about performance of the consortia overall, for example the growth in store sales, and average stores selling price measured against the retail price index. However, some KPIs are broken down to member authority level to allow each local authority to assess the extent to which it is using ESPO and in some cases to determine the extent to which they are meeting their own targets; for example, the percentage of environmentally friendly stock purchased versus standard stock is broken down to member authority level to allow each local authority to determine the extent to which they are meeting corporate targets relating to sustainability.

WASTE: PROJECT INTEGRA

In 1993 Hampshire County Council and the 13 district councils in Hampshire undertook a county-wide public consultation process to take account of the views of Hampshire residents on how to deal with the county's waste problem. The consultation process resulted in the introduction of an integrated waste management strategy, known as Project Integra, adopted by the 11 district councils of Hampshire, Portsmouth and Southampton unitary councils, Hampshire County Council, and the private waste contractor Hampshire Waste Services. Links were established within a wider network, including parish councillors, community groups and education, and these links are still being developed.

Project Integra was formed on the basis of the following seven-point action plan:

1. Action on waste minimization.
2. Action on composting.
3. Action on recycling.
4. Support for anaerobic digestion.
5. Use of recovery technologies, including incineration.
6. Three to five waste-processing facilities (not exceeding 200,000 tonnes per annum).
7. Residual waste to landfill.

Developments have been made in terms of infrastructure with the provision of:

- two materials recovery facilities (located in Portsmouth and Alton)
- three centralized composting sites
- nine transfer stations
- a network of 26 household waste recycling centres
- three energy recovery incinerators (located in Chineham, Marchwood and Portsmouth).

A county-wide promotional campaign, known as War on Waste, was launched in 1996, aimed at raising awareness about waste minimization and recycling issues. Current campaigns are more focused, being determined by information from the Project Integra research programme.

The mechanics and principles for the joint working arrangements are established in the following ways:

- A joint memorandum of understanding setting out the principles of the respective local councils' responsibilities and obligations supported by all Project Integra partners.
- A tripartite contract management agreement between Hampshire County Council and the two unitary councils of Portsmouth and Southampton.
- A formal meeting structure to include representation by all Project Integra partners at officer and elected member level.
- A proposal for a formal agreement to share income and risks from the sale of recyclables.
- A Project Integra joint service plan agreement setting out detailed objectives and responsibilities for the next year.
- A joint waste volume planning process establishing service needs and aspirations for the next five years.
- A joint promotional campaign focusing on waste minimization and recycling.

Project Integra has established an elected-member-led management board, and a policy review and scrutiny committee which came into effect on 25 July 2001. This introduces a clearer and more accountable framework to enable Project Integra to respond more effectively to the challenges of dealing with waste in the future. The agreed objectives of the management board are:

- to develop a long-term vision for waste as a resource;
- to prepare and co-ordinate the production and publication of a joint recycling plan;
- to interact with other stakeholders to promote waste minimization and to achieve an economically, environmentally and socially sustainable waste valorization programme;
- to work with and support other bodies who are in pursuit of developing, supporting and influencing the future direction of sustainable waste/resource management;
- to manage waste from outside Hampshire or from commercial and industrial sources if beneficial to Project Integra and Hampshire's residents;
- to follow the principles of Best Value;
- to produce an annual business plan to set out the future financial, marketing and service direction of Project Integra;
- to conduct any other activity in accordance within the general scope of responsibility, provided it continues to promote, develop or secure the role of Project Integra.

The policy review and scrutiny committee helps set the future agenda as well as challenging and reviewing the actions of the management board. Both the management board and policy review and scrutiny committee meetings will be held in public unless there are matters of a commercial and therefore confidential nature.

Project Integra was awarded Beacon Council status by the DETR for *Sustainable Development – dealing with waste* in December 1999. In terms of outcomes, though household waste collected for 2004–5 was 846,048 tonnes per annum (which is an increase of just over 14,000 tonnes on 2003–4), the Project Integra overall recycling rate, including composting, has risen from 7.9 per cent in 1995–6 to 27.24 per cent in 2004–5. Over 95 per cent of Hampshire's households now have access to a kerbside collection of recyclables.

E-GOVERNMENT: STAFFORDSHIRE E-GOVERNMENT PARTNERSHIP

The partnership between Staffordshire County Council, Stoke on Trent City Council, Cannock Chase District Council, East Staffordshire Borough Council, Lichfield District Council, Newcastle under Lyme Borough Council, South Staffordshire District Council, Stafford Borough Council, Staffordshire Moorlands District Council and Tamworth Borough Council was started in 2001 at the start of the IEG1 statement process. Since then it has been working on a number of e-government projects.

The major achievement has been the introduction across ten councils of a single customer relationship management (CRM) system which will give customer service advisors the information they need to sort out an estimated 80 per cent of requests at first point of contact. The CRM has a logging and tracking function which will enable advisors to report back to customers whose requests cannot be dealt with straightaway. Priorities for further development of CRM in 2006 include the adoption of government-developed authentication products which will allow customers to set up online accounts enabling them to request services which require them to prove their identity. Examples include applying for free school meals or Housing Benefit. Already, the websites of the ten councils enable customers to apply electronically for services not requiring authentication. The partners have the same data capture processes which will allow them to accept service requests for each other from a date to be agreed.

Service advisors using CRM are helped by the partnership's joined-up directory, which enables communication at the click of a mouse between more than 12,000 employees across the partners plus Staffordshire Police. The directory allows service advisors to resolve requests for customers or point them in the right direction. Customer convenience has been further improved by the fact that all partners now offer e-payments, allowing citizens to pay for council services 24/7 by internet and automated telephone payment, or by ordinary telephone call during office hours.

Partners are now developing a joint telephony system which will enable incoming calls to be routed accurately to general and specialist service advisors, and will allow partners to accept calls for each other outside office hours from a date to be determined.

The partnership ('brand' name: Staffordshire Connects) is organized and run under MSP (Managing Successful Programmes) methodology with PRINCE2 governing the individual projects. At the top they have a joint committee with its own constitution which all partner councils are signed up to. This meets quarterly and is made up of officer and member e-champions. Having a partnership of equals, where each local authority has one vote at committee level and the Chair of the committee is the chief executive from one of the district councils, is seen as an important success factor. The structure is described in Figure 4.1.

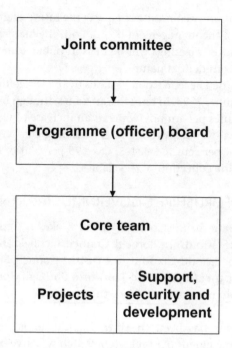

Figure 4.1   Structure of the Staffordshire e-Government Partnership

Sitting beneath the joint committee is the officer board (or programme board) which meets monthly and is made up of the e-champions from each partner authority. This board has responsibility for delivering the projects.

The partnership also has a programme director, a role that rotates every six months and is filled from the member councils, and a full-time programme manager who runs the project office which is staffed by a full-time quality assurance and technical assurance officer, and a full-time programme support officer. The partnership is also recruiting a full-time communications manager and a full-time external funding officer.

Under all this sit the projects. The executive role on each project is an e-champion and the remainder of the project management will include a senior supplier, senior customer and the project manager (some are sourced from the councils themselves, others may be consultants).

Lichfield District Council, one of the partners, said in its 2005–6 annual efficiency statement, that the joint purchase of the CRM system has already saved the partnership of the order of £445,000 on capital investment. This has led onto ongoing annual savings to Lichfield through shared maintainence/upkeep costs of £35,390.

SUPPORTING PEOPLE: WILTSHIRE COUNTY SUPPORTING PEOPLE PROGRAMME

In Wiltshire the county council acts as the administering authority and works in partnership with three Wiltshire primary care trusts (Kennet and North Wiltshire Primary Care Trust, South Wiltshire Primary Care Trust and West Wiltshire Primary Care Trust) the National Probation Service and four district councils (Kennet District Council, North Wiltshire District Council, Salisbury District Council and West Wiltshire District Council). The budget for Supporting People for services in Wiltshire in 2005–6 will be £8,284,000.

The Wiltshire programme was inspected by the Audit Commission and judged as 'good'. The inspectors found many positive features in the Wiltshire arrangements in terms of its partnership aspects including:

good engagement of all organizational partners at the Supporting People officers group and the partnership board; sound governance arrangements and partnership working around care and housing provision is well established. There have been joint working arrangements in place bringing together the county, the districts and the health sector, which pre-date Supporting People. As a result there is an understanding of the individual agendas of each organization by the other members of the partnership and a willingness to reach decisions that accommodate the interests of all parties.

There are robust legal arrangements in place covering the governance of the supporting people programme in the county. Wiltshire has adopted a partnership legal agreement to define the roles and responsibilities of the partnership board (commissioning body), Supporting People officers group (core strategy group) and the administering authority. The partnership agreement has been signed by all the relevant bodies. (Adapted from Audit Commission 2005b)

Shared services declared in councils annual efficiency statements 2005–6

Analysis of the annual 2005–6 efficiency statements indicating existing shared services are shown in Figure 4.2 overleaf. The wording is that which appears in the statements.

Other shared services

INTRA-SERVICE – INFORMAL

Derwentside District Council

In a consortium with six other councils (Chester-le-Street, Teesdale, Tynedale, Wear Valley, Sedgefield and Durham), Derwentside District Council jointly acquired an Agresso finance system that allowed each council to gain the benefits of the new system at a shared cost for implementation, consultancy and training but with each council having their own tailored system.

Kerrier District Council and Penwith District Council

The councils have worked with local colleges to develop a new NVQ training programme tailor-made for the councils' workforce, addressing horticulture and conservation and other topics on the liveability agenda. This programme will transform the single-skilled ground teams into multi-tasked and flexible operational teams. Staff will be able to transfer between the councils as needs require and grounds staff will have a network of mentors and professionals to support them.

Council	Description of shared service in the 2005–6 annual efficiency statement
Alnwick District Council	'Since May 2002 the internal audit service has been delivered via a partnership agreement with Wansbeck.'
Bassetlaw District Council	'Its recently appointed Procurement Officer working closely with another 2 districts on corporate procurement issues has, started to achieve purchasing efficiencies through collaboration with other Nottinghamshire councils.' 'Provision of high quality new leisure provision for Worksop/Retford through PFI partnership arrangements with NCC.'
Blyth Valley Borough Council	'The Council ... has a number of successful examples of collaborative working in place (for example the provision of a Joint Building Control Service with a neighbouring authority).'
Boston Borough Council	'Practical steps have already been taken such as the joint procurement of internal services with a nearby authority.'
Borough of Poole and Bournemouth Borough Council	'... signed a compact which symbolises the commitment of the two councils to improve joint working.'
Bridgnorth District Council	'The Council is working closely with South Shropshire District Council on jointly delivering the benefits service. A bid has been made to the Department of Work and Pensions to progress the collaboration, secondments are taking place to standardise processes and technology is being aligned. This is seen as a pilot scheme with potential to roll out further collaborative initiatives in corporate services.'
Broadland District Council	'Partnership with County Council for legal services.'
Cambridge City Council	'successful joint arrangements already developed in a number of areas, including occupational health, recruitment advertising, waste collection and system procurement ...'
Castle Morpeth District Council	'Since May 2002 Internal Audit has been delivered in Partnership with Wansbeck.'
Cheltenham Borough Council	'The appointment of two procurement officers in a joint-working arrangement with Gloucester City Council.'
Cherwell District Council	'Collaboration on Environmental Health service provision with neighbouring local councils and other public sector providers.'
Derbyshire Dales District Council	'Procurement of website content management system in partnership with three other Derbyshire councils.'
Eastleigh Borough Council	'the appointment, jointly with Winchester City Council, of a Procurement Officer to advise on and implement good best practice ...'
Epping Forest District Council	'The Council was a founding member of the Essex Strategic Human Resources Partnership. This is a body of HR professionals from each Council in Essex which develops and introduces strategic HR interventions in line with the new County Workforce Development Plan.'

Figure 4.2   Existing shared services identified in the 2005–6 annual efficiency statements

Essex County Council	'Law and Administration provision of services to health trusts and district councils.'
Gedling Borough Council	'Currently the Council's One Stop Shop is staffed in a collaborative way by employees of the County and District Council.'
Gloucester City Council	'Employment of a shared procurement officer with a neighbouring authority, for the implementation of procurement initiatives including E-procurement, framework agreements, procurement system re-engineering, etc.'
Greater London Authority	'The GLA has established networking and collaborative processes for joint working and has put in place mechanisms to help enable wider efficiency savings across the GLA group and across London. Some examples are: • GLA Economics – lead purchaser and provider of regional economic data • DMAG – lead purchaser and provider of population data for GLA group and boroughs • Londoner – London-wide communication by the GLA and Functional Bodies • GLA Group framework agreements – in place for web design and development, PR consultancy, London opinion polling, audio visual services, planning advice consultancy and digital mapping datasets • NOTIFY – tracks children in temporary accommodation across London • BABIE – supports the identification of accommodation for the homeless • Regional Aggregation Body – GLA/LDA company will aggregate public sector spend and broadband which should deliver 10–20 per cent savings on telecom procurement across London …'
High Peak Borough Council	'The partnership with Derbyshire County Council around Emergency Planning and Derbyshire Dales District Council with regards to the Joint Strategic Housing Function are recent examples …'
Horsham District Council	'Continue joint working with Mid-Sussex Council on procurement using shared Procurement Officer. Implement NNDR and Revenues system procured in partnership with Adur Council … Implement Financial management System, jointly procured with Adur Council'
London Borough of Havering	'The Council has many well established partnerships – for example, pan-London teachers recruitment … London Connects and London Grid for Learning. …'
London Borough of Lewisham	'in the area of Social Care, a joint tendering arrangement with the London Boroughs of Newham and Tower Hamlets has created a preferred supplier list …'
Macclesfield Borough Council	'provides Payroll services for Congleton.'
Mid Devon District Council	'the HR service is currently working with other district councils to look at combined management training and a new HR system.'
Mid Sussex District Council	'the employment of a joint procurement advisor with Horsham District Council. An ICT partnership has been established with Horsham and Adur District Councils.'
Newark and Sherwood District Council	'We have recently procured a new revenues system which was acquired through collaborative tendering with three other Councils, producing significant savings for all partners.'

Figure 4.2   *Continued*

Norfolk County Council	'The County Council has already developed an efficiency skills training programme with all of the Norfolk local councils.'
North Shropshire District Council	'Currently, the Council is utilizing the services of a neighbouring Council to carry out its Car Park Enforcement.'
North Warwickshire Borough Council	'The Council ... has partnership working arrangements in a number of areas: Internal Audit; Revenues and Benefits; Information Services; Building Control. Tamworth BC lead on procurement with Lichfield – working on building maintenance ...'
Pendle Borough Council	'sharing a legal services manager with Craven District Council ...'
Penwith District Council	'At sub-regional level, we will continue to work with the Cornwall and Isles of Scilly Procurement Steering Group to develop, and take advantage of, the opportunities for joint procurement.'
Portsmouth City Council	'joint health promotion team with the Primary Care Trust, and joint working with Hampshire and Southampton on an equipment store for social care clients, the sharing of day care facilities, secure accommodation for young people and jointly developed IT systems.'
Shepway District Council	'The Council has entered into partnerships with Kent County Council to provide environmental services more efficiently and secure an improved standard against an agreed baseline over time. The strategy is based on a service delivery partnership with Kent County Council for street cleansing, grounds maintenance, sports pitch management and residual highways services. The partnership draws on Kent County Council's expertise and efficiencies derived from economies of scale. With Dover District Council in a joint audit partnership.'
Wansbeck District Council	'securing efficiencies within a partnership arrangement with a neighbouring local authority in respect of its building control service.' 'since May 2002 the internal audit service has been delivered via a partnership agreement with Alnwick District Council.'
West Devon Borough Council	'will continue with existing service delivery partnerships with other local councils (such as the Building Control partnership with Teignbridge District Council) ...'
West Lindsey District Council	'already works with other LA partners in the delivery of payroll and NNDR administration ...'
West Oxfordshire District Council	'Provision of internal audit service to other councils in Oxfordshire and currently considering consortium arrangements. Shared Benefits training and other resources with Cherwell District Council.'
Wigan Metropolitan District Council	'Operates an Agresso finance system shared with Greater Manchester Fire Authority and a Leisure Trust.'
Worthing Borough Council	'Deliver efficiency gains from joint working with Adur District Council (shared depot, shared vehicle workshop, shared management).'

Figure 4.2   *Concluded*

The councils are also developing training centres within existing open spaces focussing on horticulture and conservation. The consortium has appointed two members of staff, funded by external money, to develop a long-term programme of partnership work.

Cheshire Out-of-Hours Contact Centre

Since its inception in 2000, the Cheshire Information Consortium has worked with the county council, district and unitary councils in Cheshire, Warrington and Halton on a series of initiatives aimed at providing better information about public services in the area, and better access to that information. This work has also involved fire, police and health services, voluntary and community bodies and town and parish councils.

The partners have provided a joint out-of-hours contact centre. The contact centre deals with simple information requests and will take and forward messages where specific local or professional expertise is required 24 hours a day.

Pan London Contract Team

This began as a response to criticism from the Social Services Inspectorate about the lack of robust contractual arrangements for children's residential care across London. A team funded by the 33 London boroughs acts as a clearing house for pre-placement contracts with private and voluntary sector providers of children's residential care, and fostering agencies. It was established in 1999 and is guided by separate steering groups for residential care and one for fostering. The objective of the pre-placement contract approach is to ensure quality and Best Value in provision, and to achieve a more efficient approach to contracting.

INTRA-SERVICE – FORMAL

Surrey Jobs

The creation of this shared service followed the opportunity created by the formation of the Surrey e-Partnership with the potential of e-recruitment seeming to offer the prospect of better recruitment at lower cost. The need was heightened by pressures on recruitment and retention, including an increase in public sector funding, resulting in greater demands from a decreasing resource pool, and high housing costs which prohibited many people from moving to the area. In addition, Surrey's proximity to London meant that employers in the public sector have to compete with London-weighted salaries. Unemployment in Surrey is low.

The objectives of the project were:

- to give an online presence at affordable prices for all partners through the economies of scale gained from a partnership approach
- to foster collective learning in the new area of e-recruitment
- to create a one-stop shop for candidates to view and access public sector jobs in Surrey which could reach a number of key groups who were currently under-represented in the Surrey public sector workforce (including ethnic minorities, the young, the disabled).

The project could also streamline and simplify the application procedure and cut the time and costs of recruitment (especially advertising expenditure). The project was expected to improve retention within Surrey's public sector by allowing existing staff to search easily and view vacancies within partner organizations, raising the profile of Surrey's public sector jobs and making opportunities more widely known (including to potential incomers to the area), and enhancing the image of public sector working by presenting it in a more attractive, modern way.

The partners joined together and entered into a partnership with a private sector partner Jobs Go Public (JGP). JGP would create www.surreyjobs. The project began early in 2002 and the website was launched on 1 July 2003.

The partners in the project include 12 district councils, the county council, Guildford College, Surrey Probation Service and a housing association. Runnymede Borough Council initially took on the role of lead authority for the project, but Mole Valley District Council has now taken on the lead role and position as chair of the board. A management board was set up for governance of the project and the product and included an HR representative from each core sub-sector of the partnership (local authorities, further education, health, crime and disorder) that had ultimate responsibility for recruitment within their organizations. Board members were appointed to also act as conduits for the other partner organizations within their respective sub-sector. The board also had representation from the private partner, Jobs Go Public, and the Surrey e-Partnership project manager, along with support from the Surrey e-Partnership. The board's role includes:

- directing joint e-recruitment and retention;
- allocating resources and proper management of funds;
- setting priorities for the partnership and allocating work;
- establishing working groups, co-ordinating their work and receiving regular reports on progress;
- maintaining policies and procedures and monitoring the use of the joint service by partners;
- promoting the use of Surrey Jobs;
- promoting externally to the public and potential partners wherever possible;
- understanding issues/problems;
- communicating and consulting with partners.

An initial investment was made from each partner to the Surrey e-Partnership for delivery of the project but partners would pay for the service directly to JGP once the site was launched. There continues to be a joint budget for project management. The costs for developing the initial solution for the shared service were in general split equally across all partners, apart from those organizations with a significantly larger or smaller workforce than the average, as it was felt that they in return would see greater or fewer benefits than the rest. The ongoing project management is supported from the shared budget whilst there is a direct payment from each organization to JGP for the service under contractual terms.

Northumberland and Durham County Councils E-Business Suite

Northumberland and Durham county councils signed a deal with Oracle to share an integrated software package to modernize and streamline their procurement and financial management systems. Northumberland County Council, which will host the application for Durham, had been using Oracle E-Business Suite since 2004 and under the arrangement Durham's finance and procurement functions will be hosted on Northumberland's systems. The plan is that Northumberland's Oracle E-Business Suite will replace Durham's Geac Smartstream finance application by 2008. Durham needed to update its Geac system but by using Northumberland's system will be far cheaper than implementing a new system of its own. Northumberland benefits by sharing the cost of maintaining the Oracle E-Business Suite software that it implemented.

The sharing is enabling the councils to share more complex, embedded systems and the councils will benefit from a reciprocal mirroring of their data centres to provide business continuity. Further down the line, Northumberland is also planning to link up with the shared customer relationship management application that Durham is using under a shared services agreement with the eight district councils in the county. Durham provides Derwentside District Council's IT services under an earlier shared services deal. As part of the project, Durham County Council will move its systems on to a new data centre. Once the data centre is operational, a joint project team of Durham and Northumberland IT staff will make it a live back-up for Northumberland's systems. At the same time, a second joint project team will set up Northumberland's data centre in Morpeth as the live back-up for Durham's systems, thereby completing the circle and giving both councils comparatively low-cost business continuity systems. Derwentside District Council will also benefit from free business continuity systems. Northumberland is rolling out a range of Oracle modules in the run up to its shared business continuity systems going live. These include training, administration, property management and enterprise asset management. In 2007, it plans to deploy a time management module, a balanced scorecard and an enterprise recruitment module – functions that will not be available to Durham initially but which potentially it could take advantage of in the future.

The final piece in the jigsaw will be Northumberland implementing the same version of Oracle CRM that is being used by Durham and its district councils. No definite timeframe has been set but Northumberland expects to be using the system within the next few years.

Pan London school admissions service

A shared school admissions Service in London was set up to co-ordinate secondary admissions based on the DfES Code of Practice for School Admissions and achieve a reduction in multiple offers, ensure more parents had their highest possible offer earlier in the process and ensure there were fewer parents without an offer of a place from a school.

The system, essentially a centralized system-based 'matching', allows single applications for schools across London involving 33 London boroughs and six neighbouring authorities through a single online portal. This improves the co-ordination of secondary admissions across London.

SERVICE – INFORMAL

Kent Benefits Partnership

The Kent Benefits Partnership (KBP) involves all of the 13 benefits councils in Kent and Medway and Kent County Council. The project aims to maximize council tax benefit take-up in the area. The partnership processes new claims for council tax benefit for pensioner owner-occupiers for ten of the 13 councils.

The team of assessment staff has access to all five different computer systems operated by the councils involved. The IT links were enabled by the Kent Connects project and by Kent County Council's ICT staff working with ICT staff in each district. Funding has been provided by all the councils involved along with a grant from the DWP performance standards fund. KBP is planning to expand so that it processes the full range of council tax and housing benefits.

Selby and East Riding

East Riding of Yorkshire Council is working with Selby District Council to support the implementation of its new computer system for revenues and benefits. The work has included training over 40 staff and support for the conversion from the old IT system to the new one. The partnership is expected to produce efficiency gains for both councils.

Blyth Valley and Wansbeck Building Control

The two councils have delivered Building Control in partnership since April 2003. The service regulates building work to make sure that it complies with the building regulations. In some cases this involves examining and approving plans of proposed work. In all cases the service inspects building work in progress and certifies that it has been completed in accordance with the regulations.

The Team is managed by Blyth Valley and comprises five staff. Application numbers rise year on year but typically the team deals with around 500 projects and 4500 inspections each year.

The partnership is a flexible arrangement which reflects historically different workloads and manning levels. Lower levels of activity in Wansbeck had made it difficult for the council to justify the employment of a full-time manager, and also created recruitment and retention problems. The solution was the equal sharing of the costs of the manager, with the quid pro quo of a commitment from Blyth Valley to provide officers to do some inspections in Wansbeck when the workload required.

Blackburn with Darwen Borough Council and Hyndburn Borough Council

The two councils are sharing staff and collaborate in providing services, including housing, economic development and transport. Blackburn and Hyndburn were driven to share people and services because they both needed to gain expertise and skills, increase efficiency, improve effectiveness and improve the employee experience by working together and sharing good practice. Other issues that drove the collaboration were housing market renewal and the city region development programmes.

In November 2004, the two councils agreed to partner on housing market renewal for a six-month period. Blackburn supplied Hyndburn with specialist advice to speed up Hyndburn's programme of work giving them part-time access to specialist expertise. Following the success of the housing renewal work, the councils decided to locate their economic development teams together at Blackburn's offices.

Partnering and sharing has developed step by step in response to specific needs. The two councils now share resources across several services including housing renewal, economic development, transport, performance management, legal services, noise nuisance, CCTV monitoring and support to local businesses.

Financially, the largest benefit from partnering is a successful joint bid for transport funding. Almost £20 million will fund improved links between them over the next five years.

The two councils also jointly fund a noise nuisance post. The councils were also successful in their joint bid for funding to improve their CCTV facilities. They won £60,000 for new digital systems that offer the improved images required for prosecutions. The councils now have CCTV facilities at the police headquarters in Greenbank. This eases communication and co-ordination with the police. The councils have implemented the same performance management system and Blackburn has also extended a database that serves information to local businesses to cover Hyndburn.

Hyndburn is to undertake the legal work for one of Blackburn's housing market renewal areas. Blackburn is making a contribution to the cost of Hyndburn's legal services. The two councils are also planning to join up their community safety teams.

SERVICE – FORMAL

East Lancashire procurement service

Coming out of the East Lancashire e-partnership, a joint procurement facility for five east Lancashire district councils was first conceived in 2003. In mid 2005, Hyndburn was hosting the service and was recruiting procurement staff on a temporary basis which could be extended with partners' support.

Staffordshire Moorlands and Lichfield district councils

The two councils have a five-year joint contract with Serco to provide IT support to both councils. The two councils shared consultancy and legal costs and managed the procurement process jointly. Each has contracted separately with Serco though the contracts are virtually identical. The contract covers all operational IT services including infrastructure, desktop management, new projects, database management and some systems development. Serco also provides a remote diagnostics service and out-of-hours helpdesk support, something that neither council was able to provide before.

Both councils have retained responsibility for the overall strategic direction of ICT services and e-government plans, to ensure that other opportunities can be exploited such as the benefits of working with Staffordshire Connects.

Both councils established internal review teams involving staff from different service areas (including IT and union representatives) to consider the requirements for IT support, to be involved in assessments and to evaluate the options open to the councils. Joint workshops took place at key stages and the final outsourcing decision was unanimous. Both councils had project boards involving elected members and key stakeholders in the management of the project, and making key decisions concerning the project and its implications. The project sponsor for each council sat on both project boards.

The contract is worth £3 million over five years and commenced in April 2003.

Macclesfield Borough Council/Congleton Borough Council

Following a Best Value review, a joint corporate centralized procurement unit led by a procurement manager was established in 2003 with the costs of this post to be equitably funded 60 per cent by Macclesfield and 40 per cent by Congleton. Two procurement assistants posts were also established reporting to the Macclesfield procurement manager. The arrangement is managed by a service-level agreement.

Staffordshire County Council shared service centre

In order to make the best use of an investment in a SAP financials system, Staffordshire County Council set up a shared service centre to process its payroll. The intention was to extend the range of services carried on into HR administration and creditors and debtors work, plus some payment of expenses and some transactional personnel activities were to be undertaken.

Even at Stage 1 of its development the shared service centre provided for the continuation of the previous payroll services provided for the Staffordshire fire and rescue service, the Stafford magistrates courts, Staffordshire Police and Staffordshire Moorlands Council, amongst its 12 customer organizations.

Northampton revenues

In early 2002 a proposal was put forward at the Northamptonshire Revenues Practitioners Group for five councils to join forces to provide business rates services in a consortium arrangement.

When the consortium began only two councils decided to participate. For Northampton, who agreed to Wellingborough undertaking the activity for them and closed down their business rates section in August 2003, the business benefits were that they did not need to replace a computer system and were able to avoid the dislocation caused by the retirement of a member of staff. The initial consultation involved discussion on debt recovery and application of discretionary relief supported by the Northamptonshire Revenue Practitioners Group.

The consortium, based at Wellingborough, provides the full range of services to customers, though payments are made to the individual councils and the details are uploaded to the consortium system daily. If customers approach the individual council service points they are dealt with as normal. Court representation and recovery are undertaken by the consortium for each council and the consortium instructs external bailiffs. All statutory returns and final accounts information is produced by the consortium for each council.

The five staff employed by Wellingborough on behalf of the consortium process around 8200 accounts.

Swindon and Kent Social Services Partnership

Swindon received a zero rating for its social services service and decided to engage managers from Kent County Council (who are an excellent rated service) to improve it.

Swindon are paying Kent £2.6 million and the ODPM pay another £1 million. Kent managers go into Swindon two to three days a week to provide advice on human resources policies and the commissioning of care packages and financial management.

They have a joint project steering group of managers and cabinet members from both councils.

Rochdale and Blackpool revenues and benefits

It was announced in June 2006 that the two councils planned to adopt a shared services model for the provision of revenues and benefits services. Blackpool will implement Anite's browser-based Pericles system on behalf of the two councils in order to deliver efficiency savings and free up extra resources for improved frontline services. The integrated system, which supports revenue collection for council tax and non-domestic rates, together with administration for housing and council tax benefits, was to go live late in 2006.

The plans build upon an existing arrangement where Blackpool already successfully provide Pericles shared services to Fylde Borough Council in a partnership that went live in January 2006.

CORPORATE – INFORMAL

Central Norfolk consortium

A group of three local authorities (Broadland District, Norwich City Council and South Norfolk District) deliver building control services using a joint committee structure. The partnership resolved the difficult issue of different staff terms and conditions in the three authorities before the partnership was set up, by reaching an agreement to harmonize, despite the staff continuing to be in the direct employment of their 'parent' councils. The partnership has increased fee income and reduced overheads, providing a return to each participating council.

East Dorset District Council

The council has funded joint posts, notably with Christchurch, including a sustainability management officer, and a health and safety officer. The council provides audit and pest control services to Christchurch District Council.

CORPORATE – FORMAL

Alnwick District Council and Castle Morpeth ICT partnership

Castle Morpeth manage a service for Alnwick providing all elements of the ICT service to both Alnwick and Castle Morpeth councils, that is, for operational, infrastructure, application support and e-government project services. The partnership was formed to provide additional capacity and resilience as well as economies of scale.

E-government is managed through a joint e-government steering group. The lead officer is the e-champion for both councils and projects are progressed after evaluation and agreement by a management team member at each authority.

AGMA (Association of Greater Manchester Councils) multi-service partnership

The development of a co-ordinated set of strategic service delivery projects began in March 2001 in order to improve services jointly across a range of administrative and direct services within Greater Manchester. This has involved the ten AGMA councils and their partners (Bolton, Bury, Manchester, Oldham, Rochdale, Salford, Stockport, Tameside, Trafford, Wigan, Blackburn-with-Darwen and Blackpool) taking a more systematic approach to joint working. To co-ordinate and manage the work, a joint service delivery steering group was created in December 2001.

Recognizing the potential added value of joint working across the region, the AGMA chief executive's co-ordinating working group identified 11 areas for joint service delivery. A lead authority was identified for each project and officer project teams were formed to take the work forward. The 11 areas were the processing of benefit claims, IT support services, computer audit, the carrying out of Best Value reviews, out-of-area education and social services, specialist legal services, construction-related professional services, brokerage services for education support services, recruitment advertising, payroll and other financial services and trading standards.

AGMA out-of-authority placements

In 2002 the chief executives of AGMA established a project to research how all the authorities could work together more efficiently to improve the quality of out-of-authority placements whilst ensuring that the placements selected were the most cost-effective. AGMA had been registering concern over the number of children and young people they have needed to place long distances from home and at significant and rising cost resulting in huge overspends on the children's services' budgets.

In April 2005, a central joint commissioning unit was established by Tameside Metropolitan Borough Council to support all the member authorities with placements for children and young people across children's services, education and social services. The member authorities are: Blackburn with Darwen, Oldham, Blackpool, Rochdale, Bolton, Salford, Bury, Stockport, Lancashire, Tameside, Manchester and Wigan.

Facilitation, co-ordination and administrative support are provided by the unit. The staff in the unit have all been appointed on a permanent basis by Tameside MBC as host authority on behalf of the partnership. The group considered that TUPE did not apply as the work of the unit was not previously undertaken by any of the partner authorities.

So far a number of improvements have been achieved, including a suite of regional contracts suitable for spot, block, cost and volume, and pre-purchase use, as well as an accreditation process, guidance information and documentation. Provider forums to support purchaser/provider dialogue, understanding and co-operation have been established and a website www.ooap-jc.org.uk provides valuable online facilities. The central unit has allowed a clear definition of out-of-authority placements in order to avoid flawed data collection and management information systems.

There is a management group on which each member authority is represented by one senior manager who may be from education services or social care services. Existing members of the management group provide guidance on the selection of the managers in order to ensure the ongoing balance of representation of the group.

Each partner authority has appointed two nominated officers to be the link between the authorities and the unit. Each partner authority has paid an equal amount for the first two years. The second year's fees have remained the same as the first without even an inflationary increase. The decision as to how funding will be split over the following years was to be made by the management group in autumn 2006. Membership is now open to other authorities in the north-west, who may be admitted subject to full payment of the partnership fee and approval of the management group.

South Oxfordshire District Council and Vale of White Horse District Council

According to the *Local Government Chronicle* of April 2006, South Oxfordshire District Council and Vale of White Horse District Council are jointly entering into a contract with Capita for revenues, benefits and exchequer services. Whilst South Oxfordshire had contracted out these services for some years and was due to re-tender in 2005, Vale of White Horse 'piggy-backed' and together they tested whether an outsourcing could have advantages over in-house provision. Capita will provide the service off site, with a saving to Vale of White Horse of £135,000 in the first year.

Adur District Council and Worthing District Council

Both councils have had a history of working together in various forms and are geographically located very close to each other. Joint working was the only option considered because the councils have an ethos of supporting the in-house provision of services. The councils believe there is real value in working together and intend to be seeking to work more and more in partnership with others over the coming years.

The councils' partnership started in November 2001, Adur and Worthing Services (AWS) was first established to bring together the refuse and recycling services of both councils to provide a unified waste collection service across the Adur and Worthing districts as a whole. The services involved are vehicle workshop facilities and fleet administration, refuse collection, recycling and street cleaning. The total value of services (excluding grounds maintenance) included in the partnership is £3.8m per annum.

The key drivers for the partnership are service improvement, cost savings (the councils were aiming to save between £400,000 and £500,000 per annum once all the phases are implemented) and capacity enhancement. Secondary considerations include the increased opportunity to secure external funding and local waste/environmental factors.

In the early stages the two councils were motivated by different priorities with cost savings being the foremost driver for Worthing Council whilst Adur Council concentrated on service improvement. The partnership has now taken on a wider importance for both councils with the realization of additional benefits and the creation of new opportunities for joint working.

The main decision-making system is the simultaneous executive meeting (SEM). Under SEM, members from each council hold a meeting at the same time and at a single venue to discuss AWS issues; they then break into separate groups for voting. The two councils have different democratic arrangements so this innovative decision-making mechanism allows decisions to be made more quickly than via joint committee reporting but still encourages full member involvement. All members from both councils receive the SEM papers and can attend the meetings. A common report format is currently being developed.

The shared workshop pilot was the first stage of the project. This has run relatively successfully since November 2002. Adur Council has undertaken work for Worthing, which has meant that one FTE post from the workshop (20 per cent of establishment) has remained unfilled since the post-holder vacated it.

The two councils are currently developing a legal agreement. Whilst some issues have been relatively straightforward to resolve, the councils have experienced difficulty in agreeing

Figure 4.3   An AWS vehicle demonstrating the 'branding' given representing both councils

terms in some areas, for example, insurance, ownership of assets and profit sharing. The legal status of the single service (PAWS Ltd) to be created has yet to be determined, the final decision being dependent on the relative merits of the traditional direct service organization (DSO) against that of the limited company approach.

Adur has also embarked on another partnership arrangement with Horsham and Mid Sussex district councils on ICT acquisitions. So far, these relate to a new, modern, up-to-date financial management system and a new revenues and benefits system across the three councils. By working together in these areas, anticipated procurement opportunities, efficiencies and economies of scale will result. Adur, Horsham and Mid Sussex have formed CenSus (Central Sussex) Partnership in which all three organizations are linking up their knowledge and experience in a bid to deliver better services to the public through increased computer capacity. This is the first venture of its kind in West Sussex and it has followed a feasibility study which identified a whole range of likely advantages.

Test Valley Borough Council and New Forest District Council

The commercial services of Test Valley Borough Council and New Forest District Council have set up a joint venture, with the aim of integrating their two direct service organizations into a single commercial services unit. A new executive joint committee, a commercial services directorate and a management team spanning both councils have been established. An incremental approach is being taken to review business systems, support service links, employee relations, performance review and service development.

Test Valley Contract Services (TVCS) has 118 employees and undertakes work to an annual turnover of almost £4 million. It trades with a small annual surplus of under £40,000. New Forest Commercial Services (NFCS) has 278 employees and undertakes work to an annual value of around £8.5 million. Historically, it has traded at an annual surplus of just under £0.25 million.

The mission statement within the business plan states the aim of the partnership as: 'To serve the community by delivering and developing high quality, cost-effective services.' The partnership objectives are described as:

* integrate the direct service organizations of TVBC and NFDC into a single homogenous business unit;

- develop an effective model of governance, management and support for the organization;
- identify customers within the community and define the services that will be delivered;
- agree improvement targets for these services in terms of quality and customer satisfaction;
- identify target areas for improving the financial effectiveness of the organization;
- develop business opportunities to increase the turnover, customer base and range of services provided;
- promote service innovation, best value and partnership working within both councils;
- identify opportunities for alignment of strategic direction and service delivery within both councils;
- maximize opportunities to promote the environmental, social and economic well-being of both communities through the services offered;
- engender a shared vision with all employees, based on service excellence, sound employee relations, openness and trust.

A joint committee has been set up under Section 101(5) of the Local Government Act 1972 and the Local Authority (Arrangements for the Discharge of Functions) Regulations 2000. This joint committee became operational on 1 September 2002. The joint committee discharges the functions relating to the operational side of the respective commercial service divisions of both councils subject to such matters being within the policy and budget framework approved by both councils. The joint committee also monitors performance of the business and is responsible for development of the service and seeking ways to maximize efficiency and quality within the business.

Three executive members from each authority sit on the joint committee. The joint committee is empowered to delegate to officers of each authority. Arrangements are in place for public participation in both the joint committee and the scrutiny committee. A joint scrutiny committee, comprising members of both councils has been set up. The respective councils, reflecting the political proportionality rules, have appointed three non-executive members from each authority. Call-in arrangements will follow Test Valley Borough Council's procedures, as they will be responsible for the day-to-day administration of the joint committee. The joint committee is only empowered to take decisions within the policy and budget framework set down by the two councils and within any margins allowed by financial regulations.

The process of combining two DSOs is being tackled on an incremental basis, commencing with the governance, identity and management of the partnership. Subsequently the focus will move to review its internal business and administrative systems, support service links, performance review mechanisms, employee relations and future service development opportunities.

The commercial agreement between the councils sets out the respective obligations in respect of the joint venture, together with the liabilities of each partner. Existing rights and responsibilities for business and contracts remain as they are. Any new business or contracts arising after the commencement date of the joint arrangements, which the councils have jointly agreed upon, are shared on a profit/liability ratio of 50/50, or as otherwise agreed. Termination and delegation are also covered by the commercial agreement.

Whilst existing employees continue to be employed by their respective councils, a new single management structure has been implemented to manage all employees within a newly formed directorate, which spans both councils. For the time being there will be no change in employees' existing contractual terms and conditions, although joint policies and procedures for discipline, grievance and capability have been implemented.

Gosport Borough Council and Fareham District Council

Following the signing of the legal agreement between Fareham Borough Council and Gosport Borough Council in October 2002, the building control services of the respective councils began working together as a single unit from 1 February 2003. The administration centre for the building control partnership was established at Fareham civic offices with a surveying and reception presence maintained at Gosport. All documentation and stationery now reflects the partnership, and the Ocella computerized system already in use at Fareham Borough Council has been implemented for processing building regulation applications in Gosport. Remote access links between the two office locations have been established. All external subscription services, such as quality assurance registration, which were previously individually supplied, have now been consolidated into a single partnership account with the anticipated savings in fees being realized.

The partnership agreement has been structured to allow Gosport and Fareham staff to remain employed by their respective employers. Three Gosport staff, including the building control manager, are now based at Fareham but routinely, surveying and administration staff carry out duties across the whole partnership area. The necessary changes in working environment and procedures have been achieved despite continued staff shortages and increasing workload. This is a strong and positive reflection of the commitment of all the building control staff to the partnership.

A partnering agreement has been established with a local company, Strand Harbour Developments, for the provision of building control advice and approval of all projects on a nationwide basis. Another large local company, Bensons Limited, are considering a similar arrangement. In both cases, the resources and unique status of the partnership were key factors in forging these links.

The joint budget for the partnership is now administered at Fareham with the close liaison and co-operation of Gosport Borough Council financial services.

The partnership management panel together with officer representation from both councils have met quarterly.

Crewe and Nantwich District Council/Congleton Borough Council

Both councils are active members of other partnerships, including the Cheshire and Warrington Information Consortium (CWIC), but see the partnership as the main operational and development vehicle for meeting local electronic government targets. This is a highly practical approach involving very closely integrated working between the two councils on a number of levels, including:

* the pooling of 2004–5 IEG funding;
* a common system for measuring BVPI 157 (e-government achievement);
* sharing of in-house ICT resources including senior management;
* adopting a joint electronic government and ICT strategy;
* jointly purchasing a new 'common e-government infrastructure' built around a CRM approach;

- the creation of a partnership management structure directly involving the senior decision-makers (chief executives and elected leaders) from both councils;
- integrating project plans, network infrastructure and ICT services.

The ICT partnership board, which is jointly funded with each council contributing 50 per cent of the board members, has a number of terms of reference. The terms include:

- the definition of the responsibilities and appointment of the joint ICT manager; receiving reports from that officer;
- examining potential areas for joint ICT working between the two councils;
- considering how new ICT systems may be procured jointly by the councils and how appropriate decisions may be made on behalf of their cabinets;
- reviewing how the ICT services of the councils might work more closely together with a view to their eventually being combined into a single unit and how their ICT project management procedures may be standardized;
- reviewing and developing the joint implementing electronic government (IEG) statement;
- overseeing joint ICT projects and the implementation of the Joint ICT Strategy;
- bidding for external funding on behalf of the councils for joint ICT projects;
- procuring joint projects on behalf of the councils and managing any joint grant funding obtained on behalf of the councils.

ConsortiumAudit

ConsortiumAudit was formed in April 2002 by the amalgamation of the internal audit sections of Corby, Kettering, Northampton and Wellingborough councils. The four councils formed an audit consortium to start to address the capacity issue along with providing an opportunity for greater economies of scale and enhanced quality. There is a formal legal agreement between the four partner councils, drawn up by the in-house legal team, which covers such matters as:

- employees;
- designation of host authority and responsibilities;
- support services;
- trading agreement;
- accommodation;
- funding;
- composition of the board;
- management arrangements;
- reporting;
- insurance;
- liabilities;
- exit strategy.

There is an agreed fee basis for days of activities and specialist services and the four local authority partners pay pro-rata contributions. There is no formal legal structure. The head of ConsortiumAudit reports to the executive board who monitor the work of the consortium through quarterly and annual budget and performance reports. There is also an annual report. The business plan is reported to the executive board and agreed with the four Section 151 officers who comprise the board membership. The head of ConsortiumAudit relates separately to each chief financial officer (CFO) as necessary and provides individual reports that include the annual audit report and a controls assurance statement. These are also reported by the consortium to the appropriate committee at each authority.

There are 15 permanent posts within the consortium. These are supplemented with staff from the private sector partner, PricewaterhouseCooper (PwC). To help integrate the consortium and PwC and to overcome recruitment difficulties, PwC also provides staff to cover two of the permanent posts within the consortium. Staff transferred under TUPE to ConsortiumAudit, which in effect meant they transferred to Northampton Borough Council since the consortium is not a legal entity that can employ staff.

Northampton has now withdrawn from the Consortium and Wellingborough have taken up the role of host of the consortium.

Consortium procurement

Daventry, Kettering, Northampton and Wellingborough have agreed to let Northampton provide procurement services to all of the councils managed by a partnership agreement. A board meets quarterly to review progress and set priorities. Specialist buyers are located at Northampton but spend time at each council so that they can understand their particular needs.

North Yorkshire audit partnership

The North Yorkshire audit partnership was one of six Best Value partnership network pilots announced by local government minister Hilary Armstrong in 1998 and is now an arm's-length consortium of three councils (Ryedale, Selby and Scarborough) to provide internal audit services. The aims were to reduce the cost of services, gain greater flexibility and professional expertise, have clear financial control and performance measurement and use Best Value concepts. The consortium was also intended to demonstrate a willingness for the councils to co-operate. Its role is to:

- prepare strategic and operational plans to be agreed with both the client and the external auditor;
- monitor performance against plan and review progress quarterly with the client;
- maintain the audit manual, adopting the Chartered Institute of Public Finance and Accountancy (CIPFA) Code of Audit Practice;
- develop and maintain a range of audit performance indicators;
- develop a computer audit.

The three partners reduced audit costs as well as improved access to specialist skills such as IT audit.

Devon Building Control Partnership

The Devon Building Control Partnership (DBCP) came into being on 1 April 2004 amalgamating the building control services of West Devon Borough Council and Teignbridge District Council into a partnership. South Hams District Council joined in August 2006. The key drivers for the creation of the partnership were improving the service, attracting and retaining staff and providing a cost-effective service so that the authorities with a sparse population and a large administrative area could achieve the same scales of economy as much larger authorities.

The formal governance of the partnership is under a joint committee comprising of two elected members from each council. It is termed a partnership board and the board delegates its powers to the management team but retains the powers to agree the forthcoming year's action plan (a costed improvement plan); to set a budget, drawing funds from partnering authorities where required; and to review the performance of the partnership (financial and performance indicators). The constitution allows for the involvement of external stakeholders on the board. Teignbridge Council is the host authority for entering into contracts and other formal arrangements that are required for the partnership.

When the partnership was established it was on the understanding that there would be start-up costs and that significant savings were unlikely to be achieved in the first year of operation; however, some savings were achieved in Year One and these were used to offset some of the costs associated with the new management structure and computer system. All non-chargeable costs incurred by the partnership in discharging non-building control functions are shared by the councils in the ratio of the relevant year's budgets. All income from the building control trading account, less expenditure, support costs and liabilities is set against the next year's action plan. Any surplus generated is distributed to each partnering authority in the same ratio as fee generated in the partnering authority's district. The service is tasked in returning a zero budget (+/–10 per cent) at the end of the financial year. The formal agreement used to establish the partnership and signed by both councils when the combined service was established, sets out how the finances of the partnership are to be dealt with. This deals with the distribution of any surpluses from the building regulation account and the way in which the non-chargeable functions are to be dealt with.

For the period of the partnership agreement, staff are seconded to the partnership. During the period of secondment the staff will continue to be employed by their commissioning council, but managed by the partnership on such terms and conditions as the partnership may from time to time determine, provided that no changes to the staff's main terms and conditions of employment shall take place which are less favourable than those applying before the secondment. When the period of secondment comes to an end the staff will return to the partnering authorities on the terms and conditions applying to their posts had they not been seconded and any additional benefits or salary enhancements applied as a consequence of the secondment, under the partnership's own terms and conditions, ceasing to apply.

SUPRA-CORPORATE – FORMAL

East London lettings consortium

This consortium provides a choice-based lettings system for member councils (Newham, Redbridge, Waltham Forest). It provides the More Choice in Lettings service for Barking and Dagenham and the Southwark Homesearch service for Southwark. It also provides an outlet for a number of housing associations. It has signed a co-operation agreement with Home Connections, a north London consortium providing choice-based lettings services to north London councils. Funded initially by ODPM as a pilot project, it operates as a not-for-profit consortium controlled by its member local councils.

Norfolk

Norfolk County Services (NCS) has grown since 1988 to now have an annual turnover approaching £60 million, and a payroll of over 4500 full- and part-time employees. NCS is managed independently from the county council, operationally and financially; it holds its own bank account and balance sheet and has the ability to retain profits. However, investment and borrowing requirements have to be authorized and agreed with the county council. NCS became a limited company on 1 April 2002. NCS sees its role as a 'market moderator' as its presence provides a credible public sector alternative to private sector delivery organizations. It provides a benchmark of the costs of delivering similar services.

In terms of governance arrangements, the NCS board comprises the managing director of NCS, an executive member, and another senior county council chief officer. The board meets quarterly but there is informal dialogue with shareholders on a regular basis. Performance is reported on a six-monthly basis. District partners have in place their own governance arrangements with proposed regular reporting to cabinet and scrutiny committees via an independent board.

NCS currently partners with two district councils:

- North Norfolk District Council (NNDC) – this partnership was formed in 2002 for ten years initially, with an annual value of £5.5m (although turnover is expected to be £6.5m to £7m, taking into account additional external work). The partnership involves the delivery of traditional 'blue collar' services.
- Great Yarmouth Borough Council (GYBC) – this partnership started on 1 October 2003 for a ten-year period. Services include refuse collection, grounds maintenance, building maintenance and engineering (coastal protection). The total annual value of services is £6m, including the management of other budgets worth £0.7m. Based on a company jointly owned by NCS and GYBC, GYB Services took on 180 staff from Great Yarmouth's borough works department. The company is far more than just a contractor; a strategic client function has been established in GYBC to monitor performance and take day-to-day decisions with GYB Services. The previous CCT contract specifications have been replaced by a new set of performance measurements, including missed collections, abandoned car removal and the average time taken to remove fly tipping, repair street lights and handle complaints. There is a contracted turnover figure for a ten-year period, with savings shared on a 50:50 basis between GYBC and GYB Services.

NCS also has service contracts with Broadland, Breckland and South Norfolk councils, as well as a number of town and parish councils. Within Norfolk, NCS provides catering services and management to 95 per cent of primary and 45 per cent of secondary schools in the county.

Norfolk County Services Transport Ltd won the three-year contract under a competitive tender from Norfolk County Council, which had successfully bid for funding from the government's £46 million Urban Bus Challenge Fund announced in 2003.

NPS Property Consultants Ltd is wholly owned by Norfolk County Council. It has contracts to deliver building and property services to the council's schools, to a number of councils and private sector clients. However in 2004, NPS moved to a more collaborative approach when it signed a deal with Wakefield Metropolitan Borough Council to create a subsidiary company called NPS North East Ltd. Wakefield have seats on the board and a share of the profits. One hundred building services and design staff have TUPE transferred from Wakefield to NPS North East with possible further recruitment of 50 completely new staff as the business takes on further contracts. They remain based in Wakefield with the company headquarters in Norwich.

Since 1994 NCS has provided both catering and cleaning at Swaffham Community Hospital on behalf of Anglia Support Partnership, an organization hosted by Cambridgeshire and Peterborough Partnership NHS Trust. In 2004 NCS was awarded the FM contract at Cromer Hospital by Norfolk and Norwich University Hospital NHS Trust. This contract includes the delivery of estates maintenance in addition to the usual hotel services. Soon after taking on Cromer Hospital, the PEAT (Patient Environment Action Team) score for the site was upgraded from 'Poor' to 'Good', and has had its on-site quality management system approved to the ISO 9001:2000 standards.

In 2004 NCS introduced Practice Support (PS), a package of services from which practice managers could select to suit the individual needs of their practices. PS can include grounds and building maintenance, cleaning and some white-collar activities such as payroll, HR and advice on legislation, legal obligations and so on.

Suffolk County Council and Mid Suffolk District Council

The two councils have created a joint venture company with BT called Customer Service Direct in 2004. A ten-year partnership has been formed and as part of this a revenues and benefits platform for Mid Suffolk District Council was created. BT owns 80.1 per cent of the company and the two local authorities each have a 9.95 per cent share, although each partner has a veto on certain key decisions. In addition, BT carries all financial risks associated with the partnership and will not start making a profit until seven years into the joint venture. The public sector partners pay a monthly charge for the shared services, based on the amount they cost before migrating to the new arrangement.

Among the improvements to service will be the creation of a single customer service bureau to manage a network of offices where the public can access joined-up county and district services, a one-stop centre for services within 15 minutes of 99 per cent of Mid-Suffolk District Council's population, a single point of access to joined-up district and council services and joined-up health and social care services, and a single telephone contact point for customers.

The scope of the partnership will include the delivery of ICT, HR, finance services (including revenues and benefits) and public access (one-stop shops, call centres and web-based services). Substantial savings will be driven out from existing budgets and used to invest £66m over ten years in improving these services. The investments will be in new/improved systems, infrastructure, equipment and business process re-engineering, leading to transformational improvement in services to the public.

Each service was monitored in advance of the implementation date of 1 June 2004 to identify baseline performance management information, which then fed into service-level agreements and key performance indicators. Nearly all of the company's staff were seconded to the joint venture from the local authorities, rather than transferred under TUPE. Only a handful of employees came from BT.

Drivers for the initiative included:

- The need to deliver business transformation and introduce new, more streamlined working processes to replace the fragmented structures that were previously in place.
- The need to improve customer service.

- Investment – Mid-Suffolk needed new finance and HR systems and BT was prepared to invest £50m in new systems, training and change management up-front.

The medium- to long-term aim is to roll-out this capability across the whole county of Suffolk, drawing in both other councils and other public bodies. The county council is undertaking a similar project with Waveney District Council and the Centre for Acquaculture and Science (CEFAS) – a DEFRA agency.

Summary

As stated above it is difficult to be precise as to the number of sharings in existence. According to local councils' annual efficiency statements (see Figure 4.2), by 2004–5 nearly 20 per cent of local councils stated that they already operated an average of 1.4 shared services of some kind and, given that they must have at least one partner, it is likely that around two in every five local councils have at least one shared service. And of those local councils who said they were in a 'partnership/shared service' a third are in a shared procurement arrangement.

Of the different types of councils either involved in sharing or planning to share, the significant majority in both types are district councils.

Based on the very limited sample of those councils who said in their annual efficiency statements that they are sharing, three-quarters of the single-tier councils are classed in the 2005 Comprehensive Performance Assessment (CPA) scores as three or four star whereas the average of all such councils is just over two-thirds (68 per cent).

In the 2003–4 CPA scores for district councils, 84 per cent were classed as fair, good or excellent. In the annual efficiency statements the percentage of sharers which are in those categories is 90 per cent.

This tends to suggest that better councils are more likely to be involved in a shared service than the overall number of councils in that inspection category.

In Chapter 7 an attempt is made to assess whether the sharings in existence have speeded improvement for those councils who have taken part in them.

5 Case Study 1: The Anglia Revenues Partnership

This case study has been written in conjunction with the management of the Anglia Revenues Partnership based on original material provided by them. Their co-operation is gratefully acknowledged.

Introduction to the partnership

In its study *The Efficiency Challenge: the Administration Costs of Revenues and Benefits*, the Audit Commission (2005a) pointed out that the Anglia Revenues Partnership (ARP) is 'already releasing over £100,000 per year to each partner'. This chapter seeks to explain how this was achieved.

The participating councils

Breckland covers a large rural area from the south-west to the centre of the county of Norfolk. The population of 120,000 is spread over an area of 500 square miles. Although mainly rural in character Breckland has five towns: Attleborough, Dereham, Swaffham, Thetford and Watton. These provide an urban mix across the region. Breckland gains its name from the heathlands, or 'brecks', which characterize the south of the area and a part of Suffolk. The south of the region also includes Thetford Forest, one of the largest forested areas in the country.

The economy in Breckland is evolving away from traditional manufacturing industries. Breckland Council has been supporting business for many years and has a desire to provide a vibrant mixed economy that provides quality sustainable jobs. The development of the ARP meets several council objectives including 'To encourage and attract quality jobs to the area and promote a sustainable economy' and responds to the following council aims: 'To foster a culture of learning and skills development among individual businesses'; 'To maximize external funding and investment opportunities for local businesses'; 'To support, grow and develop local key sectors and clusters'; 'To continue the social, environmental and economic regeneration of the area' and 'To promote the area to businesses and attract inward investment and spend'.

Forest Heath is a rural authority in north Suffolk that covers an area of 144 square miles with a population of 55,000 residents centred around the three towns of Newmarket, Mildenhall and Brandon. The population includes 13,000 United States Air Force personnel and their families based at the two airbases RAF Lakenheath and RAF Mildenhall. Whilst agriculture still employs significant numbers in the more rural areas of the district the main employers in the district are Center Parcs at Elvedon Forest, the airbases at Mildenhall and Lakenheath and the horseracing and bloodstock industries based around Newmarket.

Through the current economic development policy, a wide economic base has been encouraged around the three main centres of population in Forest Heath. This has resulted in the emergence of high-technology industries running alongside light engineering and service industries. The development of ARP meets the council's objective to provide sustainable economic well-being – to encourage and promote long-term economic well-being by attracting new investment and growth, redevelopment, training and employment opportunities.

The history of the partnership

Prior to 2003, Breckland and Forest Heath had both undertaken Best Value reviews of their revenues services and independently recognized that there were significant potential gains to be made in working with partners to deliver the services. Breckland undertook a procurement exercise to seek private sector partners as part of their Best Value process but no added value could be provided so this did not proceed.

However, as the Breckland procurement exercise ended the Forest Heath Best Value review was also being completed. Breckland shared their experiences with the private sector with Forest Heath and discussed a public–public partnership from an informed background of having worked to develop a public–private partnership.

The two councils began to develop the idea of forming a public sector partnership to achieve service improvements by combining similar skills and methods from within the individual councils and by taking advantage of economies of scale.

It was recognized early in the reviews that both councils were relatively small; as a result both councils could pay a premium to seek to improve performance. There would come a point where increasing performance would not be cost-effective and it was likely that a point would be reached where individually little or no further improvement could be made. To avoid this, the logical conclusion was to seek the opportunity to work with others to realize the economies of scale resulting from sharing expertise, ICT, staff and accommodation.

Both councils had examples on a smaller scale of the success of partnership working in this way and so were comfortable with exploring a larger shared service delivery arrangement:

- Breckland and Peddars Way Housing Association introduced a post based within the Peddars Way offices.
- The Norfolk registered social landlord pilot to allow landlords to verify benefit claims.
- Breckland and Forest Heath shared a benefits manager and fraud team leader.
- The One Project in Suffolk was a joint project between district councils, the DWP, job centre and Deloittes Touche.

Both councils also had organizational imperatives to come together – Breckland had the opportunity to reduce the cost of management through a retirement and Forest Heath were looking to whether they should invest in a new computer system. Therefore there was a mutual interest in joining forces. The coming together took place in late 2002 based initially on an informal agreement. The Partnership came into being on 1 August 2003 when councillors signed an agreement to form a partnership to deliver revenues services to both councils.

The two councils believed that they possessed circumstances that would encourage success, through their geographical position, political compatibility and shared needs. A commitment and clarity to the joint aims existed and both the members and officers demonstrated a will to succeed with this project to the advantage of both councils and their residents.

The outcome

A business plan was produced to define the gains envisaged, this was approved by both sets of councillors. The outcomes to be sought from partnership were agreed:

- Excellence in service delivery.
- Customer satisfaction with the services provided.
- Significant cost advantages to the partnering councils.
- Continuous improvement in the three elements above.
- Economies of scale promoting a robust and flexible service, capable of absorbing change.

Each council committed to achieving all of these outcomes and agreed that by making sound investment in the future, added value in terms of expertise, innovation and investment would be gained. The key objectives of the partnership were:

- to improve the revenues services for the users of the two services;
- to reduce the costs of administration;
- to see continuous improvement in the service delivery of the services;
- to offer staff development and opportunities;
- to improve the skill levels in each service;
- to achieve and maintain upper-quartile performance in the measurable Best Value performance indicators;
- to increase the number of partners and customers of the partnership to achieve further efficiency gains;
- to deliver a consistent and resilient service with the ability to ride the peaks and troughs of service delivery.

To achieve these objectives the following specific outputs were expected:

- A joint committee was to oversee service, provide joint vision and policy direction.
- There was to be a shared Academy Revenues ICT suite from one server initially based in Breckland and building on the current installation.
- IT data processing was to be provided remotely by a third-party supplier (once the partners were operating from the same accommodation) (in other words, IT hardware and software were to be provided off-site).
- Document imaging processing systems were to be shared.
- There would be joint IT support from one supplier.
- Managerial posts and operational posts were to be shared.
- All third-party services were to be jointly procured.
- There was to be a unification of processes, working practices and policies on service provision.
- Accommodation and staff were to be shared.
- There were to be shared budgets.
- There were to be single postal and cash administration access points.
- Training facilities were to be shared.

The two councils made the decision early on in the project that IT would be unified across the two councils. Forest Heath had to move off their old mainframe system in any event so the decision was taken to extend the existing Breckland contract with Academy to provide the revenues systems for Forest Heath as well. In practice this meant the migration to Academy for all Forest Heath revenues systems and a migration to Academy for the Breckland NNDR system. This became the first major shared project between the two councils and was successfully completed in August 2003.

However, from the outset, three major IT projects were instigated and run consecutively. These were:

- revenues systems and desktop unification
- electronic service delivery
- electronic document management system (EDMS).

The final one of these three projects, the EDMS, was installed in May 2006. The electronic service delivery went live in April 2004. Both of these projects were funded externally.

The only external cost that directly related to the original introduction of the partnership was the purchase of external legal assistance to draw up the contract. The rest of the work was undertaken by staff within the ARP with some expertise provided from the finance, human resources, legal and IT sections in Forest Heath and Breckland councils.

Forest Heath District Council did procure a new IT system at the commencement of the partnership but this was necessary for the authority anyway with or without partnership as their old system ceased to be supported in 2004. Although there was, of course, a significant cost for Forest Heath in purchasing new systems, they did in fact save a six-figure sum by purchasing the Academy systems in partnership with Breckland.

The development of the partnership

A project plan was introduced and agreed by both sets of councillors that instigated an overall programme of change that would last for two years and would lead to the partnership delivering the services from one building by September 2004. (This was achieved two months early on 5 July 2004.)

The project programme was split into seven project stages overseen by a project team and a project board consisting of council members and senior officers of the two councils. The programme was run on Prince II methods.

The management of the partnership

After considering a variety of options for the governance of the partnership it was decided initially to operate with a joint committee between the two partnering councils (this committee has now been developed to include East Cambridgeshire). The joint committee consists of two council members from each authority; it sits quarterly and provides the operational policy for the service delivery, sets the budget and approves the annual delivery plan. The joint committee's relationship with the host councils is slightly different in each authority because of the differing political structures in place. In Breckland the committee reports directly into the council's cabinet, and the two committee members are also cabinet members. In Forest

Heath, where the committee structure is retained, the two members report into the two committees that were previously responsible for the operation of the revenues services. In this instance it is the two Chairs of these committees who sit on the joint committee.

An operational board reports to the joint committee and forms the management team of the partnership. This board meets formally on a fortnightly schedule. As well as providing the internal management of the ARP this team also feeds into the management of the host councils providing representatives to management teams, performance clinics and so on, within each authority. A consistency of information through a monthly performance report is provided to all stakeholders in the partnership to ensure that work is not duplicated. This representation directly into the host councils does away with the immediate need for a separate client control and provides an efficient method of monitoring the performance of the partnership.

To support the partnership a series of specialized teams have been created to provide solid expertise within key support service areas. These teams provide real sources of specialized knowledge that provide the foundations for a strong organization.

Achievements

The partnership has achieved savings and these are being carried on year after year. Cost savings vary annually as additional efficiencies are driven out of the services; consequently the savings described in this case study are not specific but instead are indicative of the magnitude of savings that can be achieved.

The charge to each authority does differ and is calculated according to the population of each authority. Therefore whilst the overall charge varies the unit cost is the same to each authority. This methodology for charging ensures that each partner receives an equitable share of the savings generated by the partnership and allows for a sensible method for growth.

STAFFING

The original business plan for the first two partners estimated a staff saving of approximately £160,000 against the original separate staff budgets. In fact by the time that the shared structure was recommended and approved by the joint committee the savings seen were in the region of £170,000. This represents approximately 10 per cent of the total staff budget at the time. In addition to these savings it has been possible to absorb changes to the benefit scheme such as pensioner tax credits with the addition of no extra staff resources.

The majority of savings have come through a rationalization of management and the specialized roles that can be shared across councils. This has been achieved through natural wastage throughout the life of the partnership and has not resulted in any redundancies. In the future it is also hoped that valuable and scarce staff resources will be retained and that the partnership will be able to offer both staff development and career opportunities as it develops further.

This intention has been seen in the development of the resilience team that is available for much of the year to support other councils. When the ARP has its own peaks this team is available to support its own performance; however, at other times of the year they are loaned to another authority who pays their salaries for the time that they work with them. This provides the ARP with an efficient method of employing the right number of staff to promote excellent performance.

ICT

Savings in ICT are achieved through a reduction in ongoing maintenance costs of approximately 20 per cent per annum. Additional savings have been seen as reduced software purchase costs have been negotiated when extra costs have arisen for legislation changes.

The partnership was successful in bidding for ODPM e-government funds which have funded the successful implementation of electronic service delivery. This project has provided the ability for service users to interrogate their own claims and accounts, make payments and receive electronic bills. An increased amount of useful information has also been posted on the dedicated partnership website.

In 2005 a further bid to the DWP Improvements Fund succeeded. It was to support the purchase and implementation of a new electronic document management system. This went live in May 2006 and supports remote working across the partnership sites.

ICT SUPPORT

Now that the partnering councils are sharing the same IT platform and the same accommodation, the IT support is provided through an extension of the Breckland contract with Steria. This has given a significant reduction in the cost of IT support which is shared across the partnership.

The requirement for support at key times such as year end, new releases of software and upgrades to software and hardware, as well as for regular housekeeping and maintenance and for faultfinding, is now reduced as actions need only be taken once.

ACCOMMODATION

The third major stage of the partnership following the integration of IT and IT support has been the complete join-up of the two services into the same accommodation. Following a search for suitable property in the area or suitable land for a new build it was eventually decided to use Breckland House in Thetford. This option offered a total additional saving of approximately £75,000 over existing costs.

The staff from both councils moved into Breckland House on 5 July 2004 and they now work seamlessly on both councils' workload.

Thetford is on the border between the two councils and allows the residents of both to benefit from the increased employment opportunities that will be developed. This provided the ARP with the potential for growth and for the provision of quality jobs in the area. ARP was also able to co-ordinate objectives with those working for economic regeneration within the area as, economically, the Thetford area has an over-reliance on agriculture and manufacturing. Levels of skills and education are lower than average – a fact reflected in lower wages. However, the provision of increased opportunity for higher-skilled and higher-paid jobs to Thetford's young, energetic population and an excellent strategic location will tap into the local potential to create future prosperity for the whole of the area.

The staff, who relocated, receive the normal relocation allowance paid by their host authority with the cost shared across the partnership. There was no direct loss of staff as a consequence of the move, although two or three individuals did decide to retire at this point having reached the normal retirement age.

PROCUREMENT

The partnership benefits from advantageous rates for procurement through its larger buying power. This has reduced the cost of such services as year-end printing and despatching, bailiff services, stationery supply and printing.

Performance

The ARP has steadily improved its performance over the life of the partnership and has always moved forward in every performance measurement. But not only has the performance improved but quality of service delivery is demonstrably better as well. With time and resources to concentrate on quality the ARP has been able to promote good practice. This has been shown in initiatives such as:

* the electronic service delivery
* the landlords' forum
* the procedure manuals
* the provision of forms in foreign languages and translation services
* the employment of a bereavement officer.

The result is an excellent score in the benefits performance framework and a successful BFI report that recognized many good practices. The performance improvements in each service area is shown below.

COUNCIL TAX

It can be seen from Figure 5.1 that both councils now perform at or close to top quartile. The partnership has implemented other improvements:

* restructuring to allow for separate billing and recovery teams;
* improvement of the management of the service;
* recognizing a need to develop an awareness of other debt issues that may impact on collection;
* the introduction of earlier court dates;
* the issuing of earlier reminders;
* increasing the number of direct debit dates;
* clearing out old debt.

BUSINESS RATES

Very high collection rates for both councils have been achieved with both achieving top quartile in 2005 (see Figure 5.2). Both councils have good relationships with their business customers and this will be retained. The amalgamation of the two teams and changes in ICT systems was achieved seamlessly with minimal loss of performance. (The slight drop in Breckland's performance over the period 2003–2005 has been caused by the failure of one large taxpayer which represents approximately 1 per cent of the total collection.)

Collection rate	Top quartile	Breckland	Forest Heath
2000–2001		93%	97%
2001–2002		95.4%	97.5%
2002–2003	98.2%	96.48%	97.5%
2003–2004	98.4%	97.29%	97.1%
2004–2005	98.5%	98.1%	97.5%
2005–2006	98.53%	98.5%	97.9%

Figure 5.1   Anglia Revenues Partnership's performance in council tax collection

Collection rate	Top quartile	Breckland	Forest Heath
2000–2001		97.00%	99.00%
2001–2002		98.80%	97.60%
2002–2003		99.10%	99.20%
2003–2004	98.2%	98.84%	97.60%
2004–2005	99.2%	98.83%	98.7%
2005–2006	99.26%	98.24%	99.3%

Figure 5.2   Anglia Revenues Partnership's performance in business rate collection

BENEFITS

An indication of the current direction of travel of performance is BVPI 78a, the assessment of new claims for Housing Benefit. In 2002 Breckland was one of the worst-performing councils in the country with a performance of 122 days. This shows the improvement and indicates the real impact of partnership working for the residents of these two councils. For details of performance see Figures 5.3, 5.4 and 5.5.

The future

With the addition of East Cambridgeshire, the partnership has now achieved all of its original targets and now commences a period of growth with a new partner. Figure 5.6 documents the performance against the original objectives.

With the partnership achieving its original aims, it now seeks to extend the opportunities for increasing the efficiency gain. This will be achieved in two ways: first by the continual development of the partnership with additional partners but secondly by utilizing the skills gained to open up additional income streams. These sources of additional income will continue to drive down the cost of service delivery for the partners and will enable resources to be retained, thus increasing the resilience of the core services. To assist with this a complementary trading company was developed during early 2006 to trade the individual skills that had been developed throughout the early years of the partnership.

New claims	Top quartile	Breckland	Forest Heath
2000–2001		118 days	44 days
2001–2002		119 days	64 days
2002–2003		122 days	50 days
2003–2004		33 days	43 days
2004–2005	36 days	25 days	29 days
2005–2006	25.5 days	14 days	15 days

Figure 5.3   **Anglia Revenues Partnership's performance in administering new benefits claims**

Changes in circumstances	Top quartile	Breckland	Forest Heath
2000–2001		54 days	13 days
2001–2002		53 days	20 days
2002–2003		52 days	13 days
2003–2004		11 days	19 days
2004–2005	9 days	11 days	12 days
2005–2006	8.5 days	6 days	6 days

Figure 5.4   **Anglia Revenues Partnership's performance in administering changes in circumstances**

Accuracy	Top quartile	Breckland	Forest Heath
2000–2001		97%	93%
2001–2002		100%	98%
2002–2003		98%	98%
2003–2004	98%	97.5%	97.6%
2004–2005	99%	97.5%	97.8%
2005–2006	99%	100%	99%

Figure 5.5   **Anglia Revenues Partnership's performance in accuracy of claims assessment**

In December 2005 East Cambridgeshire District Council applied to join the partnership and was accepted as the third partner of the ARP. East Cambridgeshire is a rural authority in Cambridgeshire which covers an area of 65,516 hectares. The district is predominantly rural in character, stretching from the border with Norfolk in the north to within two miles of Cambridge in the south. It has a population of 78,000, one of the fastest-growing populations of any district in the country. The district is relatively affluent, ranking as 274th out of 354

Objectives	Achievements
Excellence in service delivery	• Introduction of electronic service delivery • Improvement to top quartile in majority of Best Value performance indicators (BVPI's) • Customer access reviewed and refined in each authority
Customer satisfaction with the services provided	• Positive customer feedback in both councils
Significant cost advantages to the partnering councils	• Cost of staffing reduced • Cost of accommodation reduced • Cost of IT reduced • Support services reduced
Economies of scale promoting a robust and flexible service, capable of absorbing change	• Improvement in benefits service performance for Forest Heath in year that systems were changed • No disruption in service during major projects including introduction of partnership, electronic service delivery, accommodation move, customer service team and contact centre development • Introduction of resilience team providing resilience to other councils
To improve the revenues services for the users of the two services	• Improved access through provision of electronic access and introduction of dedicated website • Dedicated training to customer service teams and contact centre staff • Improved performance against all indicators and measures
To see continuous improvement in the service delivery of the services	• See service performance tables
To offer staff development and opportunities To improve the skill levels in each service	• Training audit completed • Training needs fulfilled • Training diaries introduced • Professional training in progress • Professional trainee post introduced
To achieve and maintain upper quartile performance in the measurable BVPIs	• Top quartile achieved • Continuous improvement in BVPIs being seen
To increase the number of partners and customers of the partnership to achieve further efficiency gains	• East Cambridgeshire welcomed as third partner • Active discussions ongoing with other partners
To improve letters and information	• Letters reviewed at implementation of IT systems for Forest Heath • All information leaflets reviewed and reissued as joint leaflets with Plain English accreditation

Figure 5.6   Achievement of Anglia Revenues Partnership against original objectives

council areas on a scale of deprivation (with 1 being the most deprived). Generally deprivation is highest in the northern part of East Cambridgeshire; for example, deprivation relating to education, skills and training. Soham and parts of Ely are in the worst quartile for income deprivation. Areas such as Downham village and Ely East are amongst the 1 per cent most deprived in England with the key issue identified as distance to services and poor transport. The cost of housing in East Cambridgeshire is relatively high. The average house sales price (July to September 2003) was £174,935. This compares to £153,874 for the region and £161,665 for England and Wales. A key issue for the council and local residents is the availability of affordable housing.

The service delivery for East Cambridgeshire will commence on 1 April 2007 when the current outsourced contract with Capita ends. The joint committee between the two partnering councils is now being developed to include East Cambridgeshire. In due course they will provide two further members to the joint committee who will then have an equal representation to the existing partners.

Although staff will be expanded during 2006 in readiness to deliver the East Cambridgeshire services from April 2007, the addition of a third partner extends the efficiencies already gained as management and specialized roles are shared over a greater base.

The total savings increases year on year and will increase dramatically with the introduction of East Cambridgeshire. As a rough guide, each of the two initial councils has saved in the region of £400,000 per annum between them from the partnership arrangement, and it is budgeted that this saving will increase to £1,000,000 per annum with the inclusion of a third partner. This has increased each year as new income streams are introduced as well as additional efficiencies are driven out.

6 Case Study 2: The Welland Partnership

The history of the partnership

Since its inception in 1998–9 the Welland Partnership, comprising East Northamptonshire, Harborough, and South Kesteven District Councils, Melton Borough Council and Rutland County Council, has made significant progress by working together in delivering innovative solutions. The partnership has been involved in national Pathfinder projects and has also produced many joint strategies in service areas such as housing and environmental health.

The partnership itself has gained national recognition and thus has been able to influence the rural agenda. It has been recognized in the regional strategy as a sub-region in its own right and has been able to respond jointly to the regional housing strategy consultation. The partnership has also developed Welland-wide tourism and economic development strategies as part of the creation of a sub-regional strategy which seeks to preserve and enhance the rural nature of the five authorities' areas. It has also set up a payment facility so that people can pay into their council tax or rent accounts at any cash office within the partnership.

Other successes in working together have been in single regeneration budget (SRB) projects including local colleges and other organizations working together to promote education and training in rural communities in mobile facilities or community buildings. Another success was Rural Watchline, a unique crime-messaging service to increase police cross-border communication and cut rural crime – a joint project involving all Welland partners and the police forces of Lincolnshire, Leicestershire and Northamptonshire.

The partnership gained e-government funding for community portals through a £1 million Pathfinder grant, £1.4 million for a customer relationship system (content management) and £650,000 for document management and authentication.

The partners were able to secure loan arrangements for private sector grants when the grant regime altered in 2003 at preferential rates and the Welland Housing Service in partnership with its preferred registered social landlords commissioned a housing market analysis for the whole of the Welland area at significantly reduced rates, which included information at a local authority level.

Shared services

Shared service working in the partnership started with a Welland shared services group that had as an initial brief the examination of IT, planning, some commercial environmental health services and certain white-collar services. Work by Deloitte and Touche to develop a methodology for shared services, exploring the benefits and risks of a new approach to providing services, produced a proposal for sharing the revenues and benefits function. This did not go forward as the view by the partners was that the analysis was too simplistic and failed to recognize the risks and variables in the services, particularly the implications of the

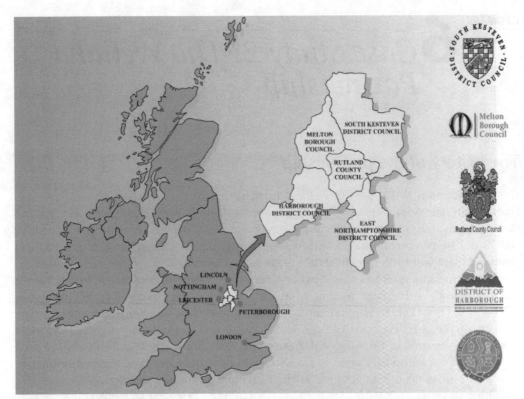

Figure 6.1   Map showing the geographical locations of the members of the Welland Partnership

differences of IT systems used. The partners put forward to councillors in early 2003 a proposal for a shared development control service. This was rejected by councillors who were unwilling to countenance a situation where their planning policies could be controlled by the officers of another council.

Some shared services were in place by 2004 – Harborough and Rutland had a single audit manager who divided his time equally between the two councils, and in building control cross-border working was formalized based on an agreement entitled 'Local Authority – Joint Working, Building Control Cross-boundary Support Service'. As a joint working group, the joint working group now employs a consultant structural engineer. A legal trainee post within legal services is funded and each council contributes four months of the training period. The first trainee has now qualified and continues to be employed within the partnership.

In 2003 the partnership sponsored a detailed exercise organized by the Welland environmental health heads (WHEH) to consider whether a shared service was possible. The services were reviewed over a six-month period and it was concluded that though there were differences in the resources allocated per council to cases dealt with, the largest council appeared to be benefiting from economies of scale – although part of this may have been as a result of the use of more narrowly experienced technical specialists, allowing routine medium- and lower-risk inspections to be undertaken for a lower staff cost.

Overall, the data analysis suggested there may be scope for the smaller councils to achieve economies of scale similar to those at the largest council, by forging partnerships or shared service delivery models. Different partners appeared to have different strengths in certain service delivery areas; therefore, there may have been opportunities to develop synergies through a shared services approach. There could be opportunities for sharing staff: as staff may live near the areas of activity, rather than the current centres of administration, they could work from home.

Eleven potential scenarios were identified, including an option that re-drew current organizational boundaries, and various combinations of two, three and four partners. Through the process of undertaking this evaluation the WHEH group arrived at the following two models of shared service delivery:

- East Northamptonshire Council with Rutland County Council and
- Harborough District Council with Melton Borough Council.

Subsequently, a crisis arose when three of Rutland's staff resigned within a period of two weeks. An urgent review of the potential for East Northamptonshire to take over the Rutland service was investigated. At the end of this it was concluded that there were no legal/logistical issues identified to prevent the sharing proceeding despite the different statuses of the councils. It was accepted that in negotiations the basis of any initial sharing must be the service by the two individual councils being initially replicated but with a five-year plan to achieve 'a significant improvement', and that that service plan should form part of any partnership agreement and should include jointly shared risks and benefits. It was recognized that there was a need for openness and transparency between the partners and that members need to be asked at the earliest stage in any proposed sharing to review how they might wish to simplify their management of the service to prevent duplication of effort.

However, the sharing was not supported because of the significantly different level of resources applied to the service by the two councils, uncertainty over the costs of support services, the differing standards required and the costs of the implementation. As a result this sharing did not go ahead but the potential for an environmental health service for all councils was included in the wider project.

The Welland Partnership shared services initiative

In December 2003 the ODPM agreed to a capacity-building grant for the partners to invest in a project to see if they could build on the services they already shared. Assisted by KPMG, the partners tried to develop a transferable methodology. The hope was that this methodology would be of value not only to the Welland Partnership councils but also any inter-authority service delivery grouping.

This project reacted to one of the partnership aims – 'To explore the opportunity to develop joint approaches to service delivery'. The partnership's *Shared Services – Principles and Protocols* contained the following statements:

The fundamental purpose … is to demonstrably improve the extent and quality and effectiveness of services provided for the benefit of residents and businesses …

The … councils are individually and collectively committed to the principle of sharing …

Each … authority will make its own individual assessment whether or not to participate in any one Shared Service Initiative …

The benefits ... will centre around what outcomes can be achieved additional to those for any one authority operating on their own. It is recognized that ... benefits will not always be cost savings ...

The partners planned to undertake a robust evaluation against their project objectives and establish the business case for change taking into account the financial and human resource implications of integration. Once done, they would develop a fully costed implementation plan including change management, risk and human resource management considerations that would lead to a procurement strategy and action plan based upon the services they chose to share.

Project decision-making was focused on the members executive panel of the Welland Partnership. The involvement of members was promoted through two seminars to which all members of Welland councils were invited and by periodic reports to the Welland executive panel representative of all councils. Individual chief executives informally briefed their own members.

The partners' chief executives met monthly in order to provide direction in overall terms as well as monitoring progress and taking executive decisions against the project programme. This included maintaining a risk register and a communications plan.

There was an opportunity for the partners to reflect on progress together with their stakeholders (that is, the ODPM, Audit Commission, KPMG) in a mid-project review and identify any shortfalls in project arrangements, resourcing or opportunities to redirect work. This was repeated at the end of the Project. Both meetings received an independent report submitted by an independent verifier from Capita.

The 'set-up' phase

KPMG provided a project manager to co-ordinate the whole project and to support capacity in the councils; researchers were engaged in particular to support the work on benchmarking. An existing cross-council group of senior managers was asked to carry out a quality assurance role in support of the chief executives group and, to support them, a skills enhancement programme was arranged covering issues such as visioning and change management. This included a visit to a shared service site.

The partners agreed that they would also examine having a non-geographically adjacent partner council in the project to see whether it was possible to share services at a distance. Selection of the councils was based on a number of criteria:

- within an Audit Commission 'family group' for as many of the partners as possible;
- whether the council had a similar or better performance profile than was the average of the partners;
- whether the council had similar or better inspection scores than were the average of the partners;
- whether the council had a similar or better CPA rating than was the average of the partners;
- whether, from a reading of their CPA report, the council had an apparently open approach to service delivery;
- whether the council had some elements of ICT compatability/convergence with the partners;

- any personal or professional knowledge the council might possess – there may be individual knowledge of a council that is particularly appropriate.

Using these criteria, the partnership was successful in recruiting High Peak Borough Council and Breckland District Council, each of whom brought into the project their 'partner' council (Derbyshire Dales District Council and Forest Heath District Council respectively). The partnership adopted the four councils as full members of the Partnership for the purposes of the shared services project.

South Kesteven District Council's key priorities for service improvement did not include shared services at the time the project started, so they decided only to participate through holding a watching brief. They did partially rejoin the project at a later stage.

The chief executives established the purpose and vision of the project as to:

- achieve a significant improvement in service delivery to local people that improves the partners' performance within five years from the project's completion;
- improve the capacity of the partner councils to ensure an enhancement of their Comprehensive Performance Assessment score within five years;
- achieve involvement of a non-geographically contiguous council in shared service delivery;
- achieve agreement on a standard methodology.

Following discussions between councils the following services were selected for investigation:

- environmental health
- collection of council tax/NNDR and benefits
- housing (landlord functions, advice, maintenance, home improvements, homelessness and lifeline services)
- internal audit
- legal services
- building control
- e-government and ICT
- procurement.

In addition some councils agreed to investigate some back-office services (HR, finance, facilities management). In order to reflect the milestones agreed with the ODPM the partners set themselves the ambitious target of starting the shared services on 1 April 2005.

During this period a series of models was prepared and adopted. The aim was to use each of the models to test which best suited each different service to support the improvement that was required through a sharing. The models used at this stage are shown in Figure 6.2.

The benchmarking phase

Though the partnership had existed for some years it was agreed that in order to consider sharing on a firm basis it was critical to establish the detail of individual services in order to compare them and identify the opportunities for sharing. It was agreed that benchmarking of each service would take place using CIPFA and Audit Commission performance data as well as internal management and self-assessment material.

Collaboration on specific and/or specialist services

A formal partnership-wide approach to jointly delivering certain aspects of a service. This could include pooled training and staff development budgets and approaches, joint trainees, the development of joint procedures and risk profiles, out-of-hours service approach, flexible working and so on, and/or approaches and contracts for the delivery of these services. Joint training, procedure development and recruitment would be undertaken.

Joint Welland service procurement model

All of the partners join together and form a common procurement arrangement to deliver services across the region. The 'central' procurement vehicle manages a series of contracts or one contract for all partners that manages and delivers all aspects of the service across the region.

Outsourcing of services between partners

One or more partners formally outsource certain aspects of their service(s), or indeed the whole service(s), to one or more of the other Welland partners. This would involve the development of service-level agreements and contracts for the outsourced services and would run on a long-term basis of at least three years. This would allow for more robust financial and service delivery planning for all concerned parties. Client-side and contract management systems would need to be established.

Lead Authority model

One of the partners would assume the lead in delivering a service for the whole of the partnership. Staff would transfer to this authority but could work flexibly across the region within various specialisms as appropriate. This would involve the adoption of the host authority's systems and procedures of operation, terms and conditions of employment, and the pooling of all budgets under the host authority.

Fewer than five partners develop a shared services model

A number of partners could fully join together to adopt a shared services model. This would involve all aspects of service delivery, including management, accommodation, service delivery, staffing and so on. This could involve the establishment of a third-party delivery entity or a lead authority.

Full joint Welland service model

All of the partners join together and form a joint venture company or special purpose vehicle to deliver services across the region. All staff would transfer to this new entity, which would manage and deliver all aspects of the service across the region.

Figure 6.2   Models used in the Welland shared service project

In order to explain fully the benchmarking process, which had been delayed within the project plan to ensure members of councils could be properly briefed and staff engaged in the process, four benchmarking workshops were held when the process and the required outcomes were explained to 37 service managers. As part of this awareness stage, benchmarking forms were completed for a comparable service judged 'good or excellent' in a Best Value inspection report for each of the services being benchmarked. These were used to demonstrate the material to be included in a benchmarking form (see Figure 6.3).

Copies of the benchmarking forms for all the services benchmarked were given to all the service managers in a service interchange process designed to give an opportunity for review of the service detail supplied and to ensure consistency in the material included in the benchmarking forms. To support the process, standard activity measures for each service were adopted in order to gain further consistency in the benchmarking.

In total 84 services were benchmarked and copies of all the benchmarking forms for each service were given to all the councils.

In order to prepare for the next stage of the process an analysis of each service against five criteria was prepared. This narrative looked at each service against a series of criteria and identified the shortfall in the current service against those criteria. These were compiled by the project manager using his experience as a Best Value inspector. The criteria were:

- meeting (national and local) objectives;
- meeting customer needs;
- service quality;
- value for money;
- performance.

The narrative which was sent only to the council concerned was then scored against each of these criteria and an overall results tabulation was prepared. An example is shown in Figure 6.4.

A copy of the results tabulation for all services was produced for each council based on the analysis of the benchmarking form. This enabled each council to judge the relative position of its service. Most importantly, it demonstrated to all the participating councils the performance gap of the services and where improvement was needed to meet the project's objectives. It also started to indicate which sort of model was likely to best meet the gap identified.

WELLAND SHARED SERVICE PROJECT (ACCOUNTANCY) BENCHMARKING DATAFORM

Description of the service – list the functions carried out	
Description of the service – management	
Description of the service – operation	
Description of the service – cost	**List all major cost components – using full year approved budget**
	Meeting Aims and Objectives
National objectives	
Local objectives	
Contribution to corporate governance	
	Meeting customer needs through access to services and responsiveness
Access arrangements (e.g. physical, web, phone, out of hours/ emergency)	
Complaints and feedback	
Fees and charging	
Information and promotion	
Services to the disadvantaged	

Figure 6.3   **Welland shared service benchmarking dataform**

	Service delivery
Service standards applied.	
Risk analysis and management	
Research and service development	
Partnership working	
Information technology	
Performance monitoring	
Quality assurance	
External accreditation	
	Value for money
Activity costs	
SUMMARY OF SERVICE QUALITY	
SUMMARY OF ANY INSPECTION RESULTS	
Performance information: Best value indicators OR Local indicators	
SUMMARY	
NOTE: There were some variations for different services. For example in environmental health and building control there was a reference to enforcement arrangements. For ICT there were questions about network security, standards and security and integration of systems. In services such as accountancy, HR and legal there was a question about the support such services gave to service delivery.	

Figure 6.3   *Concluded*

Each service head was asked to undertake a risk analysis of the issues they considered had to be overcome in order to preserve service during the creation of a shared service and to ensure the improvement if a shared service was created.

In a separate but related exercise a small number of focus groups of local people were held. Conducted by an independent consultant they looked at their views on each council's services and, importantly, their views on the creation of shared services. Copies of the individual reports on their existing services were given to each council but the overall conclusions were shared

	POOR	FAIR	GOOD	EXCELLENT
Meeting objectives	↑	↑↑	↑	↑
Meeting customer needs	↑	↑↑↑		↑
Quality of service		↑↑↑	↑↑	
Value for money		↑↑	↑	↑
Performance	↑	↑↑	↑↑	

Figure 6.4   Welland shared service project – performance gap analysis

with all partners. The headlines were that none of the customer groups was resistant to the idea of providing services differently and all recognized the need to do so. Their aspirations were for more effective, efficient and consistent services with greater value for money. All had some reservations, mostly about losing local control, accountability and access.

iMPOWER, who had conducted a study in 2003 on the potential for closer working between the partners through convergence of IT systems, compiled a report on how the possible shared services could be helped or hindered by the IT that supported the services as outlined in the benchmarking forms.

Outline business case stage

Outline business cases (OBCs) were written by KPMG for a total of 14 services. To do this the benchmarked data was cross-referenced with the risk analysis, the iMPOWER report, the customer research and views of the potential opportunities identified in the work on a joint environmental health service. Additionally there was a heavy emphasis on testing the performance gap of the collective service against the potential benefits. This, as described below, formed a critical part of the evaluation criteria to assess which model would be most likely to lead to improvement.

The format used is shown in Figure 6.5.

As mentioned above the choice of the preferred model depended heavily on the evaluation of which model best fitted the aspirations of the partners. The matrix used to undertake that evaluation is shown in Figure 6.6.

The OBCs were presented to the chief executives in an open session to which all of the service heads were invited to attend. In addition prior to the session, IDeA had been invited to independently critique the OBCs. They were asked to judge whether the content was sufficient to allow the councils to take decisions on whether to share services. The report raised concerns in respect of the lack of detail in the OBCs and said 'It is critical that the OBC/Interim Decision

OUTLINE BUSINESS CASE/INTERIM DECISION MAP

COMPILER:

DATE:

VERSION:

The service being considered to be shared	
	Management summary of business need
Functions included.	
Total budget	
Staff	
Summary of the current service(s)	
	Identified 'performance gap' to be bridged by 'shared' service
Meeting aims and objectives	
Meeting customer needs through access to services and responsiveness.	
Service delivery	
Value for money	
Performance	
	Results of evaluation of 'models'
1. Collaboration on specific and / or specialist services	
2. Joint procurement model	
3. Outsourcing of services between partners	
4. Lead authority model	
5. Less than all partners develop a shared services model	
6. Full joint service model	
	Suggested changes
Suggested changes – processes	
Suggested changes – systems	
Suggested changes – locations	
Suggested changes – organisation	
Suggested changes – costs of democracy?	
	Issue resolution
Proposals – length of sharing arrangements?	
Proposals – financial stability?	
Proposals – financial/service incentives?	
Proposals – impact on support costs?	
Proposals – impact on staff?	
Proposals – impact on ICT?	
Proposals – impact on customers?	
	5-year service plan expectations
Outcomes – improvement in service delivery	
Outcomes – performance improvement	
Outcomes – cost effectiveness	
Outcomes – quality of service	
Outcomes – improved capacity	
	Risks
Risk management assessment	
	Implementation
Summary of identified implementation costs	
	Affordability test
Capital	
Revenue	
Expected payback period	
	Other critical factors

Figure 6.5   Welland shared service project outline business case format

The Welland
P A R T N E R S H I P

OUTLINE BUSINESS CASE EVALUATION
SERVICE:

Viability

SCORE	DESCRIPTION	AWARD CRITERIA
5	(A) Excellent	As for **(B)** but will exceed the partnership's overall needs and expectations in all or the majority of the 'purpose and vision' of the service model.
4	(B) Good	As for **(C)** but will have a tendency to exceed the partnership's overall needs and expectations in some of the areas of the 'purpose and vision' of the service model.
3	(C) Average	Basically meets partnership's overall needs and expectations.
2	(D) Weak	Only meets elements of the partnership's overall needs and expectations.
1	(E) Poor	Does little to meet the majority of the partnership's overall needs and expectations.

Note: Any assessed score equal to 1 or less will discount that option as a viable method shared service partnership delivery.

The evaluation criteria will be consistently applied to all options to be assessed and include the following descriptions:

- To achieve a significant improvement in service delivery to local people through an agreed decision map for changes in service delivery that improves the partners' performance within five years of the project's completion. – PI performance.
- To achieve a significant improvement in service delivery to local people through an agreed decision map for changes in service delivery that improves the partners' performance within five years of the project's completion. – Cost-effectiveness.
- To achieve a significant improvement in service delivery to local people through an agreed decision map for changes in service delivery that improves the partners' performance within five years of the project's completion. – Quality of service.
- To improve the capacity of the partner councils to ensure an enhancement of their Comprehensive Performance Assessment score within five years of the project's completion.
- To expand and grow the capacity for shared service through collaboration with other councils.

Figure 6.6   **Welland shared service project outline business case model choice assessment matrix**

Risk

The evaluation also includes an initial assessment of risk associated with delivering the associated option including its defined benefits.

SCORE	DESCRIPTION	AWARD CRITERIA
0.33	High risk	The criteria have a high probability of not being deliverable (i.e. there is little evidence of achievement in other similar projects).
0.5	Medium risk	The criteria have a medium probability of being deliverable (i.e. there is some evidence of achievement in other similar projects).
1	Low risk	The criteria have a high probability of being deliverable (i.e. there is some evidence of achievement in other similar projects).

Evaluated option

Purpose and vision evaluation criteria	Subjective evaluation (description)	Evaluation score	Risk score
To achieve **a significant improvement in service delivery to local people** through an agreed decision map for changes in service delivery that improves the partners' performance within five years of the project's completion – PI performance.			
To achieve **a significant improvement in service delivery to local people** through an agreed decision map for changes in service delivery that improves the partners' performance within five years of the project's completion – Cost-effectiveness.			
To achieve **a significant improvement in service delivery to local people** through an agreed decision map for changes in service delivery that improves the partners' performance within five years of the project's completion – Quality of Service.			
To improve the capacity of the partner councils to ensure an enhancement of their Comprehensive Performance Assessment score within five years of the project's completion.			
To expand and grow the capacity for shared service through collaboration with other councils.			
Summary Comments:			

Figure 6.6   *Continued*

The scoring matrix

Risk bandings	Poor prospects for improvement 5.00 to 7.50	Uncertain prospects for improvement 7.60 to 12.50	Promising prospects for improvement 12.60 to 17.50	Excellent prospects for improvement 17.60 to 25.00
Low risk 3.80 to 5.00				
Medium risk 3.00 to 3.75				
High risk 1.65 to 2.90				

Figure 6.6   *Concluded*

Map documents are not seen as more than they are – a step on the way to a true business case'. However, the report was supportive of the headline conclusions of 11 of the 14 OBCs.

The OBCs were presented on 4 and 5 November 2004. The two review days were attended by the chief executives of all partners, including South Kesteven, who had announced their intention to consider being involved in shared services. Service managers were invited to attend and to make comments on their view of the OBC. These were collected separately to the discussions of the chief executives and circulated to all service managers and chief executives.

The meeting agreed for procurement to go forward as a workstream and for four services – revenues and benefits, procurement, internal audit and legal services – to be the subject of a service improvement planning group process. Chief executives chose for them to be led by service managers. Additionally, and outside the immediate project, chief executives agreed a business transformation workstream to commission a specialist adviser (iMPOWER) to write a scoping document for a change management programme that included business transformation for all partners' processes. This included full ICT convergence working towards the realization of shared services.

The chief executives did identify that it might be possible to provide some other services through the procurement route and requested the procurement group to come up with a five-year plan for procurement of services – such as payroll services and facilities management and others – jointly on behalf of all partner councils.

The chief executives decided not to proceed with proposals for sharing environmental health, ICT, e-government or HR services. Other services – such as housing strategy, housing landlord and building control – were to be worked on by interested councils outside the project.

Final business case stage

At their meeting on 26 November 2004, the chief executives agreed to the involvement of 4Ps as a means of presenting some challenge to the service improvement planning process and to lead the options appraisal process. They also agreed to the formal involvement of trades unions in the process. At the meeting the concept of a staff seminar being held in each council was agreed.

There was agreement to the format of the final business cases generation process and the chief executives agreed to meet their service improvement group members and brief them on the importance of their role and the aspirations of the chief executives. They also agreed they would hold a joint meeting with the service improvement planning (SIP) group leaders to undertake an exercise to specify the criteria for the options appraisal and the weighting be given to the scoring of the delivery models for each service stream.

The chief executives had agreed at their meeting on 17 December to a project support team critique of the SIP group process. This was undertaken by 4Ps.

On 5 January 2005 the chief executives undertook an exercise to establish their criteria for evaluation of options for the delivery models and the weighting to be given to the criteria. This exercise demonstrated the differing importance given by the chief executives to each of the services. For example it demonstrated that the most important factors for procurement were cost and service improvement, for internal audit, service improvement was most important and, for legal services, service improvement and improvement in capacity. For revenues and benefits equal weight was given to cost and service improvement.

The proforma used is shown in Figure 6.7.

After this process South Kesteven announced their withdrawal from the project because they were working to an improvement plan which gave them issues of capacity and priorities.

The first service improvement groups met and for the procurement group a process of collecting information on purchase of goods and services began assisted by Cornwell Management Consultancy using an independent consultant who specialized in procurement.

The groups undertook options appraisals to identify the delivery model they preferred for recommendation to the chief executives on 28 January 2005. They also focused on the service improvements they sought to achieve. The first draft of these and the option chosen for a delivery model were chosen. On 28 January the chief executives agreed to the recommendations of the groups.

The groups then proceeded to agree the content of the final business plans using the template shown in Figure 6.8.

The chief executives had also established a group of senior managers to review common issues to act as a backdrop to the business plans. The intention was that whatever was recommended should be in the context of the principles and protocols of the partnership (as shown at Appendix 1).

The areas to be covered were:

- the terms of any incorporation of staff in a 'shared' service;
- an agreed position on TUPE;
- the treatment of support costs – what needs to be retained by councils and what can be transferred to a shared service;
- the treatment of identified assets – write-off and amortization;
- charging for accommodation, ICT and other facilities by a 'shared' service(s) while occupying a council's facilities;
- the proposed detail of charging mechanisms for any shared service that incentivizes appropriate behaviour;
- proposals for governance of any possible shared service;
- proposals for length of partnerships, periods of notice and treatment of residual costs, and taxation or VAT issues for a new entity, such as a joint venture company or outsourcing arrangement.

Criteria	Example of approach to scoring	Weight to be applied (from 100).
Cost (N.P.V over five years)	Highest marks would be awarded to an option that produces a significant reduced cost of the service over the five-year period based on net present value (NPV).	
Cost (investment – upfront)	Highest marks would be awarded to an option that has no upfront costs to implementation.	
Service improvement	Highest marks would be awarded to an option that produces a significant improvement in BVPI performance, in customer satisfaction and in service quality.	
Legitimacy	Highest marks would be awarded to an option that has no legal obstacles, has commitment from members and staff to achieve change, minimises implications for staff and provides for a flexible and sustainable structure that can produce continuous improvement.	
Capacity improvement	Highest marks would be awarded to an option that offers increased capacity to the service through improving the capacity of management, staff and external suppliers within the council; improving the quality of officer and member meetings and the decisions they take; improving clarity of lines of accountability and responsibility; gaining positive outcomes for service users and communities through partnership working; that ultimately leads to an improvement in the council's CPA score.	
Risk – deliverability, timescales	Highest marks would be awarded to an option that offers the opportunity for ease of delivery, with minimal organizational challenge that would delay implementation and achievement of improvement.	
Risk – corporate, financial, reputation	Highest marks would be awarded to an option that offers the least risk that failure of the sharing would impact on the corporate centre of the council, impact on other services, imperil the financial standing of the council and its standing with the public and the wider local government community (including inspectorates).	

Figure 6.7   Welland shared service project outline business case model suitability option scoring format

Executive summary
- Summary of strategic alignment, business need and requirement for the project, key conclusions, options addressed, and recommendations for action/investment decisions.
- Includes decision map/process, and critical path timelines.
- Identifies stakeholder support and high level benefits of progressing with recommended actions.
- About 1–2 pages in length which can be extracted for member papers or CE briefings.

Strategic context and business need
- Who has commissioned the project and why.
- Overview and description of the services, issues faced in context of CPA, Gershon Review, ODPM drivers etc.
- How this project will support delivery of partner council strategies.
- Current state assessment/baseline study for the service – including performance, cost, quality, customer satisfaction, key benchmarks etc.
- An idea of any performance gaps as compared to better-performing/excellent councils.
- Rationale behind this project, what it will deliver, why it is needed rather than other work/activity.
- Who will be involved from within, across and outside the council.
- An appreciation of the impact and benefits of the project e.g. any citizen feedback or issues raised through CPA.
- Key messages to be drawn through to project delivery.

Project or service objectives
- Setting the scene for effective delivery requires SMART (Specific, Measurable, Achievable, Realistic and Timely) objectives driven out of the business need section.
- Where possible incorporating performance against existing measures and an indication how this will be improved or the measure changed by the success of the project.
- Establish a benefits tracking approach through clarity of objectives and desired outcomes.

Options appraisal
Option identification
In the context of what outcomes are required, identify all potential options for future service delivery. The project chief executives have already identified and agreed the following long list of options:
- Option 1: Collaboration on specific and/or specialist services
- Option 2: Joint service procurement model (outsourcing)
- Option 3: Outsourcing of services between partners
- Option 4: Lead authority model
- Option 5: Less than all partners develop a shared services model
- Option 6: Full, joint Welland service model (creation of separate service delivery entity/body)

Options assessment (long list)
- The pros and cons of each option are given in simple tabular or diagrammatic form showing why an option discounted and why and how an option selected for next stage.
- An indicative level of the costs and benefits (cashable and non-cashable) of each option is outlined to enable shortlisting.
- The 'do nothing' option as a check/balance within the process will remain from the current state assessment in Section 2.
- This process will be driven and facilitated by 4Ps, in conjunction with KPMG, with both the service improvement teams and then the chief executives group on 28 January 2005.
- This will provide a clear audit trail of how options were discounted and which are taken forward for full evaluation.

Figure 6.8   Welland shared service project final business case template

Options analysis (short list)
Following the earlier analysis and discounting of some options, a deeper and more comprehensive final business case will be drawn up around the short-listed options chosen for this stage. This will include, but not be limited to, the following information:
- performance improvements to be realized
- time to deliver
- infrastructure changes needed (buildings, ICT, overheads, etc.)
- asset transfers and implications
- cost sharing and service charging arrangements
- exit arrangements and implications
- legal and governance issues
- human resource implications (TUPE, secondments etc.)
- cost of delivery, affordability, and value for money (including payback period and overall return on investment where calculable)
- overall resource impact – capital and revenue
- quality of outcomes achievable
- financial and non-financial benefits – quantified where possible
- availability of funding
- service scope and interfaces
- identification, analysis and mitigation of key delivery risks.

Recommendation of preferred option
From all of the options assessed and analysed with reference to the specific points above, a clear recommendation will be made by the service improvement groups for the chief executives to consider on 25 February 2005.

This will form the central part of the final business case, and will be open to challenge and discussion with both chief executives and members before final endorsement is given to an agreed way forward.

This will then complete the final business case development and the project.

Figure 6.8   *Concluded*

Staff involvement groups were held in mid-January. Those attending had been selected by each council and prior to the selection their managers had been provided with briefing material. In the event the general level of knowledge was poor and the antagonism to the concept of sharing was high. The reasons for this were several but high on the list was the lack of previous involvement of staff or their representatives in the project so far.

The results of the project

The service improvement groups started work in December 2004 and presented interim views to the chief executives in January. Their conclusions were reported to the chief executives in February. Having been supported by the chief executives they were brought together for a presentation to the Welland Executive Panel of leading members.

During this process the chief executives agreed to the creation of the roles of host council and leading chief executive. The former would act on behalf of all the partners to provide a base for the shared service and be the employer for the service if secondment or TUPE was proposed. It would also provide accommodation and support to the service. The lead chief executive would act in an implementation role, project managing the establishment of the service and acting as an intermediary between the host council, the other partners and the service.

The proposals of the service improvement groups were adopted as follows:

PROCUREMENT

A 'lead authority' model was the preferred delivery model. An outline appraisal of the costs and benefits of the preferred lead authority model was based on the central procurement being accommodated in existing council offices with an overhead rate applied to salaries and on-costs to cover accommodation and infrastructure costs; the unit would use the host council's IT systems and infrastructure and would be staffed by a manager, three buyers and two support staff (only two staff would transfer from an existing council complement). No account was taken of any potential staff savings that may be achieved through councils' use of the shared service facility.

The business case indicated that the unit would produce a net annual benefit in the second year and that net cashable savings of £3 million at 2005 values could be achieved by the Welland Partnership over the first five years of operation. In addition, there would be non-cashable benefits associated with improved procurement methods and reduced risk. Future developments would be subject to separate financial appraisal

INTERNAL AUDIT

A consortium delivering internal audit for four councils was proposed. There would be a nominal host authority who would employ staff and hold budgets. Day-to-day management would be the responsibility of a head of audit, who would be one of two existing audit managers. The four councils would be paired on the basis of geography and each pair would share one of the audit managers and a senior auditor. One auditor would be based at each authority working at other councils as necessary. A fifth auditor would be deployed flexibly across the four councils. Strategic direction of the consortium and the content of the audit plans would be decided by the management board made up of the relevant Welland chief finance officers, with representation from the consortium by the head of audit. Specialist audit services which were currently procured separately by the councils will be procured jointly.

It was anticipated that:

- the total budget required for the shared service would reduce the average day rate from £228 to £199;
- the shared service would provide a staff resource that can be deployed more flexibly, enabling the risk of vacancies to be shared between the councils;
- the service would give the potential to increase the sharing of best practice and access to a larger pool of specialist knowledge, keep unproductive time and travel costs to a minimum and provide for flexible deployment when necessary, but allow staff to build up specialist knowledge of the council(s) within which they are working.

The agreed implementation timetable foresaw commencement of the shared service in six months.

LEGAL SERVICES

A consortium delivering legal services for four councils was proposed. The agreed improvement objectives were:

- to reduce duplication of effort when responding to changes in legislation, for example licensing, Freedom of Information Act;
- develop an effective performance management system, including a methodology that measures customer satisfaction, so that a process of continual improvement can be undertaken. This might include external accreditation if appropriate;
- realize the advantages of joint procurement opportunities, for example case management system, library resources;
- increase capacity to deal with peaks and troughs in service demand;
- increase joint capability/expertise, for example planning, housing benefits, employment;
- increase cost effectiveness to proactively support corporate value for money objectives;
- increase the ability to recruit, retain and develop staff.

Implementation required a framework agreement to be signed between the councils who agree to work together to identify potential for work sharing by use of internal expertise and possible joint commissioning. In addition this agreement included the undertaking of a needs analysis to establish the current outputs with a three-month time recording exercise and a case analysis.

The councils also agreed to seek to identify needs that were not currently met. They would achieve this by implementing a customer satisfaction survey and a comparative/benchmarking exercise. They agreed to identify external spending and make a decision on the level of service required in the future, and to conduct a skills analysis involving analysis of the time recording.

Of critical importance to the forward plan was the resourcing of the post of practice manager which was a fundamental first step to the creation of the service.

REVENUES AND BENEFITS

Collaboration was proposed with the following agreed improvement objectives:

- to achieve upper quartile performance in BVPIs;
- to maximize income in terms of subsidy, the recovery of overpayments, ability to bid for funds, collection by direct debit and collection of council tax and NNDR;
- to minimize duplication and write-offs;
- to ensure a service that is accessible and that people get the benefits, relief and exemptions to which they are entitled;
- to provide a customer-focused service that delivers customer satisfaction;
- jointly to evaluate emerging technology for improving service delivery, and take advantage of, if appropriate, external services/partnering;
- to improve funding and deliver staff development and to recognize staff as the most important resource;
- to investigate a joint approach to quality management;
- to reduce fraud/error in the calculation of benefits and council tax and meet the performance standards necessary to be 'at standard' and the e-government priority outcomes;
- to gain accreditation for the clarity of forms produced.

A five-year implementation programme was forecast involving formalization of the collaboration and agreement on the action plan, a steering group reporting progress to the Welland chief executives, annual reviews/quarterly monitoring and a review of key changes. An important aspect of the review was to be the identification of newly available technology

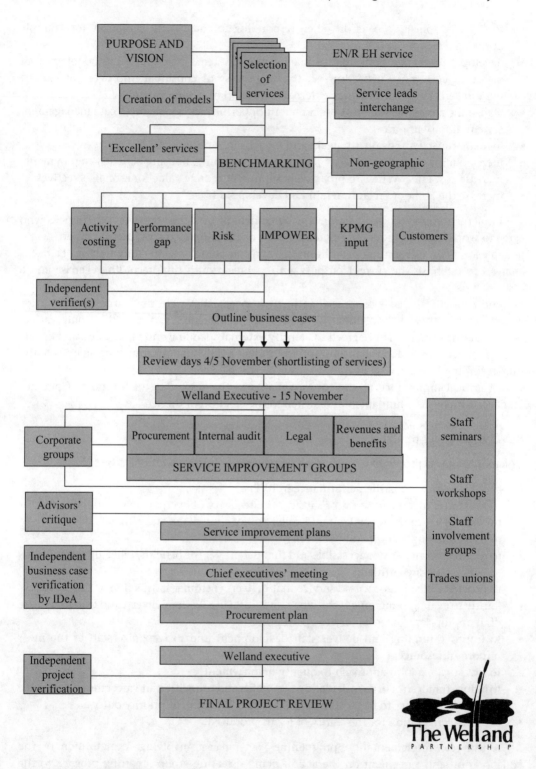

Figure 6.9   Welland shared service project diagram of project process

or reducing the cost of existing technology; another was the review and possible roll-out of proposed business process re-engineering work at Melton Borough Council.

Conclusion of the project

The project concluded on 22 March 2005 with the Welland executive panel agreeing to the proposals enshrined in the business cases agreed by the chief executives on 3 March.

Figure 6.9 contains a model of the project process.

Acknowledgement

It is acknowledged the Welland Partnership is the owner of the Welland shared services project and the outcomes including all the content and therefore the copyright for the material used from the Welland shared services project rests with the Welland Partnership.

The Welland Partnership may at any time publish a case study and tool kit in whatever medium and or through whatever channels that it chooses using the material it owns.

7 *Learning from the Case Studies*

Introduction

In this chapter the case studies will be reviewed to attempt to evaluate the potential for improvement they display. By identifying some of the learning, it will point to the issues that need to be resolved for successful development of shared services. The evidence of Chapters 4, 5 and 6 is that there are a great variety of routes available for the sharing of services. The case studies demonstrate that it is possible to share almost every service to a greater or lesser extent.

Finding the right arrangement for sharing is the key – and finding how to go about it depends on resolving a variety of political, technological and managerial issues. In the world of local government with the pressures facing individual councils the priority for sharing may not always have been high. Under the pressure to improve councils will first be concerned to put 'their own house in order' first without potentially exposing themselves to the difficulties of working in partnership or importing other councils' problems.

However, the government has increasingly found this position to be unsustainable and, given that local people are more concerned about the quality of services than about who delivers them, increasingly councils have had to explore sharing as an option.

So, if, as the government believes, shared services are a useful and potentially successful vehicle for improving services, it is important that the opportunities they provide are clearly spelt out for everyone. This chapter will seek to review the issue in four sections.

The first section will, based on the evidence of the case studies, test whether the evidence of the sharings that have taken place, suggest that sharing is a vehicle for improvement which is more effective than others.

The next two sections of the chapter will relate the sorts of considerations that have to be made in developing a project management structure as recommended by the Strategic Partnering Taskforce's *From Vision to Outline Business Case* (Office of the Deputy Prime Minister 2003c) as shown in Figure 7.1.

Though intended to prepare for a potential strategic partnership or a public–private partnership the model demonstrates the sorts of steps that need to be resolved to make for a successful shared service. It is of course possible to go from an idea to a solution informally and at great speed, but the approach recommended by the Strategic Partnership Taskforce is common throughout local government.

The fourth section will review some of the critical issues that have to be considered in managing the creation of a shared service.

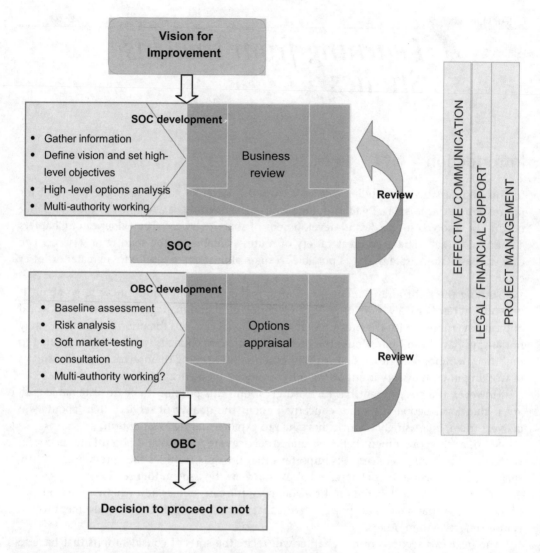

Figure 7.1   Strategic Partnering Taskforce model

Do shared services drive improvement faster than stand-alone services?

In trying to reach a conclusion it is clear that councils embark on sharing for a variety of reasons. A prime reason must be cost savings and the case studies in the previous chapters amply indicate that this is behind many shared services, such as Staffordshire Moorlands and Lichfield's joint ICT service and Macclesfield Borough Council and Congleton Borough Council's procurement service. Another example of cost saving was consortium procurement. Adur, Horsham and Mid Sussex District Council formed CenSus (Central Sussex) Partnership in which all three organizations linked up their knowledge and experience in a bid to deliver better services to the public through increased computer capacity. This is likely to produce an overall potential saving of £1.1 million across the three councils in the first five years.

But there are other reasons for sharing services, and in this section some of these are reviewed.

NON-FINANCIAL REASONS

Improving the performance and quality of the service to increase customer satisfaction

In the Anglia Revenues Partnership the aims were excellence and efficiency, promotion of electronic service delivery, economies of scale, ability to absorb change and improved customer satisfaction.

Offering greater choice to the customer

Crewe and Nantwich District Council/Congleton Borough Council's ICT was seen as the main operational and development vehicle for meeting local electronic government targets. Suffolk County Council and Mid Suffolk District Council intended their joint venture company to manage their HR, finance and ICT services and to create a new 'front-office' public access service, while East London Lettings Consortium provided a choice-based lettings system for member councils.

Improving service access

Surrey Jobs linked up all public sector bodies in a one-stop-shop approach with the aim of delivering efficiencies in recruitment processes, cost savings for recruitment and improved retention rates. The Cheshire out-of-hours contact centre aimed to provide better information about public services in the area, and better access to that information.

Offering greater opportunities for staff development, networking and sharing learning and practice across councils

The main foci of 'Crossing the Boundaries' were on sharing learning, developing common approaches to specific issues and running joint educational campaigns, joint training and joint responses to consultation on national initiatives/policy.

Sharing risk

The Pan London Contract Team, driven by criticism from SSI about the lack of robust contractual arrangements for children's residential care across London, created clear standards. The Alnwick and Castle Morpeth District Councils ICT partnership was formed to provide additional capacity and resilience as well as economies of scale.

Overall public service ethos

The North Yorkshire Audit Partnership's aims were to provide a reduction in the cost of services, to attain greater flexibility and professional expertise, to introduce clear financial control and performance measurements, to implement Best Value concepts and to demonstrate a willingness for the councils to co-operate. Norfolk County Services (NCS) has been committed to excellence in the delivery of a comprehensive range of facilities management and contract services, and strategic partnership arrangements. For Adur District Council and Worthing District Council joint working was the only option considered because the councils had an ethos of supporting in-house provision of services.

MEASUREMENT OF IMPROVEMENT

Whatever the reason for creation of shared services, they should produce some improvement in service delivery. There are three different strands of measures that can be used to test this.

First, service improvement may be measured by performance indicators both national and local. Though many have changed or been discarded and in some cases the definition has been changed, since 1998–9 there has been a reasonably consistent national body of information on councils' performance. Whilst some of these indicators deal with cost, the majority demonstrate the output/outcome performance of a council. There are difficulties here. For example, using the number of live claimants at a single point in time does not capture the full workload of a benefits section: the balance between different types of claim can make a big difference (rent rebates are much easier to administer than rent allowances) and the relationship between claims that need to be processed and the number of live claims at any one time will also vary between councils (inner city areas have a much more mobile population which will lead to many changes in claims).

Secondly, cost may be measured by the cost for carrying out certain processes. Comparisons of cost, where they are not recorded consistently, are more difficult to judge. The Chartered Institute for Public Finance and Accountancy (CIPFA) does maintain some measures but these tend to relate to inputs. Comparing service budgets is fraught with difficulty because of the definition of services which is very different across councils. For example, while staffing costs and some supplies and services costs will be clearly identifiable, as will be the cost of providing benefits administration services, councils' practices for the allocation of overhead costs, especially relating to service management and IT costs, can vary substantially.

Thirdly, service quality is a more nebulous concept but capable of measurement in terms of customer satisfaction or in the view of an inspectorate. Service improvement, though based on individual and objective statements of change is, in the round, subjective. This is because the experience of local people is individual and experiences and expectations can vary enormously. Nevertheless the Audit Commission, through its inspection and CPA judgements, has attempted to give a rounded judgement on service and corporate quality of councils. These judgements also rely heavily on performance and cost data.

An assessment of improvement

PERFORMANCE

Using the case studies we can attempt to make an assessment of performance improvement against the average of all councils:

Positive comparison

In terms of the attainment of delivering transactions electronically (BVPI 157), whereas the average of all councils rose from 33 per cent to 97.1 per cent between 2001–2 and 2005–6 – an improvement of three times in the number enabled – Alnwick and Castle Morpeth saw their combined average percentage rise by four times, Crewe and Congleton saw their average performance rise by nine times and the five councils in the Welland Partnership saw six times as many transactions enabled over the period.

There was a positive movement in the speed at which two sharing councils processed new benefits claims (BVPI 78a). The average for all councils between 2001–2 and 2005–6 was an improvement from 48 days to 34.5 days (an improvement of 13.5 days or 28 per cent). The Anglia Revenues Partnership councils saw their performance improve from an average of 91.5 days to 14.5 days (an average of 84 per cent).

Whereas the average improvement in the percentage of council tax collected by all councils (BVPI 9) between 2001–2 and 2005–6 was negligible (97 per cent to 97.15 per cent) the average improvement by the two councils in the Anglia Revenues Partnership was significantly better at 3 per cent.

There was a positive comparative improvement in the Anglia Revenues Partnership councils compared to the average of all councils in the accuracy of payments (BVPI 79a).

Negative comparison

The councils that were part of the Crossing Boundaries Trading Standards Partnership saw their average performance against a checklist of good trading standards practice (BVPI 166b) rise from 73 per cent in 2001–2 to 96 per cent in 2003–4. This compares unfavourably with an increase in the average for all councils of 67 per cent to 91 per cent.

Whereas the average improvement in the percentage of non-domestic rates collected by all councils (BVPI 10) between 2001–2 and 2005–6 was 0.6 per cent (98 per cent to 98.6 per cent) the average improvement by the two councils in the Anglia Revenues Partnership and for Northampton Revenues was less than that.

COST

Using the case studies above we can attempt to make an assessment of performance improvement in cost.

Positive comparison

Whereas the cost of waste collection (BVPI 86) for all district councils rose by an average of 45 per cent between 2001–2 and 2005–6, the average cost in Adur and Worthing only rose by 15 per cent, the average cost in North Norfolk and Great Yarmouth rose by an average of 32 per cent and that for Test Valley and New Forest by less than 10 per cent.

OTHER INDICATIONS FROM THE CASE STUDIES

Kerrier District Council previously bought all its plants for its parks service but by working with colleges and other partners to establish its own growing programme through its partnership with Penwith District Council it is estimated that council will save £20,000 a year.

East Lancashire Procurement Service claims that by mid 2005 it has saved over £200,000, invested in an online marketplace and payment cards programme as well as undertaking reverse auctions.

The Alnwick District Council and Castle Morpeth ICT partnership has made savings – from April to October 2003, e-government ICT hardware and software acquisitions via the partnership have resulted in a 25 per cent saving: some £23,000.

Macclesfield Borough Council/Congleton Borough Council achieved approximate savings in the first year of £35,000 for Congleton and a saving to Macclesfield of £107,000. These calculations did not take into account any further potential savings that may be possible such as increased buying power, e-procurement, centrally negotiated contracts, further partnership arrangements, savings accrued in staff time and lower cost of service provision.

The Gosport Borough Council/Fareham District Council building control partnership produced positive financial results. In the initial two-month period of operation from 1 February 2003 to 31 March 2003, the building control partnership achieved a surplus of £16,801 which was £14,481 more than anticipated, due to additional income of £2,230 and savings on expenditure of £12,251.

The Anglia Revenues Partnership by 2004 had achieved a net saving of £170,000 per annum against costs prior to the partnership, and accommodation costs of £70,000. The capital costs of Forest Heath not having to have invested in a new IT system of £100,000 have been supplemented by a saving on shared licences of £19,000 per annum.

The Suffolk County Council and Mid-Suffolk District Council customer centre has delivered financial savings of 25 per cent over the first three years of operation.

Taking the average number of jobs advertised by one of the middle-sized partners in 2005 (135 jobs), the Surrey Jobs sharing would have resulted in a £48,500 annual saving based on the net difference in alternative costings. Further savings have been made on IT training and developing the website.

The Pan London Contract Team has ensured estimated savings based on the contract that has impacted on price rises which were rising at an average of 9.2 per cent per annum but slowed to 3.2 per cent within three years of the contract being in place. This is estimated to equate to £11.2 million.

The cost of the internal audit service to each authority in ConsortiumAudit is less now in real terms than before the partnership.

The Northampton Revenues Consortium achieved a benefit for Northampton in that they did not need to replace a computer system and the consortium has a lower proportion of staff per household billed than other councils in Northamptonshire.

By using the Oracle software, Durham County Council expects to save around £900,000 a year on its back-office support operation once the project is fully implemented. It will also save Durham some of the capital costs of buying in the same software system from scratch.

Staffordshire Moorlands and Lichfield's joint contract will bring year-on-year efficiency savings which in their 2005–6 annual efficiency statement Lichfield say will lead to projected savings against the baseline of £46,015. The contract stipulates year-on-year efficiency savings totalling a target of £700,000 over the five-year contract life. The two councils shared consultancy and legal costs and managed the procurement process jointly. Cost savings included shared procurement/legal costs resulting in savings for each council of approximately £30,000.

Productivity benefits include:

- helpdesk support to suit business needs;
- provision of management information, enabling the quicker resolution of problems;
- improvement built into service delivery plans;
- skilled resource pool from Serco at competitive rates to ensure the councils are at the forefront of e-government through supporting new system implementations;
- change management initiatives (for example, Customer First) and upgrades on major back-office systems;
- greater reliability in the councils' core ICT systems;
- a reduction in time occupied with ICT problem resolution;
- business continuity assured as a result of better risk management and contingency planning;
- systems to support customer service meets the needs of the organizations.

The defined performance criteria are based on agreed SLAs. Performance monitoring is a contract requirement and readily accessible management information is available.

Quality

It is not possible to put quality improvements into a comparison framework but from the case studies evidence of improvements can be seen.

Kerrier District Council and Penwith District Council have increased the skills level of staff working in open space design and management.

The Cheshire out-of-hours contact centre provides customers with an enhanced service by dealing with simple information requests and will take and forward messages where specific local or professional expertise is required 24 hours a day.

The Pan London Contract Team has ensured that clear standards are set against which providers are monitored on an annual basis and helps councils by avoiding duplication and speeding up the contracting process.

The Blyth Valley and Wansbeck building control partnership has brought several benefits:

- The partnership manager has introduced consistent working practices for plan vetting and inspections across both councils.
- This includes the full exploitation of computerized systems. Fortunately both councils used the same back-office system – Uniform. Shared experience has been invaluable when the system has been upgraded
- The partnership manager has introduced a clearout of all older projects on the two councils' books, again helping to put the two services on a consistent basis
- Building control fees have been harmonized across the two councils

ConsortiumAudit has also benefited in terms of quality. Significant improvement in the internal audit services has been delivered and there are greater opportunities for staff, better quality work and greater scale, reduced management overheads, shared learning, higher staff motivation and a higher profile internally.

The Northampton Revenues Consortium achieved a benefit for Northampton in that they did not need to replace a computer system and were able to avoid the dislocation caused by the retirement of a member of staff. In addition it has enabled the retention of local accountability, standardized procedures, retained local discretion over granting reliefs and continued local customer access. Developments enabled have been the availability of customer e-payments and, in the near future, online access to individual accounts.

The Gosport Borough Council/Fareham District Council building control partnership allows for easier cover due to staff absence arising from leave, sickness and differing levels of activity across the area. The necessary changes in working environment and procedures have been achieved despite continued staff shortages and increasing workload. Major changes to building regulation legislation involving energy efficiency in all types of building have been implemented. Service achievements of the partnership since formation have included:

- The expansion of the emergency on-call surveyor base.
- Clarification and adoption of a legal basis for road renaming.
- Quality management system and procedures harmonized and registered and approved by BSI to ISO 9000-2000.
- Above-average score on the National Quality and Performance Matrix for Building Control.

Consortium procurement allows primarily for benefits of larger-scale purchasing than individual councils could achieve (total spend of £81 million (largest individual spend – £38 million)), reduced processing costs, greater expertise and enhanced availability of product sources.

North Yorkshire Audit Partnership reduced audit costs as well as improved access to specialist skills such as IT audit.

The Crossing Boundaries Trading Standards Partnership created a project called 'talkingshop' and allowed pupils, working on computers in the classroom, to interact directly with trading standards staff. By logging on to the 'talkingshop' website they are presented with a variety of consumer dilemmas that they have to unravel by researching links on the site. They then send their queries and answers to officers. In 2005 this was awarded the prestigious Brindley Medal, awarded annually at the Trading Standards Conference, for innovation and excellence within trading standards.

The East London Lettings Consortium won the Guardian Public Service Award for technology in November 2004.

Lichfield's contract with Staffordshire Moorlands has won three awards, one of which was from the National Association Outsourcing Association: the best IT outsourcing deal award.

Castle Morpeth District Council had an Audit Commission inspection of its ICT, telephony and reception services in 2000. Inspectors found the services to be 'poor'. A re-inspection judged the service as 'fair' and identified as one of the positive aspects to the services that the council has developed IT partnerships with Alnwick District Council and the Northumberland OnLine Partnership.

The Test Valley and New Forest partnership has through a merger of the two management teams reduced duplication and enabled complementary skills and resources to be used across the whole joint venture. Other benefits include a change in culture from DSO/contractor to partnership, directorate/service provider benefits to both councils in terms of Best Value service delivery, strategic service development and focus on key corporate objectives. Work is already increasing with the building cleaning and municipal property maintenance for Test Valley being taken back in-house. A unified fleet management and maintenance organization has been established, supported by a single software management package, showing immediate savings and benefits. Flexibility of labour and plant is bringing benefits across a range of operational service areas. The partnership provides more job security for the employees, particularly for Test Valley DSO staff, where the work volumes had diminished following housing stock transfer.

The Adur and Worthing PAWS partnership has raised the profile of both councils; staff consider that they may have greater buying power/leverage when bidding for external funding. Both councils feel that they have developed a shared understanding through a cross-fertilization of ideas. They are increasingly able to pool expertise in areas affected by staff shortages such as environmental health and planning. Partnership arrangements are being considered in some of these areas. Unintended outcomes of PAWS include enhanced focus on project management at a corporate level, for example, e-government.

The Anglia Revenues Partnership has been able to develop a performance culture amongst the staff, and foster a commercial culture that reflects the need to focus on the end customer.

In the Surrey Jobs sharing the website has been a great success to date with many positive impacts on the quality of the service: recruitment processes are speeded up both in the time taken to place adverts and to receive applications; there has been an increase in the number of applications which could be attributed to an improved quality of service for customers – that is, the candidates – a higher quality of candidates via the site and subsequently a higher number of appointments are made; there is greater reach to ethnic/minority groups by using the internet; positive feedback has been received from candidates, saying that the service was easy to use and better than most of the other websites encountered during their job seeking; a consistently high number of site visits from candidates and the numbers of registrations continue to grow, showing that the service is increasingly preferred by candidates to the traditional recruitment methods such as the press.

The Pan London Admissions Service claims that there are 64 per cent fewer unplaced children; 93 per cent of parents are allocated their preferred school place and 14 per cent of secondary applications are made online across London. This has led to significant cost savings, a single common interface for all London residents, borough access to a single shared service provider and an enhanced process for co-ordinated admissions in London. In addition it has improved collaboration between boroughs, provided a catalyst for reviewing processes in London and provided the infrastructure for new developments such as the 14–19 prospectus online and the development of a re-useable support and sustainability model.

The Kent Benefits Partnership (KBP) has already helped to increase council tax benefit take-up directly by around 1,500 successful claims. The team of assessment staff is also a useful potential training ground for the district councils.

The Devon Building Control Partnership is now in its second year of trading and during these two years it has introduced a new management structure and developed a centralized computer system. Already some of the above strategies are providing savings and by combining the services the partnership's performance indicators have improved and the establishment has been reduced by two full time staff.

Suffolk County Council and Mid Suffolk District Council's joint venture company produced the following benefits for the district council:

- a new contact centre was opened in November 2004 (for all council services – two more centres opened in 2005);
- a reduced turnaround times for claims;
- automated processes;
- integrated systems application with management information improved;
- the creation of training/career plans.

The percentage of enquiries resolved at first point of contact in the Suffolk County Council and Mid-Suffolk District Council customer centre has increased from the previous 41 per cent to 67 per cent during 2005. Customer satisfaction ratings of 88 per cent have been achieved. It has also consolidated and improved work processes, increased the skills and status of many employees in the joint venture through training and restructuring, introduced robust approaches to business planning and performance management, shifted resources from the back office to the front line and developed common solutions for frequent problems.

OVERALL ASSESSMENT

Though the sample is small, thus allowing only a minute amount of comparison to be made, and based on successful sharings only, it is difficult not to form the view that sharing of services appear to bring a significant number of potential benefits. The number and degree varies widely but consistently they achieve multi-layered improvement, and crucially faster than an individual council working on their own.

Believing that sharing is a good idea to achieve improvement is a crucial first step in creating a vision – critically the evidence suggests that sharing can achieve that improvement.

Creating the vision for a shared service

VISION FOR IMPROVEMENT

The Strategic Partnering Taskforce describes a vision as requiring a culture of openness and flexibility. Ideas may be linked to radically new ways to deliver the policies and objectives of the authority as set out in its community or corporate plan. Visionary leadership is essential to turn a good idea into an achievable goal but equally a sound analysis of the authority's approach to change and working in partnership is important as, whilst there is often ample support for councils which have a vision for improvement such as Best Value and keeping council tax low, there are reasons why creating a vision for sharing is difficult.

POLITICAL CONSIDERATIONS

Because councils are managed by members who have a direct link through the ballot box to local people, they will be conscious of their responsibility for managing the council in the interests of their constituents as they interpret that. They will recognize that moving away from direct provision to join up with other providers may be seen as:

- potentially jeopardizing the standards and/or quality of a service. Loss of control and flexibility are reasons often cited;

- a sign of weakness or criticism of existing arrangements, particularly amongst service professionals;
- involving a loss of local pride, a view often held by elected members.

Members may start to fear a loss of control and parochial issues, such as where the service will be based, whose staff will be transferred (because of the personal and financial issues involved) and whose approach (to methods of working, culture and style), will be paramount, meaning that reaching agreement on how the approach will be implemented becomes very difficult. There is also the issue of the capacity and interests of members. Expertise in managing large and complex organizations was not necessarily the reason that people sought election and, although the recent creation of structures that have reduced numbers of members being involved in these matters through executive roles, scrutiny and overview, it has not necessarily increased the ability of councils to act effectively. Members will also have a concern over what can be termed 'porous sovreignty' – in other words, who is ultimately in control of resources, particularly of concern in shared budgets, since this can divorce the costs of services from the tax-setting responsibilities of members.

Concern by members for the well-being of their electorate can also be a factor. Some efficiencies are only possible by shifting an imposition on to the customer. For example, oil companies cut costs decades ago by making motorists fill up their own cars. Ikea makes money while the customer makes the furniture. Members concerns are reflective of the concern of their community, particularly as customers' expectations are constantly increasing and members need to act as consumer representatives especially because of their exposure to complaints which though individual are often indicative of wider issues.

Another issue is procurement – many councils will have procurement strategies which will emphasize purchasing locally as a means of supporting the local economy, supporting local employment and increasingly reducing the environmental impact of purchasing. Suggestions of cost advantages through consortium purchasing and reliance on one national provider are less popular.

The lack of an 'honest broker' who can take an objective viewpoint in these circumstances often means the partnership stalls or even fails. For this reason joint procurement, where the individual council can still insist on local priorities rather than sharing and where an element of requirements have to be compromised, is often as far as members are prepared to commit. The consequence is that private sector intervention and delivery can be the catalyst for virtual joint working – stepping in where local authority joint working would be too difficult. Changes in political control can also cause delays.

Factors such as the grading of councils in CPA, and the possibility that weaker councils look to their better performing neighbours, may be holding back joint working on a voluntary basis. This can amplify problems with difficult previous history and past rivalries between councils, and differences in values and objectives. This is often a consequence of the scars caused by the re-organization of 1997.

This was an issue in the Welland Project where members were unhappy to think they were following an ODPM agenda and through the process were having to meet ODPM expectations of the quality and performance of services. As a result it was necessary to rethink the way the project was presented to members to overcome their concerns. The result was a set of keynote themes – these were:

- that the concept of shared services has been discussed for some time and there were examples of it starting to happen already between the partners;

- that the Welland Partners had sought to invest in this project themselves;
- that the Welland partners retained control of the project and individual service decisions;
- that the project was designed to test out the practicalities of this approach and no final decisions were to be taken unless the benchmarking and business case analysis proved conclusively that individual councils can achieve their aims in this way;
- that early work had demonstrated that each council could retain their autonomy and decision-making powers even if services are shared – each council has a common interest in improving services for local people as soon as they can, and the project provided the capacity to thoroughly review the opportunities.

In summary these can be described as 'control issues' – members feel that, by sharing, an element of the control of service delivery they exercise will be lost. However, Members are increasingly recognizing that the need is for unified service delivery, with service users having no need to understand whether the county, district or indeed other service provider is responsible for the services they receive. It is more important to focus attention on issues of how the area is as a place to live – 'place shaping' – and ensuring there are effective accountability arrangements so that people know who is responsible for what decision. This new thinking may help to increase the willingness of individual councils to share.

IMPROVING OUTCOMES FOR LOCAL PEOPLE

The vision for a new service must include a view on what would be a better, more accessible, responsive and more valuable service for local people. Local councils have not been good traditionally at improving services in such ways but this is a legitimate concern for members. Local councils are getting better at this. Many councils used the e-government agenda to improve access for local people by increasing the availability and accessibility of service channels through a better understanding of how local people wanted to interact with the council. An example of this can be shown through a survey for one council's IEG statement of 2001. The council surveyed local people to find out what they (the local people) considered was the way they wanted to be dealt with. The summary was that local people wanted:

- access
  - 'I'd like fast and simple access to as many services as I can through one contact point or one telephone number. I want to get the right person first time.'
  - 'I want to access information or services using the methods I prefer.'
  - 'I'd like to access services when I want them, not when they feel like opening.'
- service
  - 'Fast, friendly help from people I trust.'
  - 'I want to be able to trust what I am told.'
- individuality
  - 'I want my range of needs as a person met, especially if I am in a crisis. I want the council to understand my personal needs better.'
  - 'I want the council to make me aware of the opportunities, benefits and services to which I am entitled.'
  - 'I'd especially like to know what is available to me locally.'
  - 'I don't want to repeat information. I want to talk to someone who will own my problem. I want what is good for me, not the council.'

–   'If I have difficulties with literacy or language, or I am on a low income or have a disability, I'd like to have as easy access as everyone else.'

Overall, local government reacted and while in 2001, 26 per cent of services were e-enabled by March 2006 it was 98 per cent. The Society of Chief IT Managers' 'Better Connected' survey in 2006 said that top-rated 'transactional' sites are up from 38 in 2005 to 60, and that over 10.2m people visited local authority websites in December 2005 – a 40 per cent increase in visitor numbers. So far as customers are concerned, those surveyed said over the previous 12 months there was a 5 per cent improvement in the right information being found and, overall, 84 per cent now say they will return to the website compared with 7 per cent who say they will not.

Consistently, councils report increases in numbers of calls once call centres were up and running. South Hams set up theirs in October 2005 and have seen calls increase by 40 per cent. Canterbury handled 27 per cent more calls in the first six months after they opened their call centre with a high customer satisfaction rate (88 per cent) for its services to date.

These changes have had an impact on the way customers use services. Whereas in 2001 in Dorset only 21 per cent used e-mail and websites the figure in a 2004 survey was 32 per cent. Telephone use had declined. This change of access channels will also have impacted on costs – figures suggest that a personal visit costs a council £7.50, a letter £6 and a telephone call £1.70, but e-mailing, web use and texting cost only 1p. For example, Tameside's 'Customer First' functionality got 679,813 unique visitors at a cost of £0.25 per visit – compared to the call centre's 314,602 unique calls at a cost of £1.39 each.

However, because expectations are rising, local people want more – in the survey referred to earlier, people said also 'I want public services to use the most cost-effective and efficient systems to deliver information and services' and as we saw in the Welland project local people were not resistant to the idea of providing services differently: all recognized the need to do so. Their aspirations were for more effective, efficient and consistent services with greater value for money.

This provides a huge challenge for local councils.

CURRENT CONCERNS OF COUNCIL MANAGEMENT

According to the *Local Government Chronicle* in October 2005 few council chief executives think that making efficiencies is a top priority. Whilst at first sight this may appear negative, it recognizes a reality that many other issues are a higher priority. The top three priorities were 'Addressing the needs of the local community', followed by 'Meeting the needs of local politicians' and then 'Meeting central government demands'. However, the fourth and fifth priorities were 'Keeping council tax down' and 'Gershon efficiencies'.

This recognizes that, because joint working is relatively unproven as a means of service delivery, elected members and senior officers may be particularly cautious about applying it to services that have a high profile particularly in relation to national targets and central government priorities.

In summary these are reputational management issues. Senior officers, particularly chief executives, will be most concerned that investing time and energy in sharing might be at the expense of achieving other targets at the risk to their personal future career prospects.

At the present time there are still historical issues that impact on the willingness of senior managers to engage in sharing. Past attempts that failed will colour opinions and concerns about high-profile outsourcings that did not go well influence views. Another factor is the relatively low awareness of customer needs for service delivery. Despite the progress in implementing electronic government, many councils lack sophistication in providing for customer needs and this can blind them to the opportunities.

Another issue is the relative strength of people in the organization of a council to act as champion. Professional rivalries are a factor, in that the professional officer leading a department will 'know best' the needs of that department. But there is also the issue of the emphasis in both pay scales and status on the span of control, especially the size of the team. The pay weighting given in most public sector organizations to managing tasks – as opposed to people – is low. But the reality is that managing an outsourced service, because of the issues mentioned earlier like loss of direct control, is actually a harder task. This is similarly reflected in perceived status and directly fosters empire building. This makes the prospect of senior managers volunteering for the transfer of responsibility unlikely. In a survey of senior officers conducted in 2004 a quarter suggested that a reason preventing sharing was 'loss of intellectual property', presumably suggesting a desire not to lose their own personal knowledge of service delivery.

SINGLE SERVICES OR A 'BASKET'?

The evidence seems to confirm that in creating a shared service it is not sensible to be too ambitious. There are few examples of two or more services being brought together at one time. Initially this might seem attractive – the costs of creating the sharing can be spread and learning can be transferred – but most attractively the benefits gained from the sharing of one service can be used to support the potential costs of sharing a better performing service with another. This assumes that councils are a mixture of services performing at different standards.

In the event, this principle collapses quickly because members and senior managers are unwilling to risk censure from exposing services to a potential reduction in standard or increase in cost simply to achieve a sharing. This is best seen through the prism of the councils' fiduciary responsibility to its taxpayers. There is an allowance whereby 'reasonable extra costs' can be tolerated but, not unnaturally, there will be a reluctance to take a cavalier attitude to this responsibility.

Accordingly, in the search for certainty it is unlikely that analysis other than for a single service would give the clarity required and allow judgements to be made on the merits of particular sharing proposals.

This is not to say a 'basket' approach might not work, but that the evidence seems to be (excepting Adur and Worthing, Welland) that seeking to structure a wide-ranging partnership is difficult.

SOCIAL AND ECONOMIC DIFFERENCES BETWEEN COUNCILS

It was noted above that there are differences between councils because of the needs of local people. Some councils will focus on issues of regeneration as being crucial to the success of the local area; other councils see issues of cleanliness and preservation of the environment as their top priority. The result may be that different priorities take precedent and the energy of members and senior officers may be directed to that end rather than the efficiency of the services themselves.

This shows itself in the way councils are internally organized and in the councils' life-cycle. The impact of the stability of a council cannot be underestimated. Has the chief executive been in position for a while and likely to be in place for a while? Are the senior managers likely to be involved in the proposal to share directly affected or can they take a wider dispassionate view? (Managers, particularly in more traditional, hierarchical organizations, can be a barrier to joint working because such an approach can increase their workloads and challenge their positions. Because elected members do not have a clear idea of the benefits that could accrue from joint working, officers are sometimes able to dissuade them away from this course of action by emphasizing the difficulties and risks.) Has the council just had a CPA inspection and is it therefore focused on dealing with the aftermath?

The culture of the council is critical. As well as looking for the council to be open to the concept of sharing there needs to be a culture that will support the organization through the inevitable upheaval that will result. In particular, what view is taken by the trades unions and other staff representatives? Will they co-operate or be difficult? Will the staff affected themselves take a positive or negative view of the proposal?

PUBLIC SERVICE ETHOS, TRADING AND PROCUREMENT

Even today, those that work in local councils have a strong public service ethos. The lexicon of surplus (and worse 'profit' and even worse 'loss') are an anathema to members and senior officers. So to suggest opening up the council to quasi-trading activities is culturally difficult. This breeds an atmosphere of caution and risk aversion which can stifle new ways of working such as sharing.

In February 2002 the Audit Commission published a paper, *Competitive Procurement*, based on the lessons emerging from best value inspection and other research. It claimed 30 per cent of councils were unenthusiastic about procurement opportunities; 40 per cent had a mixed or ambivalent attitude and 12 per cent were striving but struggling. Many councils will instinctively feel they do not have the available resources to embark on a long, difficult and complex exercise that might be abortive and, worse, divert resources from the main task in hand, which is improvement in service delivery. Another issue is availability of skills. One of the conclusions of the Audit Commission's report was that councils lacked expertise in procurement – this would clearly prevent some councils bringing a sharing to a successful conclusion.

The government has already responded to this by the setting up the regional centres of excellence but this may not be sufficient to overcome the individual councils' needs for support to overcome the skills gap.

One further stumbling block to the growth of sharing is possible uncertainty caused by the need to apply EU procurement rules. The fear now is that councils and other public bodies could face EU legal action if they do not go out to tender when looking to share services in this way, as EU procurement law requires that large public contracts be advertised Europe-wide, to make it easier for companies to bid for contracts in other EU countries. Recent European court rulings may mean that this law also applies to arrangements where public sector organizations work together to deliver services more efficiently. The Local Government International Bureau (LGIB), the body that represents UK councils in Brussels, has written to MEPs about the issue. It has called for changes to EU directives to clarify that public sector agencies are indeed exempt from the rules where they choose to make savings by sharing back-office functions. A draft report by the European Parliament has been drawn up calling on the European Commission to clarify the procurement rules in this area. Some MEPs are also calling for the Commission to bring forward legislation to resolve the issue.

Another issue is the unpreparedness of councils to undertake 'trading' – first, because though the powers exist they are not 'core' to the council's success and may detract from the administration of services and, secondly, because they are not set up or skilled to perform such managerial tasks. Many councils may have felt there was no encouragement from the government to engage in trading. For example, according to the Association for Public Service Excellence (APSE), it only became clear when the 2003 Local Government Act took effect that it was legally permissible for local government to run shared service centres for a range of public bodies.

SETTING CLEAR OBJECTIVES

The setting of objectives requires considerable work. Doing this is critical to the success of any project, but particularly a sharing, in that it is important that the project owner – whether a leading member or officer – is able clearly to understand what the sharing is trying to achieve. Unless time is spent defining and recording the objectives and sharers can articulate these objectives, communication with staff, unions, members, stakeholders and potential partners will be difficult. Over three-quarters of senior officers in a 2004 survey suggested 'agreeing the right approach' and 'too many decision-makers involved' were reasons preventing progress on sharing.

The objectives that are agreed should be the result of detailed analysis and a thorough review. The strategic outline case (SOC) determines what is likely to be the right way forward and to show whether, in principle, there is likely to be a good business case for that approach. In many cases, lack of success in promoting a project from the good idea stage may be due to others within the organization who do not share the same vision or who may be slower to see the benefits of what is proposed, or quicker to see its shortcomings. A good SOC will help to elicit support from people who are resistant to change, who can prevent change from happening or who are best placed to assist the changes. It will ensure that the preliminary thinking is robust and well founded.

The SOC will also prepare the ground for a more detailed options analysis to be conducted and for a full business case to be prepared. Once the SOC is agreed then more detailed analysis is needed and an examination of options undertaken in greater depth. The results of this analysis together with the inherent risks of the different options need to be set out in the OBC.

The first step in setting objectives is to identify what is best to share.

Choosing the 'right' service to share

A report produced by the New Local Government Network (NLGN) in 2003 called *Crossing Boundaries* quoted from a CIPFA survey of 2001 that identified the following as services which could particularly benefit from joint working:

- standard back-office functions (IT, finance, personnel, architectural, engineering, property management);
- services where back-office functions are standardized and councils have little or no local discretion, but where local front-office branding is important (for example, benefits, council tax collection);

- technical functions that could benefit from a larger platform to share in the investment required and the business risks (for example waste disposal, fleet management and maintenance);
- specialist services where skills and expertise are scarce and expensive (for example education support services, some social services functions);
- services where clients or customers cross geographic and institutional boundaries themselves (for example trading standards, concessionary fares schemes, mental health services);

Ignoring the five most common sharing areas (which were outlined in Chapter 3) for joint working, the evidence of those that have been created and mentioned in the annual efficiency statements and in the case studies broadly confirms the NLGN analysis and shows that over three-quarters of the services shared by 2005 can be covered by the broad heading of 'back-office' services operated in support of service delivery, have limited customer interaction (with the notable exception of revenues and benefits services) and tend to be high on process.

One exception to this is building control and in this chapter and the next some of the special reasons why this should be so are identified.

So what are the factors that influence the choice of service for sharing?

LIMITED POLITICAL INTEREST IN SERVICE DELIVERY

Generally the priorities of council members are more likely to be concerned with issues such as education, housing, highways, leisure and waste management. Other services are of less concern to members and those listed in the annual efficiency statements and our case studies reflect this. This is because the outcomes from the services are relatively standard and therefore objectives are reasonably straightforward. The exception to this will be benefits, where members will be concerned at issues such as the speed of processing benefits claims and increasing the take-up of benefits across the eligible population. In this case, however, members tend to have limited room to influence what is a highly structured service. In any case many councils have developed a strategy whereby the customer service aspects are now integrated with an 'all council front-office' structure.

HIGHLY PRESCRIBED SERVICES THAT HAVE LITTLE LOCAL VARIATION

If there is less scope for disagreements about the objectives of services there is likely to be an easier progress to sharing objectives. For example, the framework for revenues and benefits services is prescribed by the Department of Work and Pensions. Building control is also based on a national set of regulations that limits local flexibility. This makes it much easier for the potential sharers to agree a service specification and there is a wealth of performance indicators available that enables each partner to get a clear idea of the relative performance of the services, their costs and the likely scope for improvement.

SERVICES WHICH ARE LOCATION INDEPENDENT OR HAVE A SUBSTANTIAL ELEMENT THAT IS LOCATION INDEPENDENT (IN OTHER WORDS, HAVE LITTLE FACE-TO-FACE CUSTOMER CONTACT)

Services which require a high degree of face-to-face contact with service users seem to offer less scope for joint working as the objectives of sharers could be widely divergent. However, services that have a high back-office element offer more scope. The examples of non-domestic rate collection in Northampton/Wellingborough shows it is not imperative for all the activities to be close to where bill payers are so long as there are adequate systems (through the internet or by telephone) for queries to be answered. ICT services can provide service from distant locations. Plan checking for building control can be done remotely.

SERVICES WHERE THERE ARE STRONG LINKS BETWEEN THE SERVICE PROVIDED BY COUNTY AND DISTRICT

Historically this explains the large number of highways functions partnerships. Of late this has been a significant factor in the growth of waste management partnerships where the roles of collection of waste and disposal of waste has had to be brought closer together to ensure government targets can be achieved. The same impact has been seen in the growth of e-government partnerships where the government's target of 100 per cent of transactions being electronically available by December 2005 required county councils and district councils to work together.

SERVICES WHICH REQUIRE A HIGH DEGREE OF INFRASTRUCTURE (FOR EXAMPLE ICT)

For some services/activities expensive capital assets are required that are used infrequently or there is a large ICT element which operates under full capacity. The objectives of the sharers will then be similar: that is, greatest capacity at least cost. Examples could be large ICT systems which support CRM systems and payroll processing. Something like winter gritting needs large stockpiles of material and vehicles in strategic locations ready for occasional use.

SERVICES WHERE COUNCILS HAVE TO RELATE TO A LARGER EXTERNAL BODY

Sometimes it makes sense for councils to work together to present a better case to an external body, for example when applying for European funding or contributing to regional planning guidance. This was a positive spur to the Welland Partnership, who were able to gain funding through working together to promote their shared objective of promoting their rural communities. Of growing interest is the development of combinations of councils working together to offer larger-scale procurement opportunities which can bring economies of scale through taking a more robust relationship to larger suppliers. Whilst it might be thought that the established network of procurement consortia had taken maximum advantage of this sort of sharing, the evidence of more and more councils (for example, Gloucester and Cheltenham) joining together to take direct action suggests these opportunities are real. The consortia themselves are now beginning to share and offer councils bulked opportunities based on the consortia itself presenting a common procurement of certain items.

SERVICES WHERE ACCESS TO EXTERNAL FUNDING SOURCES IS NEEDED

A number of sources of external funding in recent years have focused on bids from partnerships rather than local councils working alone, or bids that explore more innovative approaches. This includes the local government online programme, Invest to Save and Strategic Partnering Taskforce initiatives. The availability of funding and support has often driven local councils to consider options for joint working and put together joint bids which they may not have done if this was not a key requirement of the funding. Clearly in these circumstances objectives are shared. The implementation of joint working undoubtedly requires significant upfront investment with regard to both time and other resources. The availability of external funding and support to assist with the set-up costs is certainly an important driver. This explains the large number of councils that have worked together in e-government partnerships.

SERVICES WHERE THERE IS AN UNEVEN PATTERN OF DEMAND

This can be a very good reason for working together, providing that the peaks and troughs of demand do not happen at the same time in the sharing councils. For example, this could help to 'flatten out' the throughput of applications in areas such as building control. This was quoted as an objective of the Blyth Valley and Wansbeck building control partnership.

HIGH DEGREE OF RAPID CHANGE REQUIRED BY EXTERNAL REGULATORS/ STAKEHOLDERS

Where external regulators (such as government or the Audit Commission) are placing significant pressure on councils to change quickly the way that they operate or to significantly improve in a specific area, then there is potential for councils to work together to implement such changes and drive improvement. Examples are responding to e-government and to recycling targets where the councils share the objective of having to move quickly.

SERVICES WHERE THERE ARE PRIVATE SECTOR COMPETITORS

This is particularly the case with services such as building control. Many councils find the income generated useful in offsetting other expenditure. The services are in direct competition with the private sector and the objective the councils share will be to prevent incursion into the council's market share.

SERVICES WHERE THERE ARE PARTICULAR SKILL SHORTAGES

This is particularly the case with services such as environmental health, planning and building control. For example, currently there is a national shortfall in the number of building control professionals required to deliver the service and many councils have an ageing workforce. In ICT services, for example, councils are in direct competition with the private sector. In this situation the councils' shared objective is to ensure the scarce resources they have are put to best use. Also, having a larger portfolio means that staff could be paid more (but that there would be fewer of them) thus attracting/retaining higher skilled staff. It could also be that greater volumes allow councils the luxury of 'growing their own' staff.

THE COUNCILS' VIEW OF CHANGE REQUIRED, RISK AND BENEFITS SOUGHT

Services throughout councils vary in cost and performance. Depending on the population they serve they receive different levels of priority for investment. In considering a sharing one of the initial considerations must be the 'problem' the council wants to solve. Questions such as 'What do we want to change?', 'Why do we want to change it?', 'Who will the changes impact/otherwise affect?', 'When does the change need to happen?' and 'What will it be like after the change?' are critical to establish before discussions move into a detailed discussion of strategic fit, available options, achievability and affordability.

This discussion will result in a 'high-level' view of the service that will tend to have limited the range of shared service options available and to have established the strategic business need, established where each service is now and set business need in local service context.

Figure 7.2 demonstrates how an analysis of the perceived benefits required and of difficulty/risks will inform the sort of shared service structure needed.

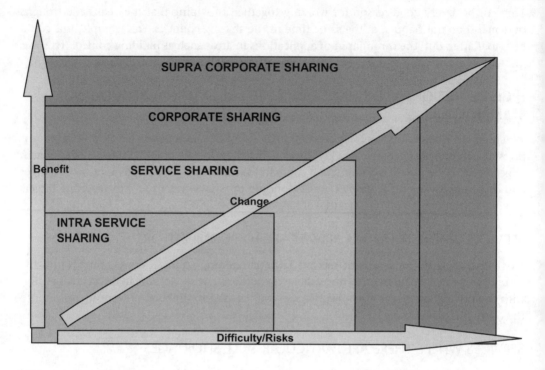

Figure 7.2   Model of the benefit and difficulty/risk relationship of sharing

The determining factor as to which is the 'best' structure to develop the shared service is not the legal powers to effect the sharing since these are common whatever the method. Nor is it the formality of the agreement between the councils since even the most informal arrangement can be governed by a legally enforceable document.

Figure 7.2 shows the relationship that a council will see in the different types of sharing between the possible benefits and the likely difficulty and risks in achieving that benefit through change. The relative degree of risk/difficulty is dependent on the degree of change attempted. The more ambitious the change, the more the difficulty and risk increases as does the possible benefits – this is because it exposes the proposed change to more conflicting issues whilst presenting more opportunities for rationalization. The early analysis that establishes what needs to be achieved will determine at what point in this continuum the 'change' needs to be fixed.

In general the guiding factors are risk transference and the degree of managerial/organizational change required to create the outcomes the sharing is intended to deliver.

Creating the outline business case for a shared service

The outline business case (OBC) develops the SOC. It will require sound business analysis of a wide range of data, judgments and assumptions, all of which must be adequately evidenced, and an appraisal of the investment required. The same areas should be addressed in the preparation of an OBC as they are in the SOC. The areas to be addressed in the OBC are:

- the strategic context
- the economic case – service need and options
- the customer case
- the commercial case
- the financial case – affordability and VfM
- project management – timetable and deliverability
- the recommended course of action.

The ultimate aim of the OBC should be to support and justify the case for the sharing to be advanced. The OBC needs to be a realistic assessment of what is possible, not a list of impractical proposals. The prime purpose of the OBC should be to provide the project team and the respective members (or the relevant approval body) with key details of the project, including the service implications, the business justification for the approach being followed and the cost of the project to the sharing councils.

Developing an OBC requires a systematic identification of information, followed by consideration and analysis of that information. Using a systematic approach, an OBC will form the basis of decision-making to allow the councils to decide if the project should proceed as planned. Once approved, the OBC gives consent to commence the sharing including, if appropriate, a formal procurement process or the development of the public/public partnership. If the procurement is subject to the EU procurement rules, the OBC triggers the need to consider placing an advertisement in the *Official Journal of the European Communities*. For some councils, a Prior Information Notice (PIN) may have been issued and published in OJEU at soft market-sounding stage, but, if not, this notice needs to be considered when the OBC is issued.

The OBC needs to show that the project is economically sound and that the preferred option represents VfM. Additionally, it needs to establish that the preferred option is the best way forward. The OBC also sets the key parameters and milestones for managing and tracking progress, and for taking a project forward in a way that focuses on achieving the objectives and outputs required.

ISSUES PARTICULAR TO SHARED SERVICES THAT NEED TO BE DEALT WITH IN THE OBC

Differences in services

Different councils have different needs for their services dependent on the needs of local people. This shows itself in the historic level of investment of the service and the demands put upon the service. Where this is significantly different in the proposed sharing services there will be increased difficulty in reaching an accommodation. In addition at any one time different services will have a different balance of performance, cost and service standards and quality. Where these are significantly different it makes it more difficult to reach a level that is acceptable to both sharers.

In addition the direction of travel of different councils and services are different. Despite the setting of government targets, the Best Value regime and particular incentives such as the Implementing Electronic Government Grant and the Planning Grant, there will often be a significant variance in performance, and there will still be some services whose performance is lagging behind.

The balance of these issues, if significant, will make it difficult to reach an agreed service specification and improvement plan, since that might require one council to reduce temporarily the level of service – a difficult concept to explain to local people and regulators.

Managing performance

If a shared service is to be created and a service specification agreed there still remains the issue of delivery and reporting. This could be a problem for those managing the service. For example in the Welland situation there was such a large difference between the Rutland and East Northamptonshire service standards and the enforcement policy that officers would, on a day-to-day basis, be required to operate a two-tier service which professional officers were unwilling to countenance.

Reporting on these issues was considered to be problematic. In this case study the requirements of reporting were very different and this would have led to significant costs (officers duplicating reports and travelling to additional meetings) that one of the potential sharing councils was not willing to bear. Despite the lack of legislative barriers, finding an appropriate governance vehicle and gaining the commitment of partners to this arrangement can take time and often slows down the development of sharing. Joint committees appear to be one of the most common governance vehicles where each member has equal voting rights. That is the model adopted by the Anglia Revenues Partnership. However, there the two councils require different reporting into their decision-making process as a means of reinforcing their retained authority as autonomous councils.

Planning horizons

Different planning horizons are an issue in setting a service specification. Most frequently this will be a factor in terms of considering the potential sharing in terms of the likelihood a sharing could deliver improvement before a council election. This would relate to whether a particular administration could complete the process and whether they could quote the improvement in election material.

This includes, for example, the differing timeframes of existing contracts and the non-alignment of Best Value review programmes, which mean that options for service delivery are reviewed at different times by individual councils, and this does not encourage consideration of a joint solution.

More basically, officers may seek to work on a sharing with one eye on their own personal situation – in at least one of the case studies the sharing was initiated because of the retirement of a senior officer.

Availability of capacity/future funding

As previously stated the implementation of joint working requires substantial initial investment to establish the appropriate infrastructure and this is often underestimated. This includes the need for certain key skills and expertise particularly in relation to project management and procurement. Project management is as good as the resources available will allow. Sharings will also require the support of legal and financial expertise and business analysis. This may not be immediately available and the costs of importing expertise can be expensive. In the Welland project the third-party costs amounted to a third of a million pounds and the opportunity cost within the councils could have well been the same.

This lack of capacity also extends to the funding required for investment in new systems and service improvements and the internal monitoring required.

No two councils are exactly alike in their financial stability. This is due to the vagaries of the Rate Support Grant calculations which can have a distorting impact on a particular council due to the changes to the criteria and the political aspirations of councils – some having a policy of low council-tax levels. Some councils, having divested themselves of their council housing, may have adequate capital expenditure programmes to invest in services, whilst others may be restricted.

The other issue is that often the services which are 'best' for sharing are those which, because of their lack of political interest, have been starved of resources in the past. This situation has created a low-performing service and this makes it difficult to create the resources from within the service to invest in improvements. On the other hand, it also makes a shared efficiency potentially the only way to make improvements.

This is equally an issue in the cost of creating a shared service. This will not be achieved at no cost. Depending on the degree of formality sought, the costs of staff and advisors and the disruption to the services while the sharing is being organized may be substantial.

Central government reporting/auditing requirements. The threat of intervention or an inspection/audit by one of the government inspectorates can be a factor in councils getting involved in sharing. This will be a concern for the 'better' council in a sharing. If the 'poorer' council's service is so poor that inspectorates were to seek to intervene, then all the work in dealing with that intervention and the improvement needed would fall upon the 'better' council at their risk. This could well be a significant burden they would be unwilling to accept.

Additionally, government departments currently require reporting to be based on the two separate council areas and therefore the shared service has to accept a cost of maintaining two sets of records.

Geography

A sharing between two neighbouring councils and councils with the same portfolio of responsibilities is on first sight easier to arrange than with a distant council or one from a different tier. But this is not necessarily insuperable. However, for it to be successful the following issues need to be dealt with.

Councils will be anxious to retain their connection to local people; this means retention of mechanisms for accountability. Setting up a joint committee at distance is difficult and brings with it the difficulty of continued involvement at a cost. Councils will want to retain local access points and the 'branding' of their council and this has to be factored in. The time and cost of travelling has to be included – despite the advances in electronic communication the use of things such as video conferencing are not widespread and not likely to be widely acceptable for use at public meetings (such as committees of members) for many years.

The Welland case study demonstrated that some services, revenues and benefits for example, could be shared (probably by the creation of a 'virtual' processing centre) as long as a local service point was created and adequate customer interfaces were available. Legal, audit and procurement services were equally possible to create on the basis that a presence was retained in the councils' locations.

STAFFING ISSUES

Hitherto this book has not referred significantly to the staff working in councils. This is not an oversight. Councils have the responsibility to deliver services for local people and this has to be their first priority. Recognition of this has freed up thinking in many councils to allow them to embrace new ways of working. But inevitably in sharing there is an initial presumption by many council members and most certainly in officers that this will mean a reduction of employment or at a least a change in employment conditions. As a result the OBC must cover this issue and seek to reach an agreement on what will happen.

The creation of the OBC may result in the following HR implications:

- Staff and the resulting processes and technology may be centralized in one location; for example, a contact centre or branch offices, or there may be more remote and home working.
- Jobs may be redesigned resulting in a selection process, training needs, changes to job descriptions and salary changes. In a shared service, some staff may face a de-motion in status while retaining their terms and conditions. In another, staffing structures would not necessarily be pared back to the minimum in order to ensure resilience to unforeseen events for example, technology failure.
- There may be changes to terms and conditions, over and above TUPE and secondment, for example, flexible working hours, place of work.
- Skills development may take place in new technology such as CRM and Workflow and/or self-serve for managers and staff. Developing existing staff may be better for morale and less costly than recruiting new staff.
- Streamlined processes and a shared service together may change the staffing requirements from generalist transactional/administrative roles to more skilled specialist or customer-facing roles. Once again, there are skills, training and development implications.

A creative approach to working hours and location may bring benefits for both the new service and employees. Job redesign may require part-time posts, which could be attractive to staff looking to balance work with other commitments. Staff who are unable or unwilling to work at the partner council's offices may be offered the opportunity to work at home or remotely; this would be made possible by technology or a split between front- and back-office roles.

Where a sharing is proposed, selecting staff for the new service needs to be anticipated. Ring-fencing posts for existing staff is often used to minimize displacement. However, this depends on the capacity of staff to meet the requirements of the new job roles. Inevitably there will be skills differences; if the new service uses the ICT systems from one council, the staff there will be more skilled than those from the other council. This presents challenges for an equitable selection procedure across all organizations. Finally, often only fractions of individual posts will be saved through shared services. In such cases, job redesign and use of flexible working arrangements such as home-working have to be used to overcome this.

Some sharing options may involve redundancies or early retirements, the costs of which must be considered at the appraisal stage as they can be extremely high. There may be differences in redundancy policies and procedures between councils and the question of which partner will bear the costs must also be decided. An approach in one partnership was that issues associated with staff not transferring to the new service should be resolved at source; that is, the transferring authority should bear the costs of redundancy or early retirement. This may run counter to the principle of shared costs and risks but was in response to an earlier partnership in which staff were transferred against their will.

While redundancies may not be necessary in order to achieve efficiency savings, other forms of staff movement also incur costs and decisions will need to be taken on who will pay these costs. The host council will also incur costs if incoming staff have more favourable terms and conditions. In the Welland case study a 'levelling-up' of terms and conditions was anticipated. In addition, one partner authority in this project belonged to a different pension fund, making employer contributions potentially a third higher for staff transferred from that authority.

In many cases, TUPE will apply. The transfer is a complex process and requires considerable work as does the harmonization which may follow. Under any partnering model option where there is a change of employer TUPE will apply (unless a redundancy situation exists). This will mean staff must transfer on their existing terms and conditions. There are regulations that must be followed involving staff consultation. Also there is legislation covering consultation, notification and information that must be available to staff (Collective Redundancies and Transfer of Undertakings (Protection of Employment) (Amendment) Regulations 1999). There is also the Two Tier Workforce Code of Practice Regulations issued in 2003; these include consultation with individual employees affected and mean that new staff must be appointed on terms and conditions no less favourable than existing staff for the same role.

Secondment avoids many of the issues associated with TUPE and has been a popular option, particularly in joint venture projects with the private sector. Staff retain the security of council employment and can move back when necessary. However, inevitably fewer savings are made in staffing costs. Moreover, if they do move back or the contract ends, they must be reabsorbed into the council or offered redundancy, which will incur costs at a later date as their old post will no longer exist and wage drift may have occurred. In short, the council who seconds the staff bears most of the risk.

There is the option to consider redeployment of staff within or across the councils when a transfer, TUPE, relocation, secondment is likely for an employee. An example may be where a member of staff does not want to or cannot practically move to another location. An employee may challenge a transfer under their contract of employment if an attempt is made to relocate them outside their current council.

Redeployment is an attractive option for members and staff as it is in the spirit of redirecting resources to the front line and can retain important skills and experience in the authority. However, it may only be a realistic option in larger councils. It may also prove to be costly once recruitment and retraining costs have been taken into account.

RISKS NEED TO BE MINIMIZED, MANAGED OR MITIGATED

There are risks in the creation of shared services. The aim of the OBC should be to identify these, review them and plan action to mitigate them. However, even whilst the OBC is being created there are risks. Though these may be temporary these should not be underestimated. In the Welland project a review was undertaken to identify these risks – essentially these temporary risks concern the need to continue service in face of the inevitable uncertainty.

Once the shared service has been created these temporary risks should have been resolved through discussion and agreed as part of the organizational protocols. The longer-term risks identified in the Welland project fell into three groups:

- *People* – Issues of relative values of each sharing council; opposition from staff after the sharing; staff retention/morale/contracts; lack of local knowledge; reliance on partners continued commitment to partnership; loss of immediate control and reliance on third party.
- *Process* – Need for clear responsibilities and reporting lines; effective communications; agreeing to common working practices including access to local information and records; prioritization protocols; data protection to ensure confidentiality and freedom of information; different policies on data and document retention; performance sanctions.
- *Technology* – Differences of IT systems; potential integration issues with other systems; security; back-ups.

In terms of resolution in the sharing, those best placed to manage individual risks should assume ownership of those risks. Councils should undertake a full risk assessment before entering into the sharing. Ongoing risks should be fully documented in terms of who should manage them. Councils should consider each risk under each category and document:

- what the risk is
- what the potential impact or effect might be
- whether the probability of the risk materializing is high, medium or low
- whether the impact would be high, medium or low
- how this risk can be minimized, managed or mitigated.

Risks with high probability and high impact demand most attention.

AFFORDABILITY

It may be a surprise to observers but there are often significant differences in the way different councils account for their services. In the Welland project there was, on the part of one council, an apparent lack of detail and clarity in the budgetary figures put forward. The reason for this was their treatment of support costs – they were not allocated precisely to individual services.

Clearly this approach does get in the way of defining affordability. There will always be the concern in a sharing that one or other of the partners may seek to make savings in the future from the shared service, thus endangering the service. This has to be resolved first by taking an open book approach and building in limits on the freedom to reduce (or, in some cases, increase) budgetary availability. This calls for the agreement on sharing to have some built-in financial stability and this may mean that questions of future affordability arise in one or other of the partners.

The way to overcome this is to prepare shared financial forecasts over the period of the proposed sharing – say five years – that relate the costs to the intended service or other benefits – in other words, a business plan. Such a financial assessment would have to include baseline information including existing costs and processes and a public sector comparator (PSC) or reference assessment which factors in the ability the partners individually has to bring about change.

THE LENGTH OF PARTNERSHIPS

All councils set their budget annually. This does not normally allow for major shifts in budget profiles. It is not possible to use such a short term in sharings where there are large numbers of staff involved on long-term permanent contracts for a particular service delivery or where there are large amounts of investment required for service delivery. Most councils plan over a three-year medium-term financial profile. This allows for investment and gives the sharing body an opportunity to profile income against outgoings and to plan for large-scale shifts in delivery that require large-scale changes such as staffing reductions or investment in new ICT.

Five-year agreements maximize the planning time but, because they exceed the financial planning horizon, they carry the risk that in the last two years of an agreement there is insufficient convergence between the service provided and the resources available. One possible approach would be to set a 'rolling' three-year contract that is renewed each year.

There should be review provisions and break clauses operating and termination of involvement would be of no less than six months' duration – 12 months would be the preferred and that 'trigger' dates should be linked to the budget cycle. Early termination of involvement would trigger the continuation of payments consistent with the residual costs being borne by the 'partnership'. These payments would be scaled to encourage continued commitment to the partnership.

FINANCIAL STABILITY IN PARTNERSHIPS

As well as the length of the partnership there is a need for both partners to be aware of the likelihood of changes. Both sides wish to minimize risk by constraining the amount of changes. Often increases due to inflation are provided for. The 'sharing providers' will seek to reduce risk by building in constraints on the ability of the sharers to reduce the budget for the service. They will seek restrictions on the amount by which a service cost can be reduced since this could produce a redundancy situation, for example. The sharers will have to consider a number of related activities; these include:

- *Indexation*: an agreed structure of how general price increases will be applied to provider service charges.
- *Change control*: how demand, structure and volume changes to services provided be managed and funded.
- *Price and performance*: how the partnership will measure, reward and penalize performance.

SUPPORT COSTS

Given the current situation whereby different councils charge support costs in different ways, it is appropriate to hold to the principle of only transferring the costs of 'direct' support and other residual support; for example, corporate software licences, office accommodation and corporate e-mail systems be absorbed by the relinquishing council. Direct costs should be charged to a shared service.

The hosting authority can charge for other costs incurred in supporting the service. But there should be no loading of the costs of the shared service. One way of dealing with this would be for the sharing councils to agree a notional support cost per person.

TREATMENT OF ASSETS

At the date of transfer there should be an agreement of what direct assets each employee needs to undertake their role. There would be an agreement by all 'sharers' as to the value of these assets which would be transferred and residual costs of assets left after the direct assets of a service have transferred would be dealt with by each 'relinquishing' council.

INCENTIVIZING THE SHARING

Ideally in all shared services, opportunities for grant aid and income (in accordance with what the market will bear) should be explored. The best way to do this is for the shared service provider to operate a trading account with any surplus being ring-fenced to the service and any deficit being shared between the partners.

The costs, implications and obligations of any related employment issues should be shared equally but there should be an obligation on the shared service manager to minimize these.

Ideally, there should be mechanisms that reward the sharers for reducing cost or improving performance or increasing volume by trading in a way that brings financial and other benefits. In this way the managers of the service have an incentive to continuously improve.

COMMUNICATION AND CONSULTATION

Developing the OBC will include the cost of communicating with staff. Ideally a joint staff communications strategy should be agreed by the participating councils and begun as soon as practically possible, making the reasons for the change clear. The OBC development should allow for staff and trade union participation but it may be necessary to avoid creating unrealistic expectations of the influence they may have on the process. It should also reflect the industrial relations climate at all the councils involved. Nevertheless, positive trade union engagement is a prerequisite for most successful change programmes. Councils must be mindful of the statutory requirement to consult on such changes as soon as possible – ideally before the final business case stage starts.

Other, non-financial, risks involved in redundancy include damaged morale among remaining staff (the 'survivor syndrome') and more able staff taking the opportunity to move on. The danger of this is the potential dip in performance that could occur as the sharing progresses. Another factor that has to be allowed for is the position of those leading change. Where in-house managers are leading change, they may be working towards losing their own job. They may feel like 'turkeys voting for Christmas' or they may be perfectly happy if the local labour market is buoyant or their personal circumstances are favourable. Unless their position is clarified through the OBC stage there is a danger they could disrupt the process.

There is a balance to be drawn between 'top-level' communication and ground-level communication which will contribute to the ownership of the project but can appear to be disjointed, lacking clarity, structure and timeliness. This is complicated if the methods of communication are not consistent amongst the sharers as the common message will become diluted.

PROJECT COSTS

Previously reference has been made to the costs of creating a shared service. The use of a third-party facilitator can help to overcome potential conflicts. This facilitator can play the role of 'honest broker' and if it is felt an arbitrator is needed then this will be a further cost to the project.

Another cost in a sharing at the OBC stage would be if each of the sharers retained an independent advisor to advise them individually on the consequences of the sharing.

Managing the creation of a shared service

In developing a shared service there are some practical management issues that have to be explored in order to ensure the shared service can achieve its outcomes. This is the theme of *Service Transformation through Partnership* published in June 2006 by the Department for Communities and Local Government, which was based on the key recommendations for local councils from the Strategic Partnering Taskforce's final report (Office of the Deputy Prime Minister 2004a).

The essential first steps of partnership include making sure that you are mapping the right course, having buy-in from all stakeholders, assessing all options and having a viable business case. These are the areas that are often skimped.

MAPPING

The strategic fit between organizations needs to be closely aligned, although not necessarily identical. Use of the ODPM's Partnership Assessment Tool (2003) can assist potential partners in gauging the degree of compatibility and strategic fit on which to found a durable relationship. In many sharings, trust has to be built and this is best developed on the basis of shared needs and challenges.

The number of partners involved at the start of the project should be examined carefully. Too many partners can slow down decision-making and progress and it may well be that there are initial 'founding' partners who start the project, with other partners joining later. Commitment and enthusiasm are essential. Generally collaboration between two authorities is difficult and hard work, but is an effective business model between equal partners. The collaboration of more than two authorities and more than two tiers becomes exponentially more difficult.

BUY IN

The way that organizations work together will depend on the strength of relationships at a number of levels and on organizational culture. The ability of partners and potential partners to compromise and to give some ground for the greater good is essential to forming a strong rapport that will facilitate progress.

Strong and consistent leadership is the foundation of successful shared service partnerships. The leadership needs to be supported by simple and effective management structures to ensure that objectives are clear and unambiguous and that their implications fully understood by all partners; responsibilities are clear and are recognized at the highest level of partner organizations; the right skills are accessed at the right time; rapid action is possible when required; and decisions are properly made and are open to scrutiny.

Excellent governance of a project is essential for a partnership to be established and managed effectively. A governance agreement should be in place at the beginning of a partnership and in advance of a more formal contract. The best governance arrangements are where all parties are clear about the purpose of the project and the role of those involved. The authority and its elected members remain accountable for services, regardless of the provisions that are made for delivery. Entering into a partnership with clarity of responsibility for delivery can provide an effective way of discharging that responsibility.

An effective communications and consultation plan needs to be put in place to keep all stakeholders, including staff, informed of the objectives and progress of the project. The views of employees, their representatives, service users and council tax payers are vital to ensuring the deliverability of, and focus on, the shared service objectives. Consultation might also form a useful part of reviewing and monitoring the progress of the project – a quality assurance exercise. This should be undertaken by a third party and provide a useful check that the project is on track to meet the councils' objectives.

A clear timetable should be drawn up for each project and the responsibilities and roles of each partner should be clearly stated so that it is clear as to what must be done by whom and when this must be done in order to meet these timescales. If there are significant delays in the project, for instance if there is difficulty obtaining information from partners or if a large proportion of partners drop out, there should be mechanisms to deal with this.

Both sharers may want to establish internal review teams involving staff from different service areas (including IT and union representatives) to consider the requirements, to be involved in assessments and to evaluate the options open to the sharers. Joint workshops can take place at key stages. Both sharers could have project boards involving elected members and key stakeholders in the management of the project, and making key decisions concerning the project and its implications.

This can help overcome fear of change and reduce the impact of inaccurate rumour and speculation, poor communication within partners and lack of understanding of workload implications and timetables. Despite good project management the partnership will have a life and timetable of its own – not everyone will immediately buy into the partnership, and some opposition can be expected – the partnership challenges people's comfort zones and cherished routines.

ASSESSING OPTIONS

Formal reviews should be undertaken at key stages to ensure the validity, feasibility and deliverability of shared service delivery projects before proceeding to the next stage. This applies equally to public–public and public–private partnerships. During the project, continuous improvement should be supported by the use of a formal process.

It is worth considering an incremental transformational approach to partnership working where the scope of the relationship can be enlarged over time. The benefit of this approach is to reduce the risk to all partners of contractual commitment to a wide range of services before the fundamental ability to work together has been tested.

There is no substitute for proper project planning. More time spent at this stage of the process will assist with the future development of the project whilst any short cuts will inevitably mean a future delay. Project planning requires an assessment of current practices/performance, data collection, consideration of needs, consultation with interested parties and an appraisal of key options before embarking on the chosen process. The project plan should detail when, how and in what order the project will be implemented.

Project management is the key to successful delivery of any project and needs to be undertaken properly for the establishment of a partnership to be successful. Particular attention is needed to identify a dedicated project manager at an early stage of a project. The project team should be equipped with individuals who have the necessary skills base to lead and deliver the project on behalf of the councils. The initial stages will require procurement expertise whilst the latter stages will involve negotiation and commercial skills. Councils should therefore ensure the project team contains the right mix of skills to ensure the objectives of the councils are fulfilled.

During the process of creating a shared service there is a need to review the details of the service to be shared. This includes challenging the partnering authorities' support costs, streamlining the management structure so more resources are directed to the frontline; introducing peripatetic and flexible working practices; removing barriers and bureaucracy to speed up decision-making and allow for cross-partners working; offering new professional services, sharing workloads; completely reviewing every procedure, practice and document; ensuring that risk assessments, value for money assessments, service plans, action plans, business plans, performance plans, marketing plans and polices are all up to date.

VIABLE BUSINESS CASE

If there is no economic case for joint working and collaboration then a principal reason is absent and it will be much harder to justify any business case for change. The economic case is always strengthened where processes are relatively straightforward. Quantification of the economic case is an important early step in joint working and collaboration.

The business case for joint working or collaboration between councils is usually based on the tenet of economies of scale; in determining the potential, councils should go through a number of steps:

1. The scale of the authority's present activity in the area of potential partnership.
2. Assess the synergy in the areas of the review being undertaken.
3. What is the potential for stripping out inefficiency and/or make greater use of underutilized assets or dispose of surplus assets?
4. Assess the process costs of developing and working in partnership and consider whether adding more partners above an agreed starting point increases the costs out of proportion to the benefits gained.

One of the main responsibilities for the councils is to manage the partnership arrangement or contract. Understanding the client's key responsibilities and applying effective risk management throughout the partnership will help to ensure that the benefits are realized from the partnership. Understanding and developing the key skills for the role of client will make a significant difference to the relationship and the performance management of the partnership.

Summary

Hard evidence is still difficult to find. As such the certainty that sharing will automatically bring benefits is not evident. Clearly there are some benefits appearing but they are not universally quantifiable in terms of reduced cost or improved performance. However, the growth in the number of sharings and the positive attitude of those taking part is sufficient to encourage others to share.

The evidence of economies of scale being achieved is limited but there is more evidence of duplication of effort being avoided and there are certainly claims that sharings have brought greater organizational resilience and capacity. There seems to be greater clarity in the services shared and a willingness to share financial benefits which suggests 'open book' accounting is common. Whilst the use of common standards is clear in sharings, whether this represents the use of best practice is not clear and there appears to be limited service re-engineering. There appears to have been little assimilation of objectives, procedures and systems between different partners. The sharings appear to be based generally on increased formality in the relationships and also often appear to be incrementally organized to develop in scope and formality over time. There is little evidence of a positive impact on improvement judgement of external inspectorates.

There is little evidence (obviously, since these are all successful sharings) of political difficulties in creating these sharings and no evidence of loss of public accountability and difficulties with reporting issues. Staff issues have been resolved and there have apparently been few problems with 'branding' these services. There appears to be no difficulty with the relationship of these shared services to the remainder of the council.

The evidence for improvement against the headline and comparable published indicators is weak, partly because the services shared to date do not line up readily with a large number of indicators. What evidence there is, is limited.

However, the evidence available confirms that the reasons for sharing are more varied than simple improvement in a particular indicator. Some of the case studies expect to deliver significant efficiency savings in the medium term, but it is not yet possible to evaluate the likelihood of delivering these savings. The evidence is a little better with some of the older sharings, such as procurement consortia and e-government partnerships, but these are not solid comparisons: in the case of procurement consortia involvement is voluntary and there are examples of councils joining and leaving at will or only partially participating, and in the case of e-government there was an element of coercion (inspired by access to resources).

However, the Audit Commission published a national report (2005a) called *Efficiency Challenge: The Administration Costs of Revenues and Benefits*, the key findings of which were:

> *those councils prepared to be more innovative in delivering revenues and benefits services can make considerable savings, without lowering service quality. Improving direct debit take-up rates alone could generate savings in transactional and administration costs totalling £15 million per annum within five years.*

> *Partnership working, either within the public sector or with the private sector, offers councils the greatest potential for efficiency savings if they are prepared to overcome the perceived barriers. Partnership working between two district councils is already releasing over £100,000 per annum to each partner. If this approach were extended across the country it could generate substantial savings.*

> *The case studies in this report show that other initiatives, such as home working and modern IT systems, offer further scope for efficiency improvements. And for London councils, where costs are higher, the relocation of back office functions outside London presents a considerable opportunity for cost reduction.* (pp.4–5)

The Efficiency Review target of 2.5 per cent equates to £75 million per annum by 2007/08 for revenues and benefits. The study has demonstrated that there is scope for achieving efficiency savings of much more than this amount. Savings of this order are particularly important to help councils minimize pressure on high profile frontline services such as education and social care.

Major reductions in cost may take some time to achieve because existing arrangements are complex. However, councils that approach this task with enthusiasm should secure savings that will allow them to protect or invest further in frontline services to the public. (p.47)

Sharing is not solely about achieving cost and efficiency savings; it can lead to a range of other benefits and in some cases these are seen as more important. The other benefits that arise are identified above in our case studies. They can be categorized as:

- improving the performance and quality of the service to increase customer satisfaction;
- offering greater choice to the customer;
- improving service access;
- offering greater opportunities for staff development, networking and sharing learning and practice across councils;
- being able to attract external funding that individual councils acting alone may not have been able to secure;
- councils that are collectively working together feeling they can have a greater influence and profile over external stakeholders such as the government office than if they act alone;
- sharing risk.

This report presented an extremely positive view of the benefits of sharing services. The analysis of the case studies in this book demonstrates that sharings bring benefits. That latter analysis has to be given the caveat that it is drawn only from successful sharings and the results are limited and disparate.

But taken together the case for sharing seems to be unquestionable. The question must be – is this evidence and the reasons behind it sufficient for the idea of sharing to spread? This will be addressed in the next chapter.

8 *The Shared Services Scene in Late 2006*

Introduction

The general picture is that local government has been successful in making improvements in service delivery. The ODPM's preferred measures of cost-effectiveness suggest that overall there was a 10 per cent improvement in the quality of local government services between 2000–1 and 2003–4. But this figure masks some disparities. There is strong evidence that current policies have helped lead to improvements in the quality and effectiveness of services, but there has been much less impact on efficiency, access to services and public satisfaction. But it seems that some of this improvement may be due to additional funding rather than more efficient service delivery. In the case of public satisfaction current policies may even have had a detrimental effect because of the way in which they have raised public expectations whilst highlighting poor performance. There is also evidence to suggest that council tax increases have dented public satisfaction with local government.

The rate of improvement has varied between services. Centrally determined targets, PIs and funding appear to have had the greatest impact in services such as waste management, benefits and revenues and housing management. This seems to be because business processes in these services are fairly uniform and can be relatively easily re-engineered by deploying new technologies. By contrast far less improvement is evident in services like education, social services and planning, where there is probably less scope for simple technological fixes.

There is some evidence that the current approach stifles innovation. Councils complain that there are few incentives for them to experiment with new approaches. The system appears to them to be weighted towards 'playing it safe' (that is, doing the things that they know that inspectors are looking for). As a result the current approach has had the greatest impact on the worst performers. There has been much less impact, it is argued, on the best councils. It has 'raised the floor', but had far less impact on the 'height of the ceiling'.

But cost efficiency is occurring. According to the ODPM a backward look at the achievement of local councils efficiency work shows that in 2004–5 councils achieved total savings of £757 million of which £559 million were cashable. According to the *Local Government Chronicle* in 2005–6 the amount of savings increased to £1.2 billion in savings, an increase of 63 per cent over the previous year.

Of most interest to this book is that between 2004–5 and 2005–6 the savings in corporate services (the areas most likely to be shared) have increased from £103 million in 2004–5 to £206 million in 2005–6, and in procurement, the area of activity most frequently referred to as an area of sharing, they have increased from £57 million to £114 million. Together from representing 21 per cent of savings in 2004–5 they represent 35 per cent in the proposals for 2005–6.

But still the government wants more – in the November 2006 pre-budget statement the Chancellor increased the annual efficiency savings required between 2007 and 2010 to 3 per cent per year. According to a poll in the *Local Government Chronicle* of 4 January 2007, over half of chief executives questioned do not believe they can make these savings without services being affected. In the report it was said nearly four out of five councils questioned called for incentives (set-up costs) to set up sharings.

The analysis of the annual efficiency statements in Chapter 4 and the case studies in Chapters 5 and 6 give a tantalizing glimpse of the actions being taken to share services across local councils. Undoubtedly under the stimulus of the Gershon agenda the pace has, and is, quickening. In July 2005 the Local Government Association published a three-year action plan which included a proposal to amalgamate back offices, taking a lead in procurement and personnel issues, and sharing call centres.

Councils' current plans in terms of shared services

In its study *The Efficiency Challenge: The Administration Costs of Revenues and Benefits* (2005a), the Audit Commission looked at what, from the evidence of those councils that had made change, were the 'enablers for change' (in revenues and benefits). See Figure 8.1.

These factors suggest that councils have in place the mechanisms for a significant increase in sharing. If this is correct, it should be possible to see the evidence in the annual efficiency statements now required from each council. In Chapter 4 it was possible to 'baseline' where councils claimed to be in 2004–5 and so, analysing the statements for 2005–6 and 2007–8 (forward), it is possible to see the likely growth in such arrangements. Any claimed savings or benefits are highlighted. These are shown in county groupings as that is the focus for the vast majority of sharing arrangements.

There is evidence from other sources that suggests some local councils want to take the idea to a wider context in the hope they can deliver greater benefits. These examples are described below.

EVIDENCE FROM THE ANNUAL EFFICIENCY STATEMENTS

Buckinghamshire

For 2005–6 all the Buckinghamshire councils have agreed to work together on a number of joint working/procurement initiatives. By 2007–8 these general intentions have solidified but are still unspecific except in the case of South Buckinghamshire District Council who say 'Procurement support will continue to be delivered by a neighbouring authority ...' and Aylesbury Vale District Council who are working with the county council to provide a joint one-stop shop within Buckingham with shared services and infrastructure.

Cambridgeshire

Cambridge City Council and Huntingdonshire District Council were both liaising with other Cambridgeshire councils to identify and pursue opportunities for joint working and in 2005–6 South Cambridgeshire District Council were to enter into a partnership agreement with Cambridgeshire County Council for them to carry out Category 1 responsibilities required under the Civil Contingencies Act. By 2007–8 East Cambridgeshire District Council are to join the Anglia Revenues Partnership; South Cambridgeshire District Council are arranging for

Awareness

The awareness of the efficiency agenda has now grown and councils are starting to consider issues in relation to revenues and benefits. The need for better-publicized success stories is clear, as the view of councils is that there need to be very significant savings in order to make change attractive.

IT

Many councils now operate with electronic document management (EDM) systems. This modern IT platform provides an opportunity for work to be transferred quickly to staff at a variety of locations. Systems and structures that will help to enable change are now in place in many councils. Home-working initiatives are in place in some councils, using EDM is helping to improve productivity through better output and reduced sickness levels.

Most councils now have a front/back-office approach to delivering the service. This was not the case five years ago, and provides an opportunity, if councils wish to follow this route, of relocation of back-office functions

Government and council initiatives to modernize other IT interfaces through e-government are making progress. Websites are improving and providing more interactive services. Specific projects such as the National Benefits Project provide the potential to improve efficiency, and in council tax collection, the e-government project Valuebill offers further opportunities to councils. The Office of the Deputy Prime Minister (ODPM) e-innovations fund is being used to help councils trace people who move house and have a council tax debt outstanding. The ODPM has approved a bid sponsored by Mid Sussex District Council to develop a national solution in conjunction with the Institute of Revenues, Rating and Valuation, TDX Group and Agilisys.

IT systems need not be a barrier and examples are emerging of effective partnerships using different IT systems. The Kent benefits partnership provides council tax benefit assessments for ten councils using five different IT systems.

Attitude

Where innovative projects have taken place, we identified a very positive approach to change with staff empowerment, high-quality managers, and a strong commitment to change from the top of the organization. Performance nationally has improved over the last three years and more councils are achieving the level of stability required in order to take new initiatives to improve efficiency.

High-performing councils have greater capacity to break down the process so that delays and blockages can be reduced or removed. This is not always the case if a backlog of work exists as much time is spent problem solving and therefore there is less capacity to examine alternative solutions.

External influence

Inspection and assessment have enabled change. Poor BFI reports have led councils to make significant changes in the way their services are delivered. There are examples of councils using the CPA framework so that learning is shared.

Figure 8.1   Enablers for change

Source: Audit Commission (2005a, paras 51–6)

Cambridge City Council to provide a Cambridge sub-office. Cambridge City Council, which already has joint arrangements developed, in areas such as occupational health, recruitment advertising, waste collection and system procurement, is introducing a parking enforcement agency on behalf of the county council.

Cheshire

Cheshire County Council claimed in the 2005–6 statement to be working collaboratively with partners on the provision of shared services (including the police, the fire service and other local councils) and Vale Royal Borough Council will implement a new Housing Benefit and council tax system in collaboration with Crewe and Nantwich Borough Council and Ellesmere Port and Neston Borough Council. By 2007–8, Macclesfield Borough Council say they will have a partnership with Congleton Borough Council on environmental health services, a joint procurement unit and a joint payroll with Congleton and a joint building control partnership with Congleton and Crewe and Nantwich borough councils.

Cornwall

In the earlier statement Caradon District Council and Kerrier District Council both were exploring solutions to procuring goods and services through co-ordinated county-wide procurement initiatives. North Cornwall District Council was to develop a corporate debt recovery and bailiff services contract in partnership with Restmorel Borough Council and Caradon District Council (which was to be let in 2007–8). Penwith District Council were to procure new revenues and benefits processing software in conjunction with the North Cornwall revenues and benefits partnership (Caradon, North Cornwall and Restmorel district councils) and Restmorel Borough Council are to enter into a joint management arrangement with another council for the management of building control.

For 2007–8 Penwith District Council have a partnership arrangement with Kerrier District Council to collect abandoned vehicles and the cost of this new arrangement is considerably less than the previous contract. A new pest control contract is being let jointly between Penwith and Kerrier councils to offer a larger contract and therefore potentially benefit from economies of scale.

SAVINGS FLASH*

Penwith District Council's partnership arrangement with Kerrier District Council to collect abandoned vehicles has improved collection/removal from three days to three hours and the savings equate to approximately £4,000 per annum, plus a considerably improved service.

County Durham

Chester-le-Street District Council shares a corporate procurement manager with Derwentside District Council. Sedgefield Borough Council have joint working with a neighbouring council in provision of managed ICT services. Teesdale District Council is currently working with Wear Valley District Council with the aim of establishing a shared service delivery for the Housing

Benefits function and jointly with Wear Valley District Council has appointed a procurement officer.

Derbyshire

The 2005–6 statements contained general statements of intention from several councils including High Peak District Council (who during 2006–7 will market test the Parks Service and Streetcare preferably through a joint service arrangement) and Derby City Council.

Notably, Bolsover/Chesterfield/North East Derbyshire councils had developed an overall joint working project managed by a high-level member and officer steering group. Internal audit was identified in early 2005 by the three authorities' joint steering group as an area of potential joint working and collaboration which by mid-2006 had developed a joint business case for a full shared service. The shared service is due to start on 1 April 2007. In addition, the three councils were looking at sharing building control and procurement services. In addition Chesterfield and North East Derbyshire district councils were planning to implement a joint-use customer services centre and to market test a joint building cleaning service. Derbyshire Dales District Council were planning to purchase vehicles through a joint arrangement with Derbyshire County Council to whom they had transferred provision of information technology services. They were also members of the East Midlands legal services partnership.

Devon

Mid Devon and South Hams District Councils reported in the 2005–6 statement they will be exploring the possibility of joining together with neighbouring councils to deliver services in new ways. Torridge District Council and North Devon Council were looking at combining separate sports courses for young people to provide a better level of service using the same database and save money on staff and administration costs. By the time of the 2007–8 statement Teignbridge District Council reported that during 2005–6 the council entered into a formal understanding with South Hams District Council that both councils should pursue partnership opportunities as 'partners of choice' and work has already commenced on joint working on personnel and payroll, joint consultation unit and building control services. In future they expect to work together on finance, revenues and benefits, legal property services, ICT, customer services, personnel and payroll, waste and recycling. Additionally, Teignbridge intend to restructure joint management of Devon Building Control partnership and pursue joint management arrangements with South Hams and Mid Devon District Councils for internal audit. West Devon Borough Council said that work is already underway for joint working arrangements on personnel, payroll, staff training, benefit fraud, building control and consultation with other councils.

SAVINGS FLASH*

The Teignbridge, South Hams and Mid Devon district councils' internal audit service is expected to save Teignbridge £4,000 in the first year rising to £14,000 per annum.

Dorset

At the time of the earlier statement Bournemouth Borough Council and Poole and Purbeck district councils were looking for areas of sharing. Six of the eight councils in the county had agreed the objective of merging their respective building control organizations into a single entity with North Dorset and Christchurch considering joining. The perceived benefits are:

- economies of scale – savings through management and IT systems;
- improved flexibility – ability to move staff resources to meet particular peaks;
- improved recruitment – offer of a larger more professional body;
- improved work experience – promotional structure and larger operating area;
- improved customer experience – uniform practices through a single entity.

In the later statement West Dorset District Council were expecting to develop and implement partnering arrangements for a revenues and benefits service and Poole expect a greater emphasis on joint service delivery with neighbouring Bournemouth Borough Council.

The details of the shared revenues and benefits service between Weymouth and Portland Borough Council and West Dorset District Council were made public in October 2006. Both provide a similar service and have similar caseload and collection issues due to their location. However, at certain times of the year each faces different customer needs, especially in the area of benefit processing. As the councils both use the same processing system for the revenues service, staff are already trained on the same system and tend to be carrying out the same daily functions, just on different sites. The Department for Works and Pensions has recently approved funding of £309,000 for this partnership.

The key objectives of this project for Weymouth and West Dorset are:

- improved services for its customers;
- reduced costs of administration; continuous improvement in service delivery;
- staff development opportunities;
- improved skill levels;
- achieve upper quartile performance;
- an increase in the number of partners and customers of the partnership.

As WestWey1 the joint service will have a partnership board consisting of both members (from each council) and key officers (again from both authorities) to oversee the partnership operation. Cost savings will be achieved with the West Dorset District Council service manager taking redundancy and the fraud manager post at Weymouth and Portland District Council, currently vacant, not needing to be filled as the duties can be absorbed into the already formed Dorset fraud partnership. The partnership aim is to operate a processing centre from one site and use the same IT hardware and software wherever possible. This joint use of accommodation and IT will create a saving that is only possible through partnership. Total cost savings have been estimated as £168,000 in the first year.

The funding offered by the Department for Work and Pensions represents approximately two-thirds of the costs they consider will be incurred by the councils in setting up the partnership totalling £469,000. This includes project management, servers and server set up, hardware installation, migration of software, home-working and interconnectivity, procedures/process alignment, document alignment and templating and training.

Durham

Only Sedgefield Borough Council referenced shared services in the 2005–6 annual efficiency statement, particularly mentioning the potential of working with Wear Valley and Teesdale to consider joint service provision of waste collection services. In the 2007–8 statement Teesdale District Council claimed to be currently working with Wear Valley District Council with the aim of establishing a shared service delivery for the Housing Benefits function having jointly appointed a procurement officer. In addition a Durham County Accord has been established within which councils in County Durham are committed to working together for the benefits of the community.

East Riding of Yorkshire

In the 2005–6 statement East Riding of Yorkshire Council believed a public–private partnership starting in 2005–6 for corporate and transactional services would bring added efficiency gains as well as an opportunity to work in collaboration with other councils. Selby District Council has information services supplied by the East Riding of Yorkshire Council. Selby District Council is working with North Yorkshire County Council for the delivery of key services where existing council capacity is limiting service quality.

East Sussex

There were significant statements of intent on collaboration in the 2005–6 statements by East Sussex County Council, Eastbourne and Lewes district councils (both looking at revenues services and support services) and Rother District Council. In early 2006–7, the delivery of revenues/benefits services by all councils in East Sussex is being independently reviewed as part of an ODPM-funded joint improvement programme.

By the time of the 2007–8 statement Hastings and Rother district councils were in partnership on emergency planning and were exploring the joint provision of building control services. A successful bid to the government office of the South East Capacity Fund involves all councils in East Sussex developing opportunities for the joint provision of back-office function across more than one council, starting with the revenues and benefits service and legal services.

Essex

Several of the councils in Essex made positive statements about joint working in the 2005–6 statements including Epping Forest, Maldon and Rochford district councils.

The later statement indicated that progress had been made: Basildon District Council is to provide managed insurance services for Castle Point Borough Council; Chelmsford Borough Council will provide an NNDR collection service for Rochford District Council.

The Epping Forest District Council statement mentions the council was a founding member of the Essex Strategic Human Resources partnership. This is a body of HR professionals from each council in Essex that develops and introduces strategic HR interventions in line with the new county workforce development plan. Successes have included two bids for ODPM funding to develop a cohort of future leaders, and three county-wide advertising campaigns aimed at attracting staff to work in Essex councils. In both projects the authority has achieved more than it could have done on its own by pooling resources, attracting external funding and sharing expertise to deliver innovative programmes.

SAVINGS FLASH*

Chelmsford Borough Council projects a net income of £18,800 for the provision of an NNDR recovery service for Rochford District Council. Further improvements to the rate of collection of council tax and NNDR are projected to result in an interest saving for the council of £11,800.

Gloucestershire

There were limited mentions of collaboration in the 2005–6 statements though Gloucester City Council was examining the feasibility of joint working with other local councils for the provision of council tax and Housing Benefit administration. There was little extra detail in the 2007–8 statements although there was mention of a Gloucestershire procurement partnership.

Greater London

In the 2005–6 statement Enfield was pursuing joint highways procurement with Barnet and Haringey. Kensington and Chelsea, meanwhile, were undertaking joint commissioning of rough sleeper services with Hammersmith and Fulham. Other councils, including Hackney, Kingston upon Thames, Lewisham, Newham and Sutton London boroughs, said they were exploring opportunities for working with other local councils.

By the time of the 2007–8 statements a new contract for the management of abandoned vehicles had been prepared, tendered and was being let for Barnet, Enfield and Waltham Forest London boroughs.

The London boroughs of Barnet and Enfield had awarded a joint PFI street lighting contract, providing the councils with a renewed and enhanced infrastructure, fully managed and costed for 25 years, which, compared to the public sector comparator figure, represents an annual saving of £2,000,000.

Greater Manchester

The 2005–6 statements were written with the background of the work of the Association of Greater Manchester Authorities on shared services. The later statements similarly referred to the work of AGMA without referencing specific detail.

Hampshire

Basingstoke and Deane Borough Council's 2005–6 statement talked of collaboration with neighbouring councils in procurement of waste and recycling services, Havant Borough Council identified revenues and benefits as an area for collaboration and Hart District Council was investigating partnering arrangements with neighbouring councils, particularly in the areas of building control, legal services and the waste collection service.

For 2007–8 the Isle of Wight Council was looking at a potential merger of adult services with PCTs and NHS trusts. Southampton and Eastleigh councils have a partnership agreement on licensing services and in addition discussions are at an advanced stage regarding the potential for further partnership working in respect of building control and environmental health, with other areas such as waste collection, planning and a customer relationship management system (CRM) also being explored. The two councils have an out-of-hours noise service partnership.

Several councils mentioned the Hampshire Collaborative Working Group which examines how services can be shared across local councils in Hampshire.

Herefordshire

In 2005–6 Herefordshire Council made a general statement on seeking to build on existing successes by continuing to identify opportunities for alternative service provision through strategic procurement and develop partnerships or consortia as appropriate.

Hertfordshire

East Hertfordshire District Council and Welwyn Hatfield Council made general statements in the 2005–6 statement. For 2007–8 Stevenage Borough Council said their CCTV partnership with East Herts District Council would bring economies of scale. Watford Borough Council has a memorandum of understanding with Three Rivers District Council providing the basis for expanding the existing joint working arrangements with some initial savings having already been identified as a consequence. Welwyn Hatfield Council have seen a reduction in their external audit fee and internal audit agency costs through partnership working with two other local councils.

Kent

The 2007–8 statement shows that an internal audit partnership exists between Dover and Ashford district councils and these councils share a legal trainee. Tunbridge Wells and Sevenoaks district councils share a joint equality policy officer.

SAVINGS FLASH*

Shepway District Council is to remove a post of audit manager at a saving of £32,000 because of the existence of the internal audit partnership with Dover District Council.

SAVINGS FLASH*

Canterbury City Council claim staffing, IT and legal cost savings in choice-based lettings achieved by joint commissioning with other Kent Councils of £35,000 and £8,000 from a joint ICT disaster recovery plan with other councils.

Lancashire

In 2005–6 Fylde Borough Council intended to implement revenues, accounting and benefits technology with Blackpool Borough Council. Lancaster City Council is actively seeking partnership working and Pendle Borough Council are developing joint working with other local councils; for example new contact centre (six district councils and the county council) and sharing a legal services manager with Craven District Council.

For the 2007–8 statement Fylde Borough Council were able to say that in 2006–7 they will implement a series of joint service reviews in partnership with Wyre Council using business process re-engineering as a means to furthering partnership working, improving service provision and reducing costs. Also they would also complete the business case for amalgamating the revenues and benefits staff with those of Blackpool Council. In addition a rationalization of the Fylde waste partnership with Wyre Council will be undertaken early in the year to secure further efficiency savings. South Ribble Borough Council was also having internal health and safety at work support provided by Preston City Council.

SAVINGS FLASH*

In 2007/8 Wyre Borough Council predicted a total of £34,560 in savings through operation of a payroll contract and a property maintenance contract for other councils and appointing a shared procurement officer with Fylde Borough Council.

Leicestershire

As in 2005–6, the later statement contained a number of councils having general intentions but Melton Borough Council expected to have implemented a Welland procurement unit (including Harborough), hosted by the council and part-funded in 2006–7 by the East Midlands Centre of Excellence. The principle of the joint procurement unit is to achieve cashable savings for the five partner councils. During 2006–7 a shared internal audit service will also be implemented. Oadby and Wigston District Council expected that with effect from 1 April 2006 the council will share a procurement officer with Blaby District Council and continue sharing an arts and heritage officer with that council.

Lincolnshire

There was significant activity outlined in the 2005–6 statements for Lincolnshire councils – East Lindsey District Council progressing a joint building control service; and South Holland and South Kesteven district councils looking to the joint procurement or joint provision of a select range of services, in particular revenues, legal and building control. West Lindsey District Council had commissioned consultancy work to evaluate the possibility of working with partners to deliver key projects such as CRM and IT support services. By the 2007–8 statement East Lindsey District Council was able to say the joint building control service with a neighbouring unitary council was delivered in 2006–7 with 10 per cent savings in 2007–8 and future year savings of £10,000 from a joint legal library arrangement. They also expected to implement a joint building control service. West Lindsey District Council intend to further develop partnership working with North Kesteven District Council which has been an integral part of being able to bring the councils ICT service back in house. This includes a Web manager post for joint management of both the North Kesteven and West Lindsey website. West Lindsey, East Lindsey, South Holland district councils, the county councils and Business Link are providing business support to rural businesses throughout the three districts. North East Lincolnshire Council had a joint procurement partnership with North Lincolnshire Council.

Norfolk

In the 2005–6 statements both Breckland and Broadland district councils identified clear intentions to seek sharings. By the 2007–8 statement Broadland District Council had formed a building control partnership with two other councils and provides energy conservation services to South Norfolk Council and provide a care and repair service for Broadland residents. They have jointly contracted out their internal audit service with two other councils, one of whom provides the client side. They have jointly gone to the market for banking, insurance and treasury management services.

Northamptonshire

Daventry District Council in the 2005–6 statement intended to implement an agreement with a neighbouring authority to undertake payroll functions. East Northamptonshire Council was to implement the outcomes of the Welland ODPM capacity building bid for shared services by implementing a shared internal audit service with Welland partners and develop a joint procurement function and implement a shared server arrangement with Harborough District Council and share ICT staff support. In the later statement Corby Borough Council referred to the Northamptonshire 'Mrs Barker' shared services project, funded by the East Midlands Centre of Excellence.

Northumberland

Alnwick, Berwick Upon Tweed, Blyth Valley and Castle Morpeth councils all said in the 2005–6 statements that they were looking to extend collaborative working in conjunction with other organizations within and outside Northumberland. By the 2007–8 statement Alnwick District Council was operating a joint customer service centre on behalf of itself and the county council without increasing its own staffing and receiving a contribution of £10,000 from the county council. Wansbeck District Council claimed that a viability study is currently being carried out for a shared street-scene service with Blyth Valley Borough Council. Castle Morpeth Borough Council detailed its two partnerships: ICT with Alnwick District Council and internal audit with Wansbeck District Council.

North Yorkshire

By 2007–8 Hambleton District Council were looking to implement a joint procurement unit in partnership with other district councils in North Yorkshire and Craven District Council had a shared management arrangement regarding the council's legal services with one other council.

Selby District Council is working with North Yorkshire County Council for the delivery of key services where existing council capacity is limiting service quality.

Nottinghamshire

Nottinghamshire was evidentially well advanced in the 2005–6 statements, which included Ashfield District Council exploring vehicle-related services – maintenance, spares, consumables and servicing – and building control services. Bassetlaw, Broxstowe, Gedling, Mansfield, Newark and Sherwood and Rushcliffe were all exploring the possibility of collaborative arrangements with other local councils for some corporate services.

By the 2007–8 forward statement Newark and Sherwood District Council had recently implemented a new revenues system acquired through collaborative tendering with three other councils, and were in the process of developing a joint procurement unit with two other councils. Rushcliffe Borough Council had appointed a joint procurement officer with Gedling Borough Council and were looking to provide a joint debtors service for Gedling with Gedling providing payroll services to Rushcliffe. The two councils also plan a joint clinical waste collection service. Bassetlaw District Council is looking for collaboration and co-operation with councils both in Nottinghamshire and beyond the county boundaries, and was working with the IDeA and two councils (one in Nottinghamshire, one in Lincolnshire) on developing partnership working opportunities. The Nottinghamshire chief executives' group continues to lead on general collaboration opportunities; the most advanced of these is the joint building control initiative. A procurement unit between Bassetlaw District Council and two other Nottinghamshire councils is being developed.

Oxfordshire

For the 2005–6 statement, West Oxfordshire District Council identified that the councils in Oxfordshire have now considered principles for shared services and have identified those back-office services with the potential for joint provision at an early stage. Work in legal services was fairly well progressed in terms of joint commissioning/call-off arrangements for external bought-in work and the possible sharing of surplus capacity, whilst internal audit consortium arrangements are now under active consideration.

By the time of the 2007–8 statement, Vale of White Horse District Council claimed to had moved beyond joint financial services to assessing the feasibility of Vale of White Horse and South Oxfordshire district councils jointly providing internal audit, legal and democratic services. Wychavon (in Worcestershire) and West Oxfordshire district councils have agreed to jointly employ an expert environmental health officer to deal with common contaminated land issues for one year only, saving each council approximately £17,000. Jointly with Oxford City and Cherwell District Council, West Oxfordshire District Council is a registered IRRV NVQ Assessment Centre, which allows for reduced costs in training their own staff and has the potential for generating income from other councils. Cashable efficiencies of at least £10,000 from 2006–7 are expected.

Rutland

In the 2005–6 statement Rutland County Council detailed work in a joint review with Melton Borough Council by BT on front- and back-office operations to eradicate any duplicate effort and re-process in business processes in the collection of council tax and the establishment of a joint procurement unit led by Melton Borough Council. In the later statement the council mentioned that the Welland shared services procurement initiative will become effective in 2006–7 and there will be a shared audit service additionally.

Shropshire

In the 2005–6 statement Bridgnorth District Council and South Shropshire District Council were looking to jointly deliver a benefits service, while North Shropshire District Council was exploring the possibility of Shrewsbury and Atcham Borough Council providing a management service for car parking enforcement, internal audit and pest control/dog warden services. By the time of the 2007–8 statement Bridgnorth District Council and South Shropshire District Council had received support from the Department of Work and Pensions to make a joint benefits service happen; North Shropshire District Council were considering a partnership arrangement with a strong procurement partner – that is, Merseyside Fire and Rescue Service – and South Shropshire District Council was working with Shropshire County Council in the provision of a finance system, a payroll service, HR and IT provision and an e-marketplace solution.

Somerset

In the 2007–8 statements Bath and North East Somerset Council said they were collaborating with five other councils to host an e-auction for the provision of agency staff. Sedgemoor District Council was working with West Somerset District Council on joint building control service provision and Taunton Deane Borough Council to provide a 24/7 CCTV service. South Somerset and Taunton Deane district councils were in the South West Audit Partnership with two other councils. Taunton Deane District Council was one of five councils sharing a housing needs survey officer.

SAVINGS FLASH*

Sedgemoor District Council says the partnership working with West Somerset District Council on building control will save them £25,000 a year.

Staffordshire

Two councils made general intentional statements in the 2005–6 statements but by the 2007–8 statements Staffordshire Moorlands District Council was involved in a system of e-procurement and a number of the councils were involved in the Staffordshire e-government partnership and involved in the re-negotiation of the telephone call charges contract.

Suffolk

Babergh and Waveney district councils made general intentional statements in the 2005–6 statements. By the 2007–8 statement Suffolk Coastal District Council was looking to implement a partnership to increase the efficiency and effectiveness of legal services across Suffolk and to reduce costs, and Waveney District Council and Great Yarmouth Borough Council have begun partnership working in the legal team. Babergh District Council has a shared procurement officer and Forest Heath District Council is involved in the ongoing development of Anglia Revenues Partnership, which received Beacon status in March 2006.

Surrey

General statements in the 2005–6 by several councils were continued in the 2007–8 statements but particularly significant was the reference to the East Surrey Improvement Partnership consisting of three local councils – Mole Valley District Council, Reigate and Banstead Borough Council and Tandridge District Council.

Warwickshire

General statements in 2005–6, such as Nuneaton and Bedworth Borough Council examining partnering arrangements for support services and Warwickshire County Council working in partnership with Stratford on Avon District Council on parking provision, were firmed up in the 2007–8 statements. These included Nuneaton and Bedworth Borough Council entering into a partnership working arrangement with other councils in Warwickshire for the provision of computer audit services and North Warwickshire Borough Council having partnership working arrangements in internal audit (with Rugby), revenues and benefits, information services, building control and procurement.

West Sussex

In the 2005–6 statements:

- Adur District Council was working in collaboration with Worthing, Horsham and Mid Sussex district councils. Adur was to implement a revenues system in partnership from June 2005 with Horsham District Council and procure a corporate electronic document and records management system with Horsham and Mid Sussex district councils for implementation during 2005–6. It was also planned that a joined-up revenues service with one management structure across the three districts of Adur, Horsham and Mid Sussex would be achieved by April 2006, and this was successful.
- Horsham District Council will develop joint working with Mid Sussex and Adur councils based on one centre of ICT support and development. It will continue joint working with Mid Sussex Council on procurement using a shared procurement officer, implement an NNDR and revenues system procured in partnership with Adur Council and investigate further efficiencies through combined tax collection. It will implement a financial management system, jointly procured with Adur Council, and implement partnership arrangements with Crawley Council on building control services.
- Mid Sussex District Council is being assisted by the employment of a joint procurement advisor with Horsham District Council. An ICT partnership has been established with Horsham and Adur district councils and is being developed into the joint delivery of services. A joint revenues collection service (council tax and NNDR) will commence from the end of 2005.

- Worthing Borough Council will deliver efficiency gains from joint working with Adur District Council (shared depot, shared vehicle workshop, shared management).

By the time of the 2007–8 statement:

- Worthing Borough Council was carrying out a joint pay and grading review with Adur District Council and working jointly with neighbouring councils to procure an integrated HR and payroll system. Worthing was also developing joint initiatives and sharing of staff with Adur District Council on a range of services including economic development, engineering and building control.
- Crawley Borough Council has appointed a procurement advisor jointly with Horsham and Mid Sussex District Council and have a building control partnership with Horsham District Council.

SAVINGS FLASH*

Horsham expect the sharing of a procurement officer with Crawley Borough Council and Mid-Sussex District Council to bring a saving of £7,200.

SAVINGS FLASH*

Worthing District Council says implementing a joint staff structure review will save £24,450 in 2006–7.

SAVINGS FLASH*

Worthing District Council claims that developing a range of joint working initiatives, primarily with Adur District Council in areas including building control, engineering services and economic development will generate cashable savings of £50,000.

Wiltshire

General statements were made in the 2005–6 statement but by the 2007–8 statement North Wiltshire District Council was expecting joint procurement of IT hardware. Kennet District Council anticipated their payroll service would be outsourced to the county council, resulting in a reduction in staff resources, negating the need to replace the existing payroll system and bringing the bank contracts of the councils into line, with a view to jointly procuring the banking services of the councils. West Wiltshire District Council is leading work to join up building control services across Wiltshire and elsewhere.

Worcestershire

In the 2005–6 statements several councils made general intentional statements based on the existence of a 'shared service vehicle' (four key areas have been identified as priorities – revenues and benefits, ICT services, payroll and waste management). By 2007–8 a detailed business case was being prepared for a revenues and benefits shared service within Worcestershire; Worcester City Council were developing a partnership approach in the procurement arrangement with other councils, such as Malvern and Bromsgrove; and both Wyre Forest and Wychavon district councils were expressing interest in continuing the provision of internal audit services to neighbouring and other local councils within the county. A procurement service is currently being provided for Bromsgrove District Council, and both Wyre Forest and Wychavon district councils have also expressed an interest.

Yorkshire

In the 2005–6 statement East Riding of Yorkshire Council believed a public–private partnership starting in 2005–6 for corporate and transactional services would bring added efficiency gains as well as an opportunity to work in collaboration with other councils. By 2007–8 Calderdale Metropolitan Borough Council cited IT as one of the service areas in which Calderdale is working in partnership with neighbouring councils and another major area was procurement. For Waste Disposal, Calderdale is exploring a possible partnership with neighbouring Bradford Metropolitan Borough Council. Selby District Council is working with North Yorkshire County Council for the delivery of key services where existing council capacity is limiting service quality and working with the East Riding of Yorkshire Council who support the delivery of information services to the council.

Future routes for sharings – local councils doing it for themselves

Just as the pace of sharing is quickening, so the ambition being displayed by councils is growing. It is clear that, left to themselves and faced with the pressure exerted by the Gershon agenda and the work and financial inducements of the centres of excellence, as well as their own initiative, local councils will create new opportunities for sharing way beyond what has gone before. The following are a number of recently publicized proposals.

'CORPORATE' SHARING

South Hams and Teignbridge district councils

South Hams and Teignbridge district councils in Devon are moving forward with plans to merge a number of their services. The first services include audit; ICT management, desktop support and helpdesk; design and engineering; finance; legal; personnel and payroll. Phase 2 will include property; revenues and benefits; and waste and recycling – management, administration, vehicles and enforcement; Phase 3 will include customer services; ICT – major systems merger; and waste and recycling – operations. The potential exists for significant annual savings of approximately £1.2m per annum across all of the identified services set against the costs of implementing these arrangements, estimated to be in the region of £1m. The mergings would be completed by March 2011.

Officer working groups will be set up for each service. These will involve the relevant heads of service from both councils together with other key staff. These groups will work under the leadership and guidance of the specialist advisors to develop the service business cases. A joint steering group will be responsible for ensuring that the work of the working groups is undertaken objectively and transparently and that appropriate independence and challenge are built in. It is likely that any structure will need to be operated, ultimately, as a separate entity, with a senior officer to act as a director. The structure is also likely to be modular in nature as it will be built up over a period of time. It will also need to be able to take on new functions should the need arise at a later date. There will be a joint committee as the governance model.

Cornwall

It was reported in the *Local Government Chronicle* on 26 October 2006 that all of the districts and the county council in Cornwall have signed up to joining up revenues and benefits, legal, building control and grounds and maintenance services.

The East Surrey Improvement Partnership

In the section on Surrey above the initiative by Mole Valley, Reigate and Banstead and Tandridge district councils (as the East Surrey Improvement Partnership) is mentioned as is the planned joint work in procurement, media services, legal services, archiving and advice and benefits. However, there is clearly more to this than just the achievement of Gershon savings. As reported in the *Local Government Chronicle* on 17 November 2005, the chief executive of Tandridge said 'If we can work together to improve services then the unitary argument is an academic discussion. We think [restructuring] will be a bureaucratic solution that undermines the achievement of efficiencies. People get focused on identities and drawing boundaries, not performance'.

The East Surrey Improvement Partnership, governance of which, as a principle, includes both members and officers, has as its objectives the improvement of the quality and value for money of service to communities, resilience of service delivery, contribution to the local and central government efficiency gains programme, exploring opportunities for trading in the medium to longer term and the creation of a stronger voice for the area on strategic issues and the value of local authority services.

It has adopted some underlying principles such as not compromising the independence of decision making in each council or dilute identity; any development should accommodate existing partnership arrangements and they would continue to explore partnership/joint working with other public, voluntary and private sector partners as long as they look first to one another for partnership.

They expect that partnerships should provide benefits for all three councils and where a project, within the programme, is between two of the partners an opportunity must be left open for the third to join at a later date and there should be concentration on outcomes and benefits rather than processes, including customer service and quality standards.

The partnership was seeking quick results with tangible achievements from 2006–7.

The Inter-Authority Partnering Unit (I-APU)

Kent County Council established in 2004–5 what is called the Inter-Authority Partnering Unit (I-APU). The I-APU is a delivery agent for Kent County Council and potentially other excellent authorities for longer-term partnership agreements, which it described as franchises, that deploy experienced local authority management practitioners and best practice to deliver radical service improvement outcomes within poorer performing councils. The I-APU wants to develop local government franchising as a new public service process. The I-APU (the franchisor) plans to grant a licence to an excellent authority (the franchisee), which entitles the franchisee organization to distribute their best-practice 'products' under the I-APU name. Local authorities that are under-performing can elect to work with a chosen high-performing local authority from the I-APU. The first franchising agreement is already in place between Kent County Council and Swindon Borough Council.

Cumbria Local Strategic Board (CLASB)

The purpose of the Cumbria Local Strategic Board (CLASB) is to promote the role and voice of democratically accountable local authorities; to provide a means to promote the interests of Cumbria regionally nationally and internationally; to identify, consider and pursue opportunities for collaboration on service delivery and efficiency; to ensure the member authorities are engaging effectively with each other and partners in delivering public services to the community; to identify opportunities and increase their collective capacity for shared learning and development across authorities; and to facilitate, by its work, a more effective engagement by local government with the strategic partners.

Working to the board, the responsibility of the Connected Cumbria Partnership (CCP) is to develop and facilitate partnerships for the facilitation of service modernization and efficiency and to take a shared approach to initiatives, to recommend a programme of work, to actively seek opportunities to reduce costs and/or improve service through joint working.

The CLASB structure includes a strategic board, a chief executives' group, the Connected Cumbria Partnership and Achieving Cumbrian Excellence (ACE) Task and Finish Groups. Procedural rules allow any two authorities to proceed unilaterally. If any authority declines to participate it is not a veto to others proceeding and authorities may opt out of a particular service or in at a later date. CLASB operates by a scoping report being presented by officers to CLASB, followed by an ACE member/officer seminar, followed by a report back from the seminar and recommendations. CLASB then appoint a sponsor and a brief is given to CCP and a multidisciplinary team develop the business case and project initiation document. CLASB considers the business case and Project Initiation Document and initiates the programme. Services being reviewed include procurement; building control; human resources – recruitment; property rationalization; licensing and single IT client.

Adur and Worthing district councils

In 2004 exploratory work was undertaken to establish the advantages and disadvantages of amalgamating the two councils. This was the first time that two independent councils had looked at merging outside a local government review. However, on 14 June 2005, Adur District and Worthing Borough executive committees recommended that a full merger of the councils did not go ahead. On the basis of their analysis and risk assessment they decided that a full-scale merger project was too onerous on existing and short-term resources. However, they re-stated their strong commitment for further service partnerships between the councils, such as the successful Adur and Worthing services project, as these have a better chance of success in the shorter term. As part of their recommendations to each of the councils they proposed further work to identify the areas of joint working that might progress next. The members of both councils were unanimous in emphasizing the importance of these conclusions.

In 2005 Worthing's chief executive left. Having considered the different options available the council decided to recommend the appointment of Ian Lowrie, the existing chief executive of Adur District Council, to work for Worthing for 2.5 days a week till the summer of 2006. Commenting on this a leading Worthing member said 'we have had discussions with leading councillors at Adur and they are completely positive about this shared arrangement. Like us, they see it as an excellent opportunity to re-examine our partnership working to see if it can deliver even more benefits for the council tax payers of both councils'. Although by June 2006 Worthing had decided to appoint a permanent chief executive rather than continue the arrangement, in March 2006 the two councils appointed a joint strategic head of human resources for the duration of a pay and grading review demonstrating they are still working ever closer together.

Lincolnshire shared services partnership

The Lincolnshire shared services partnership has been formed with Lincolnshire councils agreeing a 'partnership framework': a formalization of shared services work that has been taking place across the county for a number of years. The programme is supported by the East Midlands Centre of Excellence. Nine services have been identified for further exploration. These were selected through a series of workshops and evaluation processes. The decision about which services formed the first phase was based upon a range of criteria including how the service fits within the strategic priorities of the partners, how difficult/easy it would be to implement shared services in the particular service area and the likely impact on customers. Services included within this group of projects are building control, ICT support, legal services, procurement, property management and training.

The partnership anticipates a number of benefits, such as communities to have a closer relationship with service providers, regardless of who is delivering them; seamless, high quality and efficient services tailored to local needs; less red tape and bureaucracy; more resources invested in frontline services and removing the confusion about which council provides services to local people.

The partnership is also expecting some benefits for staff with more opportunities to tailor their jobs around their lifestyles, more scope for flexible working, more opportunities for career development and opportunities to get involved in service redesign.

The partnership also intends a programme of transforming services which are largely customer facing. The plan is to develop outline and detailed business cases for each of these services during 2007. This group includes customer services, revenues and benefits and street scene.

A member board will oversee the programme. This is responsible for the strategic direction of the programme. Beneath this sits the programme board which is comprised of officers. This is responsible for the progress of projects within the programme. The chairman of the programme board is the programme director and the co-ordination of the programme will

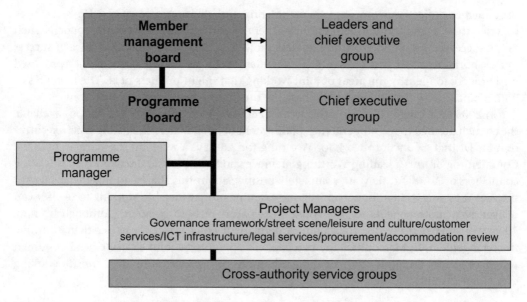

Figure 8.2   The Lincolnshire shared services partnership management structure

be provided by a programme manager. Each project area or workstream will be managed by a project manager and will have a sponsor on the programme board.

The shared services programme is split into three tranches. The first is the strategic framework. This covers projects which are designed to ensure the correct infrastructure is in place across the county. The second deals with the infrastructure: ensuring the right information systems and communications infrastructure are in place to support shared services; and the third is about property – in the fullness of time planning accommodation holdings across the county to provide the most appropriate locations for services and users. See Figure 8.3.

These are long-term projects, with initial strategic work planned to be carried out during 2007.

Activity	Outcome	Target date given in East Midlands Centre of Excellence bid
Framework for neighbourhood governance across Lincolnshire	Framework developed	April 2007
	Framework implemented	April 2008
Baseline analysis	Map existing: – computer systems – ICT networks – contracts for services – office accommodation – service standards	Dec 2006
Migration strategy for business systems	Migration strategy	Oct 2007
Property rationalization strategy	Property rationalization strategy	Dec 2007

Figure 8.3   The Lincolnshire shared services project initial strategic workplan

The shared services tranche is concerned with the horizontal integration of existing council services. Six services have been identified as potential shared services within the first phase of the programme and work is progressing to determine whether or not a shared service in these areas across two or more councils within Lincolnshire would be beneficial.

The process for deciding what form a shared service might take involves a project team made up of people from each authority who are working in the service in question. They are carrying out a number of steps (see Figure 8.4) which explore different options in increasing detail.

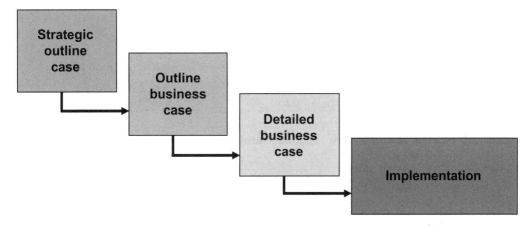

Figure 8.4 **The Lincolnshire shared services project workstream plan**

The target dates for completing the implementation of the preferred options are procurement – April 2007; legal services – June 2007; training – October 2007; property management and building control – October 2007; ICT support – March 2008.

Service transformation is the final tranche of the shared services programme. The aim is to take a completely fresh look at the way a service is provided and to think radically about how it could be improved, perhaps by delivering it in an entirely different way. There are three large services within this tranche, (see Figure 8.5) and the project teams will be undertaking the following stages in assessing how the service may be transformed. A preferred option will be identified by March 2008.

'SUPRA-CORPORATE' SHARING

Greater London 'mutual' insurer

According to an article in the *Local Government Chronicle* in September 2006 the London Centre of Excellence has provided a set-up grant to allow the 32 London boroughs, the City of London Corporation and the Greater London Authority to set up a mutual insurer owned by the councils. This, according to the consultants' report, has the potential to make savings of 15 to 20 per cent on average on councils' premium spend across their liability and property coverage.

Activity	Outcome	Target date given in East Midlands Centre of Excellence bid
Customer services	Feasibility study	Jan 2007
	Outline business case	March 2007
	Detailed business case	Sept 2007
	Implementation plan	March 2008
Street scene	Feasibility study	Jan 2007
	Outline business case	March 2007
	Detailed business case	Sept 2007
	Implementation plan	March 2008
Revenues and benefits	Feasibility study	Jan 2007
	Outline business case	March 2007
	Detailed business case	Sept 2007
	Implementation plan	March 2008

Figure 8.5   The Lincolnshire shared services project service transformation workplan

East of England revenue and benefits

According to a report in the *Local Government Chronicle* in April 2006, the Eastern Region Centre of Excellence was due to present a report to 46 member councils in that month recommending migration of benefits administration services to a maximum of six sub-regional benefits processing facilities. A single benefits advisory service would support customers. The argument extends to council tax administration where delivery from a single regional facility would together with the reformed benefits administration deliver efficiency savings of £9 million over three years. This is based on bringing together 2587 staff across the region that administer revenues and benefits at a cost of £117 million per year, collecting £1.9 billion in council tax and £1.4 billion in non-domestic rates and paying £886 million in housing benefit and £209 million in council tax benefit. This approach is not without its critics – according to the *Local Government Chronicle* the assistant borough treasurer of King's Lynn and West Norfolk District Council, which dropped out of the project early on, argued that centralized processing centres do not have a good track record and a 'small drop in collection [of council tax] could easily wipe out any efficiency gains'.

On the 24 August 2006 the *Local Government Chronicle* was reporting that the initiative could be in danger due to a lack of funding from central government. Required was £25 million in initial costs. And on 19 October the *Chronicle* reported that there were serious questions being asked by some of the councils involved – one chief executive claiming the concept, data and numbers 'are flawed'. Another chief executive argued that based on the feasibility study presented by external consultants 'not one of the 14 councils present [at a presentation of the proposals] would be keen to go down this road'.

Improving Services in Somerset (ISIS)

Somerset County Council and Taunton Deane Council are appointing a commercial contractor to provide strategic service delivery for corporate support services (finance, IT, HR, property services and revenues and benefits) and customer access. Somerset Police are looking to join. The plan is to establish a joint venture company vehicle with the founding authorities being original shareholders.

The programme objectives have been developed and agreed jointly by Somerset County Council and Taunton Deane Borough Council:

- to improve access to and delivery of customer-facing services
- to modernize, reduce the cost of and improve corporate, transactional and support services
- to help modernize and transform the overall workings of the county council and Taunton Deane Borough Council
- to invest in new world class technologies to improve productivity
- to create an excellent working environment and a more sustainable employment future for staff
- to generate economic development by attracting a partner willing to invest in Somerset.

The base programme scope is centred on corporate support services currently provided by the County Council's resources directorate and includes the majority of functions in finance, ICT, HR, customer services and property services, together with elements from legal services, and Somerset County Services.

The efficiency savings for the local authorities are in the order of millions of pounds and will be quantified during the first phase of the project.

Summary

The evidence is that sharings are increasing, and both the range and pace of change is quickening. No longer are sharings simply between one council with its neighbour; more and more ambition is being shown. An analysis of the annual efficiency statements above – accepting all the uncertainties inherent – is that between 2004–5 and 2007–8 the number of sharings will have at least doubled.

In July 2006 the Department of Communities and Local Government published a report, *The National Procurement Strategy – Two Years On*, and this claimed that 59 per cent of councils (31 per cent in 2004) were involved in joint commissioning of services (not including health and social care), 32 per cent were involved in creating a shared procurement function, 29 per cent were creating other shared corporate service functions and 25 per cent were working on other shared services.

It appears that the number, scope and type of sharings are increasing. No longer are sharings only between one council with its neighbour but rather there is more and more ambition being shown. The vast majority of the new sharings will be based on some form of county-wide or intra-county grouping.

This clearly continues and strengthens the relationships forged in the highways and IEG partnerships and the new supporting people arrangements. It also recognizes the pressure the government has placed on councils to work together through local area agreements.

So, on the basis of this evidence, the age of sharing has arrived. However, will local councils continue to be free to develop sharing by themselves?

9 The 'Fifth' Wave

Introduction

As we have seen in the last chapter local government seems to be achieving what the government wants through 'Gershon' savings and creating more joined-up service delivery. But it seems that the progress made is not adequate for the government's liking – the need for keeping the lid on public sector expenditure, the unpopularity of the council tax and continuing low levels of satisfaction with councils (according to MORI the national average overall satisfaction with councils declined from 65 per cent in 2000–1 to 55 per cent in 2003–4) in the face of rising expectations have persuaded the government that more needs to be done.

We will look at this through, first, the evidence that local councils are not moving fast enough themselves, secondly, the Local Area Agreement initiative and, thirdly, three national initiatives the 'Transformational Government: Enabled by Technology' strategy of November 2005 and 'Direct.gov.uk' and '101'.

Local councils are not moving fast enough

A survey undertaken by RSM Robson Rhodes and summarized in the *Local Government Chronicle* on 28 September 2006 suggested that many councils were unambitious, despite 89 per cent of respondents saying their council sees 'sharing services' as an 'opportunity'.

The survey said only 20 per cent claimed to have a fully operational sharing project and when asked what their basis was for selecting partners, 87 per cent mentioned geography (thereby limiting the potential 'pool' of partners), 41 per cent saying compatible information technology and 32 per cent saying political leadership.

Sixty-seven per cent of respondents think that the central government's enthusiasm was the main driver for shared services and 43 per cent think the main driver behind shared services was saving money, but they had little idea how much would be saved. Almost as many respondents, 33 per cent, said that 'improved service levels' were likely to be the main benefit. Fifty-three per cent of respondents rated their capacity for dealing with shared services to be 'strong' or 'good' with the remainder only 'OK' or 'weak'.

And, according to a report in the *Local Government Chronicle* of 14 December 2006, the report published by the New Local Government Networks, *The Politics of Shared Services* (Brand 2006), claims the take-up of shared services has been slow and limited because many councils 'remain unconvinced'.

These results would tend to support the argument that local councils are not well enough focused on the issue. But as we described in Chapter 2, the potential for sharing has been available for over 30 years, the missing ingredient has been the will to share whether derived from a positive impetus or necessity.

Some barriers still remain, however. The survey in the Audit Commission report (2005a) revealed that many councils see a number of barriers to changing their current working arrangements (for revenues and benefits). See Figure 9.1.

Risk aversion
- The fear of failure is high and prevents councils adopting a different approach to delivering the services. For example, there is still a strong awareness of some of the bad experiences of services that have been contracted out in the past.
- There is a strong view that there is a high risk that the reputation of councils will be damaged if things go wrong, particularly for councils that have good existing levels of performance. Poor performance has a much higher profile than the cost of delivery, particularly in benefits, and is a significant issue for councillors too.
- Councils value the existence of the service delivered and tailored locally and some see a more central approach to delivery as a threat to local accountability.

Service policies
- Local policies vary. This is seen as a barrier in relation to council tax collection issues, where some councils adopt a harder approach to collection. Others have strong social inclusion policies that can impact on the cost of both services, for example, a comprehensive approach to benefit take-up would increase the costs of benefits, but this conceals the wider community benefit of helping raise income levels.

Partnerships
- Some councils are unwilling to work with others for a variety of reasons such as lack of trust or poor relations between the organisations, at both political and managerial level.
- Larger councils already benefit from many economies of scale and are therefore reluctant, in some cases, to look at partnerships to increase the capacity of smaller councils, and further improve efficiency for themselves.

Staffing issues
- A centralised back office would be unacceptable to many councils if it was located outside their area as it would mean a loss of local jobs. This issue was reflected in all types of council and is preventing more in-depth partnership work from taking place.
- It is often down to individual managers to lead the change agenda, where there is no drive from the top of an organisation. This is difficult, as managers have potentially most to lose (their jobs) in any potential joint working arrangement.
- Recruitment and retention of staff at management level are further pressures that can prevent a move to change. One council we visited had experienced five changes in senior management for revenues and benefits in five years. Many councils, particularly London boroughs, have difficulty recruiting and retaining staff.

IT systems
- Incompatibility of IT systems between councils is seen as a barrier to change. The revenue and benefits market is served by a number of different software suppliers and, although the systems need to comply with regulations, each one is different. Staff within councils therefore need to develop different expertise to use each system. However, there are examples of organisations in the public and private sector working together effectively with different systems for these services.

External pressures
- Where significant change has taken place, it has tended to be driven by problems. For example, a poor inspection report, or Comprehensive Performance Assessment (CPA) rating.
- Pressure prevents innovation and forward thinking – revenues and benefits are subject to regular external changes through legislation. Add to this local pressures created by staff restructures, relocation and new computer systems, all very recent in one council we visited, and there is limited capacity to deal with other significant changes.
- While all these barriers are real issues, we found that councils are not making a robust evaluation of the alternatives. As a result, local taxpayers may be paying a premium for the existing method of service delivery.

Figure 9.1   Barriers to change

Source: Audit Commission (2005a, para. 47)

Benchmarking
- Examples of innovative practices are often not accompanied by a thorough cost-benefit analysis. This makes it more difficult to share the benefits and encourage others.
- Within councils there is a lack of trust in some of the benchmarking, particularly in relation to costs. Councils are not maximising the benefits of benchmarking and there is no clear purpose to much of this activity. Benchmarking groups are more active in some areas than others. The Greater Manchester Group has produced some useful data that can be used to identify the relationship between process and performance. Other groups operate in a fairly competitive spirit, and this can prevent a more joined-up approach being adopted. There is evidence that in some areas councils have stopped participating, meaning that councils cannot maximise opportunities to share initiatives, such as procuring a new computer system together.

Figure 9.1　　*Concluded*

These issues have been explored earlier in the book and they do not, in themselves, present an insuperable barrier to sharing; rather they are the product of a desire to avoid failure through exposing the council to risk from uncertainty. This unwillingness to 'stretch' is also evident from the lack of joined-up sharings being organized across the public services to include health and police, even in areas as basic as back-office services.

There is also a lack of evidence of large-scale migration of such services to the ready-made shared service centres provided by the private sector – this is not to say this doesn't happen but the amount and frequency are low.

One example where this has happened is Hertfordshire County Council's payroll service. Serco provide payroll and pensions services from their Hertford Shared Service Centre which has approximately 75 customers and processes over 1.4 million payslips a year.

The centre also provides finance and ICT shared services, but the initial contract was signed with the initial client Hertfordshire County Council by Serco (then ITNET) in 1993 for Hertfordshire County Council and approximately 75 other clients. These range from small voluntary and community organisations, such as Hertfordshire Action on Disability and Redbourne Parish Council and many Hertfordshire schools, to other larger councils, public sector agencies and private sector organisations, including GSL Global (formerly Group 4), Hertfordshire Police Authority and Orbit Housing Association. Since then other major contract wins have included:

- 1998: London Borough of Brent;
- 2002: London Borough of Islington's schools payroll contract;
- 2003: Healthcare Commission;
- 2004: Travelodge;
- 2004: Little Chef.

The original objective was to improve value for money for Hertfordshire County Council, providing a better quality of service at reduced cost. The following were achieved:

- transformation of services from using traditional, separate legacy-based applications to fully integrated SAP applications across payroll, HR, accounting and procurement;
- transformation of the pensions service through implementation of best-of-breed pensions administration application in AXISe, including the latest integrated imaging, employee internet and workflow applications;

- improvement in capability of staff through training and development; payroll staff are trained or in the process of training to IPPM payroll administration standards;
- the winning of new pensions and payroll contracts. Now there are over 75 public and private sector customers. Some of the larger customer payroll contracts served by the Hertford teams include: BASF (800 employees), Premier Brands (5,639), Group 4 (7,400), Alstom (800), Travelodge (4,000), Little Chef (3,800), Canon UK (2,500), London Borough of Brent (13,000), Hertfordshire County Council (33,000), Hertfordshire Pensioners (19,000), Hertfordshire Constabulary (4,000), Police Pensioners (1,400), Hertfordshire Probation (300) and Orbit Housing Association (1,000).

Benefits to the county council include reduced cost per payslip, increased accuracy rate and a reduction in payroll staff numbers of 12 per cent. This reduction was achieved through natural wastage and against the background of a 30 per cent increase in employees paid through new business in the same period.

The private sector is very keen to run the shared service centres on behalf of public bodies. Capita is already marketing service centres that bring together contact centres, council tax collection, business rates collection, payroll, pensions, HR activities and housing benefits processing. Its two existing shared service centres, in Coventry and Cumbria, support a dozen councils.

Local Area Agreements

During 2000–1 the government piloted Local Public Service Agreements (LPSAs) with 20 local councils who agreed to deliver improved outcomes for about 12 key areas of activity which reflect a mix of national and local priorities. In return for this they were given greater freedom in the means of delivery, and financial incentives. Thus a council would agree, for key areas of activity, to exceed the performance required by its Best Value obligations in terms of quality, quantity and/or timescale. LPSAs can therefore be seen as a tool for local councils to deliver even better outcomes for local people than they would otherwise expect to achieve.

Local Area Agreements (LAAs) were launched in July 2004. They are intended to deliver improved local service outcomes through better co-ordination between central government and local councils and their partners. While central government will continue to set high-level strategic priorities, the aim is for central government departments to devolve detailed day-to-day control of programmes and funding streams, and move towards stronger partnership working with local councils. The LAAs are agreements negotiated between local partners and government offices (GOs) (on behalf of central government), specifying a range of agreed outcomes shared by all delivery partners, with associated indicators, targets and funding streams. Twenty-one LAA pilots were announced on 4 October 2004, and 20 LAAs were signed off by the Deputy Prime Minister on 22 March 2005. On 22 June 2005, the Deputy Prime Minister announced a further pilot phase of 66 agreements.

A process evaluation of the negotiation of pilot Local Area Agreements for the ODPM in June 2005 found that local councils, partners and GOs have largely welcomed the LAA initiative and the majority remain positive about the scheme and its potential. Appendix 2 summarizes the researchers' findings.

Their most relevant findings were the considerable enthusiasm for the overarching principles behind the LAA scheme, the difficulty of making it work in two-tier council areas and the fact that local partners have signed up jointly to pursuing outcomes that reflect key priorities for government; this formal joint ownership – and the joint performance management that will flow from the LAA – are important advances. Also that the process of developing their LAA has helped to build amongst local partners a shared understanding of priorities across each locality that require joint action – it has involved hard choices, whereas many community strategies fudged these.

The researchers consider that implementation of the agreements has the potential to deliver more appropriate and higher quality local services. The important thing here was that these improvements were in higher-level sharings such as joint commissioning of services between health and social care with greater involvement of local people; for example, joint working between partners at county and district levels to reduce homelessness for families and vulnerable young people and bringing together all youth support agency funding into a single virtual pooled fund to tackle the needs of disaffected young people not engaged in education, employment or training (NEETs) in the most disadvantaged neighbourhoods.

The researchers said many agreements contain proposals for new ways of working that could have been put in place without the LAA, but required the process as a catalyst to reach agreement between partners. The process has begun to strengthen local strategic partnerships, given focus to existing theme partnerships and helped to stimulate the establishment of new ones where necessary. It is clear that, at local level, the process has in general cemented existing relationships and opened the doors to new ones.

Researchers considered that the LAA process provides a vehicle for other public sector bodies to share in the process. The involvement of health and police in LAA development has clearly helped to get all to recognize the shared agenda in which they are involved. It would not take much more joint working for all these bodies to come to appreciate the advantage there could be of working together more formally in terms of sharing management of back-office services.

Commenting on the agreements Phil Woolas, Minister of Local Government in October 2005, said:

> It is very clear to me – having looked at the early rounds of local area agreements, having studied the agreements across England, having local knowledge in my own constituency, having looked at all of the evidence – that local area agreements are in my view the most significant change in public service and local funding that we have had since the Second World War. I believe the possibilities that they open up for local service delivery are profound and I think they have deep and broad consequences for national government as well.

Introducing the White Paper *Stronger and Prosperous Communities* (Department of Communities and Local Government 2006) in the Commons, Ruth Kelly, Secretary of State, said the amount of money to be channelled through LAAs was to increase from £500 million to £4.7 billion in a single 'pot' that can be used in whichever way the partners decide although the expectation is that it will be used on activities or services related to agreed targets or which closely reflect the original purpose of the grant stream.

'Transforming government'

The government published *Transformational Government, Enabled by Technology* in November 2005 (Cabinet Office e-Government Unit 2005). This strategy set out a vision for government in the twenty-first century, requiring three key transformations:

1. 'Services enabled by IT must be designed around the citizen or business, not the provider, and provided through modern, co-ordinated delivery channels.'
2. 'Government must move to a shared services culture – in the front-office, in the back-office, in information and in infrastructure – and release efficiencies by standardization, simplification and sharing.'
3. 'There must be broadening and deepening of government's professionalism in terms of the planning, delivery, management, skills and governance of IT enabled change.'

The strategy takes a broadly based approach to shared services, identifying eight areas where action is needed:

1. *Customer service centres* – to provide both central and local government services in a more customer-centric manner.
2. *HR, finance and other corporate services* – which together cost up to £20 billion a year across the 1,300 government organizations that each have their own service functions.
3. *A common infrastructure* – to bring together the GSI, the Government Gateway and Government Connect.
4. *Data Sharing* – between agencies to help deliver better services and guard against fraud and other misuse.
5. *Information management* – tools to analyse and spot patterns in shared data, enabling more-informed management decisions and better policy-making.
6. *Information assurance* – measures to combat the increased security risks that follow from wider sharing of data.
7. *Identity management* – rationalizing the existing numbering systems in government and moving towards a federated approach.
8. *Technology standards* – to enable systems and architectures to dovetail together.

This strategy has become closely linked to two major strategic change programmes: the Capability Reviews and the Comprehensive Spending Review of 2007.

The Capability Reviews are taking place under the direction of the head of the Prime Minister's Delivery Unit, and will be consistent with the strategy. A further discussion document – *Transformational Local Government* – was published by the ODPM in March 2006; it looks at the strategy from a local perspective and is aimed at promoting wider debate of how change will take place across English councils.

The Cabinet Office on behalf of the Chief Information Officer (CIO) is working closely with HM Treasury to ensure that the potential of transformational government is realized in the Comprehensive Spending Review and that proposals for expenditure and reform are consistent with the strategy. In the 2006 Budget statement the Chancellor announced he had asked Sir David Varney, Executive Chairman of HM Revenue and Customs and former CEO of O_2, to advise him on the opportunities for transforming the delivery of public services.

Sir David Varney published his report to the Chancellor of the Exchequer on *Service Transformation: a Better Service For Citizens and Businesses, a Better Deal for Taxpayers* on 7 December 2006. Acknowledging the achievements made in the past decade, Sir David's report identifies major opportunities to strengthen public service delivery to make it more accessible, convenient and efficient to meet changing citizen and business expectations.

Launching the report, Sir David Varney said:

The service sector has an increasingly important role in the economy and public service delivery needs to evolve to meet the emerging challenges. There are opportunities to deliver better public services through joining up service provision across the public sector, and by engaging more directly with users in the design and delivery of services. Over the next ten years there are opportunities to provide better public services at a lower cost to the taxpayer, if the Government takes these opportunities, then I believe the UK can create a world class public service economy with interactions with citizens and businesses that deliver real value and resolve problems first time.

The key proposals were:

- develop a change of circumstances service starting with bereavement, birth and change of address by 2010, to drive citizen- and business-focused cross-government working;
- improve Direct.gov and Businesslink.gov so they become the primary information and transactional channels for citizens and businesses, reducing the number of departmental specific websites, providing the Secretary of State for the Department for Work and Pensions (DWP) and the Paymaster General respectively with responsibility for the services;
- improve public sector contact centre performance by establishing performance targets and best practice benchmarks, reducing operating costs by 25 per cent releasing £400 million;
- take forward proposals to develop a cross-government identity management system to enable greater personalization of services and to reduce duplication across government;
- build on a proof of concept project to share data between HM Revenue and Customs, DWP and 12 local authorities;
- establish new citizen and business contact roles and functions within departments to drive increased skills and capability to respond to citizen and business needs and to increasingly co-ordinate service delivery from a government perspective;
- develop better-co-ordinated and focused face-to-face services, through a cross-government estate strategy, underpinned with departmental plans for increased third sector delivery of these services and more mobile working;
- establish service transformation as a top priority outcome for government, underpinned by a detailed delivery plan and quantitative performance indicators which form the basis of a published annual report on service transformation.

He also identified, although not as a recommendation, a vision for service transformation which sets his recommendations in context and has significant implications on the direction of sharings. See Figure 9.2.

'Direct.gov.uk' and '101'

'DIRECT.GOV.UK'

The government have created Direct.gov.uk and trailed it heavily in advertisements on national television and radio. Available through the website are such services as:

In 2020, people throughout the country can access public services that are tailored to their personal needs and preferences.

For self-service, an individual would go to their local area, public services portal, where they would ring the single non-emergency number. They get through to their local contact centre and if they wish to, they can walk into a convenient, local one-stop shop. This single point of access triggers a comprehensive, fast and accurate service both locally and nationally.

Local public services teams reach out to people who would otherwise find themselves excluded from public services, carry out a single assessment of their needs and means and commission appropriate services for them.

The requirement is greater in those communities facing the biggest socio-economic challenges.

Citizens identify these local public services teams with their council. Behind the scenes, central and local governments coordinate a network of public bodies, private and third-sector partners to provide seamless access to these services.

The front-line delivery of services is also integrated. Older people, children and young people, workless people and other customer groups can choose packages of public services tailored to their needs.

Public, private and third-sector partners collaborate across the delivery chain, in a way that is invisible to the public.

The partners pool their intelligence about the needs and preferences of local people and this informs the design of public services and the tailoring of packages for individuals and groups.

Value for money is a central principle in the design of public services, but this does not mean there is a uniform solution in every community. There is room for difference and experimentation to drive improvement. The culture of government is to seek out duplication and opportunities for efficiency, ensuring resources can be directed to where they will most add value and benefit to the public.

Measured benefits, services and facilities are shared between all tiers of central and local government and other public bodies. The public do not see this process. They experience only public services packaged for their needs.

Figure 9.2   A vision for service transformation

Source: Sir David Varney's report to the Chancellor of the Exchequer on Service Transformation: a Better Service For Citizens and Businesses, a Better Deal for Taxpayers

- *education and learning* – early learning, schools, material for teenagers aged 14 to 19, university and higher education, student loans, adult learning; motoring – driver licensing, learners and driving tests, buy or sell a vehicle, taxing and MOT, online services;
- *home and community* – home buying and selling, planning, environment, recycling, water conservation;
- *employment* – looking for work, employees, working hours and time off, redundancy, jobseekers;

- *money, tax and benefits* – benefits and tax credits, pensions, taxes, debt, National Insurance, managing money, council tax;
- *health and well-being* – medical records, health services, smoking, NHS Direct, strokes, first aid, emergencies, seasonal flu;
- *travel and transport* – journey planner, passports, bus travel concessions, taxi safety, safety (speed) cameras;
- *leisure and recreation* – green spaces, museums and galleries, cycling, events in the UK, gardening;
- *crime, justice and the law* – crime prevention, prison and probation, anti-social behaviour;
- *rights and responsibilities* – identity theft, data protection, death, citizenship, consumer rights, complaints.

It also includes a 'Life events' section dealing with different types of people such as:

- *parents* – having a baby, childcare, Your Money, bullying, maternity leave;
- *disabled people* – Disability Living Allowance, rights, home, work, money;
- *over 50s* – working, learning, retirement and pensions, health;
- *Britons living abroad* – working abroad, returning to the UK, health abroad;
- *caring for someone* – Carer's Allowance, support, working and caring;
- *young people* – learning, leisure, work.

Users of the website are able to access the service they require by entering their postcode or the name of their council to get into their council's website.

'101'

'101' is the government's idea to have a single non-emergency number available across England and Wales by 2008. The intention is that this number can be dialled by those reporting vandalism, graffiti and other deliberate damage to property, noisy neighbours, threatening and abusive behaviour, abandoned vehicles, rubbish and litter, including fly tipping, people being drunk or rowdy in public places, drug-related anti-social behaviour and problems with street lighting.

The Single Non-Emergency Number (SNEN) was announced by the Home Office and the communications regulator Ofcom. The service has been commissioned to free up the 999 service ('70 per cent of 999 calls made in 2004 were not emergencies') so it can handle emergency incidents more efficiently. The new number has been designed to improve the delivery of non-emergency services. It will be provided by local councils and police forces working together and will initially be launched in five 'Wave 1' areas in summer 2006. The first wave involves partnerships between police forces and local councils in the Hampshire Police force area, Northumbria Police force area, Cardiff in South Wales, Sheffield in South Yorkshire and Leicester City and Rutland County in Leicestershire.

Calls to 101 will be charged at a fixed rate of ten pence per call whether from landlines or mobiles.

The second wave of projects has, according to the *Local Government Chronicle* on 16 November 2006, has been put off for a year due to concerns over the costs and success of earlier pilots. The Home Office has confirmed the delay in order to assess the first wave. Councils have suggested that Phase 1 pilots were too costly and a superintendent of Hampshire Constabulary was quoted as saying that 'Customer satisfaction is still low for tasks such as noise nuisance, graffiti removal and harassment type incidents because the expectation is for a quicker response service. There needs to be more public awareness and knowledge about when to call which service, and that is taking time.'

Where next?

If we accept that local councils are not moving fast enough for the government we can see the 'fifth' wave has the feel of an integrated push to achieve sharing by putting all of the elements in place to increase the amount of sharing of service delivery in local councils. The success of the Local Area Agreements has convinced the government that by applying pressure through targets (as it did in the National Health Service – though the success of these has been questioned) on a county basis, linked to the continuing individual council targets of the 'Gershon' approach and the inducements offered through the Regional Centres of Excellence, all framed in the White Paper, sharing can be made a virtual necessity for local councils.

And just to make sure, while this process rolls out, the government has provided the mechanisms through 'Direct.gov.uk' and '101' to ensure the public have the access to public services.

Whilst there appears to be no escape from this process, the speed, format, methods and outcomes are at present unclear. The final chapter will try to forecast what could happen.

10 *The Future for Shared Services: The 'Sixth' Wave?*

Introduction

In October 1998 the Public Management Foundation published *The Future for Public Services 2008* – two scenarios over a range of topics were postulated, including the following references to citizens, that seem (although they were written up as alternatives) remarkably prescient:

New technology has allowed different organizations to pool their databases and give access to a wide range of services through a single gateway. The same process has allowed those who consume services to have far greater influence over how they are shaped: it is now unusual for any public service to be offered without measuring both its outcomes and the views of its users.

And:

There can be no doubt that ... more information does not necessarily mean a more informed public – and levels of understanding about the strains under which public services have to work are rudimentary. Those who use services are certainly more vocal than they have ever been. The problem is often that they demand more than can be delivered ...

If that scenario describes well the situation local councils now find themselves in, what is likely to be the situation in another ten years? In the 'Transformational Government' strategy, the year 2011 is identified as the date for the final phase for the strategy but clearly much has to happen to achieve this. The Discussion Paper issued in March 2006 without being prescriptive outlined what a 'transformed' local government scene would look like:

There is no slick, concise definition of 'transformation'. However, it clearly should be defined in terms of the citizen and user of local public services, not in terms of the organizations that provide them.

Our vision is that people will be able to say the following about local public services:

- *'I feel a sense of engagement in local decisions and ownership of the outcomes.'*
- *'I know who is responsible for which services and I can hold them to account.'*
- *'I feel that local policies and services are tailored to my needs.'*
- *'I can see that the public services are being responsive and creative in their approaches to local problems.'*
- *'I perceive local public services as accessible, easy to use, comprehensible (I know what they can and can't do) and joined-up when they need to be.'*

- *'I feel that local public services are doing things in the most efficient way.'*
- *'As a business, I understand the legislation that affects me and the support available to me locally.'*

To achieve this is a huge task but clearly cannot be achieved if service delivery is organized as it is now. However, the government have given a significant boost to transformation with the launching of Direct.gov.uk and the 101 number. This is because they provide potentially a 'virtual' route to service delivery divorced from any concept of local council structures and responsibilities.

In April 2006 the Department of Communities and Local Government posted on its website 'All Our Futures: The Challenges for Local Governance in 2015' written by the Tavistock Institute with SOLON Consultants and the Local Government Information Unit which suggested that in 2015:

> *Increasing expectations of efficiency, effectiveness and transparency from public sector services and administration ... [and] growing external markets for public service provision and the need for new and varied range of suppliers both private and voluntary ... implies that who delivers services in the narrow sense – who empties the bins, who provides adult education – may not be that important. But who organizes, who makes the strategic choices – and whether strategic choices are and can be made at all – about service delivery will be immensely important to public policy outcomes.*

If the scenarios outlined here were to come true, the world of local councils would be very different. The picture it paints is one that has often been speculated on – the council as an 'enabler' rather than a service deliverer. What does this mean for the 'local government brand' – will the individual and collective 'brand' be enhanced or degraded? Can local democracy survive? Will the public really be concerned? What would be the place of shared services?

There seems little doubt that all of the elements are in place to increase the amount of sharing of service delivery in local councils. However, the speed, format, methods and outcomes are at present unclear. This chapter tries to review the available evidence on the likely trends to try to draw some conclusions.

The key question is whether a top-down centrally driven strategy is needed to encourage (or compel) councils to work in partnership with each other and other providers to achieve economies of scale, or whether individual councils (and/or networks of councils) in fact need to be given greater operational freedom to enable them to develop new partnerships and to embrace new forms of commissioning and service delivery. The Gershon Report assumes that government needs to compel/encourage councils to share back-office functions in order to reap economies of scale. Meanwhile the government's ten-year strategy for local government emphasizes the importance of choice, more personalized services and devolution of control over services to local communities/neighbourhoods, implying that there are advantages to be gained from local control and smaller scale delivery.

There was a hope that the government's White Paper of late 2006 would provide a steer.

The White Paper – *Strong and Prosperous Communities*

At the beginning of 2006 the government launched a consultation of local government designed to test opinion of the future shape of councils, the perceived view being that they hoped to create a new structure to start from 2009.

Throughout 2006, the debate was conducted across government, surviving a Cabinet reshuffle and, according to those in 'the know', the wrangling between the Prime Minister and the Chancellor. Supporting it were the ongoing deliberations of an inquiry being led by Sir Michael Lyons.

Issues being heavily trailed included 'double devolution', in which councils could be rewarded with extra responsibility and freedoms, provided they agree to hand specific functions, from street cleaning to park maintenance, to neighbourhood deliverers; larger strategic councils and smaller town or parish councils with beefed-up powers able to engage citizens in local issues, whether anti-social behaviour, economic regeneration or difficult health issues; new city-region partnerships around conurbations such as Greater Manchester and the West Midlands and new unitary status for some councils.

Strong and Prosperous Communities was published on 26 October 2006 with the aim 'to give local people and local communities more influence and power to improve their lives.'

It covers a wide range of issues including requiring councils to change to one of three strong leadership models including fixed-term directly elected mayors or leaders; giving overview and scrutiny committees of councils new powers to review the actions of key public bodies; inviting a small number of councils keen to seek unitary status to apply; reforming the current standards board and implementing a more locally based conduct regime.

Other issues covered are strengthening the ability of councillors to act as champions for their community via a new 'Community Call for Action'; reviewing the barriers to increasing community management and ownership of underused local community assets; making it easier to set up a tenant management organization; devolving the right to set up parish councils to local government and giving communities in London the same right to establish parishes as elsewhere with councils able to determine local byelaws and enforce these through fixed penalty notices without agreement from central government.

It also includes an intention by the government to work closely with those local councils who have already come forward with proposals to help promote their further economic development – whether in city-regions or elsewhere, recognizing that there is no one-size-fits-all model and a package of reforms of Passenger Transport Councils and Executives to strengthen leadership and enable a more coherent approach to transport in the biggest cities are proposals also included.

Revising the Best Value duty is an issue also included to secure the participation of citizens and communities in the delivery of local public services; providing better and more timely information on the quality of local services, including annual publication of local councils' performance against national outcome indicators and a set of indicators on citizen satisfaction; establishing a clear set of government priorities, with 1,200 national indicators slashed to a single set of around 200, measuring issues of nationwide importance including where minimum standards are essential; agreeing through Local Area Agreements, a single set of around 35 specific improvement targets for each local area, plus the statutory targets for childcare and educational attainment; risk-based assessment, enabling targeting of inspection where it can add most value and putting in place a new framework for strategic leadership in local areas are ideas also referenced.

Chapter 7 of the White Paper is entitled 'Efficiency – transforming local services' and deals at length with a number of issues. The full text is shown in Appendix 3.

This chapter lays out a number of important implications for sharing between local councils in the context of the Transformational Government strategy and a clear statement that ambitious efficiency gains will be required as part of the 2007 Comprehensive Spending Review. In order to help meet these the government will encourage greater service collaboration between councils and across all public bodies.

The White Paper believes 'the goal for continuing two-tier areas is to achieve ... shared back-office functions and integrated service delivery mechanisms'. More generally, the White Paper states that in order to deliver the transformed services and value for money that communities want, councils will have to challenge traditional methods of delivery, rooting out waste, in order to drive efficiency. One way in which this is to be done is by 'securing more collaboration between local councils and across all public bodies, where this improves effectiveness and efficiency, and ensuring that administrative boundaries do not act as a barrier to service transformation and efficiency'.

To do this the White Paper expects 'all local councils must adopt a strategic approach to service delivery'. It says 'The Cabinet Office discussion paper *Transformational Local Government*, produced in collaboration with local government, set out a number of prerequisites for driving service transformation' and 'We are currently reviewing the transformational government agenda and how channel delivery can be made more responsive to citizen and business need. Combined with proposals in this White Paper, the findings of Sir David Varney's review [see Chapter 9] will seek to provide further opportunities for local and central government and other providers to work more closely together on customer centred services.'

The White Paper is not content to leave local councils alone to determine the way forward, pointing out that there has already been research on the relationship between positive attitudes towards competition and improved service performance (*Long-term Evaluation of the Best Value Regime: Summary Report, Communities and Local Government*, 2006) and the White Paper says there will be a report on developing the local government services market. Working with local government, commissioners and providers, the paper will explore opportunities to develop and shape the local government services market, to encourage a diversity of suppliers across the public, private and the third sectors. This will include considering ways to stimulate new markets in order to secure alternative provision and enable both commissioner and user choice in areas of local government which are currently uncontested or not fully contested; and increase the capacity and competitiveness in existing supply markets, including streamlining procurement processes and cutting red-tape. The White Paper says that the third sector – voluntary, community and social enterprises – will be a key part of this mixed market, bringing with it a wealth of expertise and experience with user groups, as well as innovative and cost-effective approaches to delivery.

What are the likely consequences?

TYPES OF SHARING

Sharing will increase. The issue is whether it will be more of the same, or organized by different groups of councils, or maybe a different type of sharing. This is fundamental to the aim in the White Paper that to 'deliver the transformed services and value for money that communities want, councils will have to challenge traditional methods of delivery'. Figure 10.1 demonstrates an 'evolutionary scale' of sharings. This shows how 'shared services' move service delivery from single services organized for the convenience of the service provider (in this case by traditionally organized local councils) to being organized with the customers' requirements as paramount.

SERVICES ORGANIZED FOR CUSTOMERS BENEFIT

SERVICES ORGANIZED FOR STRUCTURAL CONVENIENCE

365 Local Councils traditionally organised.

SHARING OF NEW OUTCOMES – e.g. achieving economic and social well-being	Transformed
SHARING OF NEW SERVICES – e.g supporting people	Agile and Responsive
SHARING OF NEW CITIZEN CENTRED SOLUTIONS – e.g. implementing electronic government	Integrated
SHARING FOR SPECIALIZATION – e.g. Contact Centres	Competent
SHARING FOR RESOURCE MANAGEMENT – shared services for specific services e.g. procurement	Resource wise

Figure 10.1   Model of the 'evolutionary' scale of shared services

This model also describes the types of attributes shared services display when they display organization for customer benefit. Services that have been shared between local councils to date are rarely 'integrated' and almost never 'transformed'. Those that are 'agile and responsive' are currently usually the result of external influence.

So the challenge for the future is to create shared services that achieve the higher-level outcomes, while still being competent and resource-wise. But where will the impetus come from?

In a recent report the New Local Government Network said there were still many major obstacles to shared services becoming the norm in the public sector and argues that a lack of joined-up thinking may prevent the shared services agenda achieving its ultimate goals. Clearer strategic leadership is needed, supported by more comprehensive central data, local government sponsors and greater incentives. It is obvious that the government will be behind the setting of the agenda, and therefore will be controlling the pace of the agenda. There are likely to be three main thrusts. First, local councils doing it for themselves with the pressure applied through the use of efficiency targets such as a flat-rate financial target aided and abetted by bodies such as the Regional Centres of Excellence and the Improvement and Development Agency. Secondly, there is likely to be the use of target-setting through an adoption of an

LAA model such as an 'Improvement' grouping or county-based grouping of councils – this approach could include other public sector bodies. Thirdly, there will be the manipulation of the market with local councils finding the private sector as the only way to achieve the targets set for them.

Finally, and if the other routes do not deliver change at the pace required, there is the regulatory, legislative and structural reordering route – a case of last resort.

LOCAL COUNCILS DOING IT FOR THEMSELVES

Based on what has gone before and what is intended in the annual efficiency statements the number of councils involved in a 'sharing' is bound to grow. Although it is difficult to be precise the rate of progress is quickening. On the basis of the statements in the annual efficiency statements there appears to be a doubling of sharings every two years.

Local government generally is becoming more ambitious with larger and more extensive sharings, with more councils involved and a widening range of services. Local government is overachieving the government's efficiency targets but there is no certainty this can continue unless councils display more ambition and include more parts of the public sector.

This is because the type of sharing does not appear to be changing. As far as one can tell, the intended sharings are focused at the lower end of the 'evolutionary' scale. Even where larger groupings of services for sharing are being explored, such as in Lincolnshire, the grouping and aims are familiar. This, as the government's 'Transformational Agenda' proceeds, will become unacceptable as requirements for joined-up working become even more stretching and intensive and there may well come a point when the government loses patience with the failure of councils to move up the 'evolutionary' scale.

LOCAL AREA AGREEMENTS

Chapter 7 of the White Paper lays out a number of important implications for sharing between local councils in context of the Transformational Government strategy and says that in order to deliver the transformed services and value for money that communities want, councils will have to challenge traditional methods of delivery, rooting out waste, in order to drive efficiency.

One way in which this is to be done is by 'securing more collaboration between local councils and across all public bodies, where this improves effectiveness and efficiency, and ensuring that administrative boundaries do not act as a barrier to service transformation and efficiency'. It gives support for the development of county-wide sharings and in some cases regional collaborations.

The White Paper says the 'freedom' offered to local councils to achieve improvement through LAAs will be balanced by 'an ongoing challenge on efficiency across the public sector, as well as what is achievable within local councils, which will be at least as ambitious as the current spending review period. We will embed efficiency as part of the new performance framework and we will explore ways of using the framework to monitor local councils' performance in this area and challenge poor performance. One option would be for local partners to come together to agree an efficiency target as part of their LAA which they would then work jointly to achieve.'

Together these ideas give a very significant boost to the concept of sharing being organized on a county-wide level. Just as it is clear the LAAs to date have impacted on the nature of service delivery at the higher end of the government's aspirations for joined-up service delivery, the White Paper sees the use of more all-embracing LAAs working at a more basic level.

One can easily foresee a target for the delivery of a set of services, for example, revenues and benefits to be set relative to the cost of providing that service per taxpayer or benefit recipient and the county grouping to be set challenging targets that force them to collectively work to achieve it in order to earn the additional resources success will attract. Similar scenarios for other services such as cost per customer enquiry would be equally valid.

This would be a powerful way of achieving the required impact for the government. Target-setting has had, despite well-publicized hiccups, a fundamental impact in the health service and in the police and increasingly local councils have had to follow where the government has led – waste, recycling and e-government being the prime examples. Particularly attractive is the notion that this allows for local discretion and local decision-making, thus absolving ministers from having to make hard choices.

Also, this allows the government to set targets that effectively reflect national aspirations for a 'national standard'. And this is important – despite widespread cynicism about politics generally, in a survey quoted in the *Local Government Chronicle* on 25 May 2006 (YouGov/ LGIU), although two-thirds of people say they cannot influence decisions and do not trust their councillors, 80 per cent of local people would rather have decisions taken by their elected councillors than quangos. In his interim report, Sir Michael Lyons (Lyons Inquiry into Local Government) illustrated the range of support there was amongst people as to whether there should be set public service standards. Whilst a majority of people thought there should be central government standards for the NHS, fire and rescue services, police and education, the majority supported having 'local government decision' on refuse collection, leisure services, planning and development control, social housing, public transport, social services and roads. And three times as many respondents were happy to see different standards in different areas.

THE 'MARKET'

It is certain that councils will increase their use of the private sector shared service centres in existence. Examples of such centres are the Liberata Centre at Barrow-in-Furness doing work for nearby councils; the Middlesbrough HBS Business Centre, which does work for Redcar and Cleveland Council as well as Middlesbrough Metropolitan District Council; the HBS Business Centre in Lincoln, which primarily supports Lincolnshire County Council but also does work for Lincoln City Council; and the Blackburn with Darwen Capita Centre, which also provides services for 20 other councils (such as processing benefits payments for Westminster), acts as an additional call centre for the Criminal Records Bureau and processes BBC television licences.

One commentator has suggested that the amount of central services that are currently outsourced is only 14 per cent of the potential market and there is therefore plenty of room for growth. The same commentator suggests that the private sector's involvement in councils will treble by 2015.

Another analyst says shared services is poised to become the single biggest new opportunity for software and IT services (S/ITS) suppliers to the UK public sector over the next five years. They predict that the total S/ITS market for shared services in the public sector will grow at a compound annual growth rate of 29 per cent between 2005 and 2010, taking the market size from £351 million in 2005 to £1.6 billion in 2010.

There is no area of service that is 'off limits' to the private sector but inevitably the earliest efficiencies are likely to be achieved in areas in which the private sector are experienced, such as finance, revenues and benefits, e-government or frontline services (for example, running customer contact centres and call centres), HR and payroll and pensions.

It requires no legislative change for the growth of the use of the private sector by local councils – when in the White Paper it says there will be a report on developing the local government services market:

> 'to … explore opportunities to develop and shape the local government services market, to encourage a diversity of suppliers across the public, private and the third sectors …'

this is a very clear hint that the government will seek to open up the market further by reducing the cost of tendering, forcing the creation of larger contracts and reducing the amount of risk in contracts (for example, changing the rules on pensions). The private sector is likely to react by being much more concerned to offer services higher up the 'evolutionary' scale rather than just being interested in 'traditional' service based offers.

THE LAST RESORT

The government has an impressive set of sanctions at its disposal. Obviously the financial control is paramount as the government still retains the power to 'cap' councils who set too high a council tax to make up for any shortfall in the level of government grant.

The government as we have seen can take advantage of its ability to set targets (as in recycling and e-government) and to dictate organizational structures (as in Supporting People).

But it also has the regulatory sanctions. This would be applied at first through the Audit Commission's role of inspecting and auditing councils, and already through the Comprehensive Performance Assessment process it has the ability to reward councils with increased freedoms for achievement of high performance or intervention and monitoring for failure.

The government has shown itself willing to increase the standards required through the CPA judgements by tightening the criteria, thus requiring better performance from councils to retain their scoring status, and adding in extra elements for judgement such as 'value for money' and 'service user focus and diversity'. There is talk of 'sustainability' being added. In the *Local Government Chronicle* on 16 November it was said that the Audit Commission are to take a tough line with councils that fail to embrace the drive towards shared services. The Chair of the Audit Commission, Michael O'Higgins, said shared services should be driven at the local level. He is quoted as saying:

> I would encourage key authorities to take the lead to get [shared service projects] going. If [a shared services project] is shown to be working and any local public body hasn't signed up, we would want to know if they were making comparable savings from another method and if not, why not.

Finally, there is the structural route. Whilst the current government seems unwilling to set out on a wholesale restructuring it also seems unwilling to prevent restructuring from happening if certain criteria can be met. According to the *Local Government Chronicle* of 7 December 2006, almost half of the 34 English county councils are likely to seek unitary status. In the event 9 applications were approved, this would reduce the number of councils in

England from 388 to fewer than 330, having a significant impact on the number of potential sharings as, effectively, for those councils that come together sharing of service delivery is part of the package. Should the government feel the pace of sharing elsewhere is not quick enough it would not be averse to forcing the ends it wants.

Another stimulus to a restructuring would be if conglomeration of services becomes so common that some councils, probably smaller districts, have too few unique functions being delivered individually for them to sustain themselves. They themselves would seek a new status that lessens the exposure of locally elected representatives to management responsibilities: in other words, they would be approaching the situation where the council only meet a few times a year to set policy, check progress and award contracts.

SO WHAT WILL HAPPEN?

Looking forward to 2015, it seems inevitable that the pace of sharings will have continued to increase. There is much greater probability that there will be a focus on county groupings, not necessarily because that this is the optimal size or volume for sharings but because increasingly the focus for local councils work will be their county group (in pursuance of effective LAAs). There will undoubtedly have been an increase in the share of activity carried out by the private sector.

However, I fully expect that, by 2015, there will be a 'patchwork quilt' of service delivery across local councils. There are three reasons for this.

First, the pace of change is uncertain. The White Paper does present a clear hint of how the government intends change should happen, but translating this into clear action may not be easy. I would not expect this part of the White Paper to be controversial. However, progress may get caught up in the inevitable slow down in thrust caused by the Prime Ministerial change in 2007. Some commentators have speculated on the ending of the Department of Communities and Local Government and the setting up of a new intermediary body.

It may therefore not be until late 2007 that local councils are given clear guidance about the implications for LAAs and are able to focus on creating shared services on a county basis. In the meantime many councils will have develop bilateral arrangements in order to meet their Gershon targets and the emerging Transformational Government agenda and will be unwilling to risk quickly unpicking those arrangements in favour of a county arrangement. Other councils will be involved in the creation of their unitary councils and have little time for sharing activity.

As it takes generally between 18 months to three years to achieve a sharing it is unlikely that it will be much before 2010 that county-based shared services could become a reality under LAA targets.

Secondly, the nature of the change is uncertain. Many local councils will come under pressure to create sharings in order to meet their efficiency targets. This will come from a variety of sources. The private sector will see the White Paper as presenting a real opportunity and will be making strenuous efforts to create an 'offer' to councils. This will be based on extending the use of existing shared service centres at the 'transactional' end of the market.

They may also face competition from some successful NHS shared service centres such as the Anglia Revenues Partnership. It is also possible that the external pressure on all local councils will be enough to do away with traditional rivalries and persuade some councils to allow the county council (or a large unitary council) to take on some of their back-office services such as payroll where the larger council can offer significant economies of scale irrespective of the likely coming together to share LAA targets. There are those who are advocating that local councils join together to form not for profit organizations, which would present an intermediary form of organization that allows local councils to retain activities within the public sector. One advantage of this form or organization is that surpluses can be re-invested in the organization. This opens up the possibility of some sort of internal market in local government where, as Kent County Council have suggested, councils trade between themselves to deliver services for each other. I think this is a less likely scenario than one in which effectively the private sector uses its infrastructure and contacts to trade across local government and the other parts of the public sector.

Thirdly, the public reaction (and consequentially that of local councils) is uncertain. The White Paper stresses the need for local councils to get the public involved in the creation of service delivery and whilst local people may be interested in the mechanics of arranging services such as social care and education they may well have limited interest in back-office services. The implication of this is that it is likely that such services as accountancy, personnel, ICT and revenues and benefits are regarded as transactional and will continue to be most frequently shared whilst other services – higher up the 'evolutionary' scale – are retained more closely under the control of councils until all the details have been worked through. This is because, as the White Paper pointed out, the need to tackle difficult cross-cutting issues and maximize the value for money of public resources requires that services should be designed around the needs of the citizen and the community, not around the processes and structures of individual agencies. In these services the need to engage other services such as health will be time-consuming.

However, if the model of the private sector is followed it may only be a few years before some council's service delivery is offshored and whilst this may well be a sensible economic move, the likely outcry may well temporarily slow progress and cause some to question the wisdom of such efficiencies.

It is inevitable that the pace of these three strands will vary across the country and whilst the headlines are clear – sharing will increase faster than in the past and be more ambitious – it is impossible to predict the 'final' outcome.

The 'final' word?

The White Paper makes it clear that the structure and size of individual units of local government units will be less important than ensuring that they have the appropriate incentives/sanctions for partnership working and measures to build up the local capacity (in terms of skills and technical competence) needed for councils to commission and procure services in ways that offer best value.

It might be that the optimum solution will be a combination of top-down incentives (and/or sanctions) and greater operational freedom at local level. And more than likely it will reflect thinking on the probability of what is best for different services. But getting the right mix is not likely to be straightforward.

The case for strong centralized control as a means of achieving economies of scale is probably not as strong as it once was. In the past there were heated debates about which scale of operations offered optimum technical efficiency in service delivery (see for example the discussions associated with successive waves of local government reorganization). But the size of individual councils may be far less important now than it was, as councils are increasingly commissioning and sharing rather than delivering services individually (leading to economies of scale that can be achieved on a wider customer base). New technology increases the opportunities for new forms of delivery across boundaries, which do not therefore depend for the efficiency on the scale of operations in one locality. The increased emphasis on partnership working opens up new possibilities for councils to work together and/or with other service providers to reap economies of scale.

For example, revenues and benefits could be reorganized by setting up regional processing centres (perhaps controlled by the Department of Work and Pensions), or environmental health services could be restructured as county or regional services linked to the Food Standards Agency. For those standardized services there could be common national standards set for cost, performance and quality thus ensuring common standards throughout the country. Other services where the public would accept local variations can stay local.

In other words, there is a real possibility that the organization of delivery will become much more complex and varied. There is no doubt the number of providers of services could increase; for example, the public could get benefits from one provider and refuse collection from another. Even if the number of service determiners (local councils) stays the same, for the public that would become an irrelevance as they would have the means (one-stop shops, customer call centres, Direct.gov.uk and 101) to access any service in the same way irrespective of the provider and wherever they are so that the number of interactions that people will have to engage in to get service delivery will stay the same.

This will be a real challenge for local councils – just how do they retain their identity and their relationship with local people in a situation where they are purely 'enablers' and others are delivering services. For sharing services as a concept, the future is more certain – there will be more, and local councils will find it as a prime method of delivering services. The 'sixth' wave could be the tidal wave that engulfs and changes local councils for ever, ending for once and all the role of direct service providers they have held for over a century.

1 Welland Shared Service Project – Principles and Protocols

These are the principles and protocols agreed by the Welland Partners in May/July 2003.

Introduction

The purpose of this protocol is to provide guidance to the partner councils when considering how to apportion costs between the partners when embarking on partnerships activities.

Given the nature, variety and complexity of the partnership activities this protocol does not seek to be comprehensive. It offers guidance on the procedures to follow to ensure that all partners are aware and have agreed the basis of the cost sharing. It also provides a number of options for cost sharing depending on the particular type of partnership activity being undertaken.

General principles

- Agreement
  Prior to the incurring of any expenditure all partners must agree as part of the planning and appraisal process a budget for the particular activity and how any residual costs will be shared. As part of this process it will also be necessary to agree any individual budget holder responsibilities. The agreement will be recorded in writing and a copy provided to each partner by the lead partner. Any subsequent changes to the agreed basis of cost sharing will only be allowed following agreement by all of the partners.
- Authority to act
  It will be the responsibility of each partner to ensure that any Officer or Member acting on behalf of a partner in agreeing the basis of any cost sharing is appropriately authorized. An agreement by an Officer or Member who purports to have such authority shall be binding on that partner.
- Finance officers
  Prior to any agreement any proposals for cost sharing shall be submitted to the Welland Finance Officers for comment who may suggest amendment or an alternative basis for cost sharing.
- Adjudication
  In the event of failure to agree either between the partners or with the finance officer, the Welland Chief Executives' Group will adjudicate and may call for such information as is considered necessary to reach a decision. A unanimous decision will be binding on all the partners

- Lead partner
  Where appropriate one of the partners will be appointed as the lead partner and will be authorized to incur expenditure up to the amount and for the purpose approved for the particular activity. The lead partner will ensure that proper records are maintained of all transactions and that any amounts recharged to other partners are supported by such information as the partners agree, between themselves, shall be provided.
- Overspends
  It shall be the responsibility of each partner to notify the other partners if at any time it becomes apparent to them that the final cost may be in excess of the agreed budget. The partners shall consider if such additional costs are justified and if agreed on what basis such additional cost should be shared. Any costs incurred in excess of an approved budget shall be borne by the partner incurring those costs unless the prior approval of the other partners has been obtained except that retrospective approval may be granted, depending on the circumstances, by the other partners or one or more of the other partners may agree to meet some or all of the increased cost.
- Financial reporting
  The lead partner will ensure that financial reports are provided to all the partners on a regular basis and not less frequently than quarterly. The reports should as a minimum provide information on the budget: amount spent to date, commitments and known or anticipated variations that could affect the cost of the activity including any contributions in kind.
- Contributions
  Partner contributions towards the costs of activities will normally be in cash but in some circumstances it may be appropriate to allow a partner or partners to make their contribution in kind or a combination of cash and in kind. In assessing whether an in kind contribution should be allowed it will be necessary to decide if the contribution in kind of one or more partners is much greater than that of the other partners. This could relate to the input of staff time, office accommodation or provision of equipment tools and materials etc.

Basis of cost sharing

- Equal shares (1/5 share per partner)
  It is appropriate to use this basis when the benefit to each partner is broadly the same in cash terms. When all partners are involved this would be a 1/5 share per partner.
  For example: Welland-wide research, strategies, cross-cutting work, joint posts, Welland Partnership promotion.
- Council tax base
  It is appropriate to use this basis when the benefit to each partner is proportionate to its size (the proportion to be determined at the point in time when the basis of cost sharing is agreed by reference to the previous year's CTV1 Council Tax Base).
  For example: shared services, marketing and promotion, joint posts, etc.
- As determined between the partners
  If it is not appropriate to use either of the above bases the partners must determine on what basis the costs are to be shared having regard to the benefit each partner will receive.

For example: surveys undertaken on a Welland-wide basis but with varying quantities between partner councils, caseload numbers, attendees at events, attendees at facilitated training, number of council houses, number of day visitors etc.

Review

This protocol will be reviewed at least annually to reflect any changes resulting from the ongoing experiences or changing nature of the partnership.

2 'A Process Evaluation of the Negotiation of Pilot Local Area Agreements' for the ODPM in June 2005

Researchers found considerable enthusiasm for the overarching principles behind the LAA scheme, although different aspects of the initiative were of importance to different players. Expectations were sometimes high and, perhaps because of the tight timescales, LAAs generated both excitement and energy. However, many participants remained confused about the purpose of LAAs throughout the process. Others were clear what they wanted from the process but were sceptical as to whether it would be delivered, and a growing pragmatism was widespread.

The researchers considered there was no doubt that the process was much more difficult in two-tier areas, but even here some lead councils in particular made it work effectively. The problems in these areas are not only different in scale – with many more partners to be engaged and a greater diversity of needs and priorities – but also in kind. Many organizations operating at below-county level perceived the LAA as a threat, a centralizing force rather than a move towards localism. With few special funding streams, the debate had quickly to move into the much more difficult arena of mainstream programmes. However, the potential benefits of the LAA are also qualitatively different, in terms of better targeting of resources, removal of duplication and achievement of critical mass.

In terms of outcomes the report found local partners had signed up jointly to pursuing outcomes that reflect key priorities for government; this formal joint ownership – and the joint performance management that will flow from the LAA – are important advances. However, the targets are not 'stretched' against some notional 'no LAA' situation, and it will not be easy to quantify how much difference the LAA has made. The process of developing their LAA has helped to build amongst local partners a shared understanding of priorities across each locality that requires joint action. This understanding builds on but is in general more focused and more explicit than that in the Community Strategy (in a local area) – it has involved hard choices, whereas many Community Strategies fudged these. While government expected most localities to have this vision at the outset, it has in fact been a beneficial outcome of the process in many localities. The process has made partners realize how many of their issues are cross-cutting, and to appreciate the need for joint action to take a preventative approach and to tackle inequalities. In two-tier areas, the extent to which the agreement has been able to reflect a differentiated picture of truly local needs is limited, but it has brought the beginnings of a more strategic approach. The process has stimulated local partners to start to consider what additional joint actions are required to deliver the outcomes to which they have agreed, although this work has some way to go in most cases.

The researchers consider that implementation of the agreements has the potential to deliver more appropriate and higher quality local services. There are many examples in the agreements of things that should improve the lives of local people. Examples include: joint commissioning of services between health and social care with greater involvement of local people; joint working between partners at county and district levels to reduce homelessness for families and vulnerable young people; proposing to regularize and extend a pilot's health trainer work and to link it to the recruitment of young people from deprived communities; developing a new Partnership Framework Agreement for joint health and social care delivery and commissioning that also provides the basis for similar formal arrangements between other parties in the LAA; and bringing together all youth support agency funding into a single virtual pooled fund to tackle the needs of disaffected young people not engaged in education, employment or training (NEETs) in the most disadvantaged neighbourhoods.

Judging the extent to which the LAA initiative has led to innovation is not easy the review concludes. Many agreements contain proposals for new ways of working that could have been put in place without the LAA, but required the process as a catalyst to reach agreement between partners. It is often difficult to tell which of the apparently new ideas were in fact already planned. For many the opportunity to do new things in the first year is very limited, given the timing of the agreements and existing commitments.

The focus for all the pilots was on effectiveness rather than reducing costs. Some interviewed for the report saw that redeployment of resources might bring greater efficiency for instance by reducing duplication, achieving economies of scale, targeting resources where they can have the greatest impact and this seemed to be particularly true in two-tier areas where spreading resources across many relatively small crime and disorder reduction partnerships can lead to inefficiencies if they do not work together. Others saw efficiencies from co-location of staff, unified assessment processes and shared management arrangements enabling more funds to be channelled into frontline services.

It is evident from the report that the LAA process has the capacity to help to build stronger and more effective partnerships. The process has begun to strengthen local strategic partnerships, given focus to existing theme partnerships and helped to stimulate the establishment of new ones where necessary. In some instances, the process has accelerated the establishment of a public sector board and local partners felt that it is this that would make the difference; in others this option was considered but rejected or postponed.

It is clear that, at local level, the process has in general cemented existing relationships and opened the doors to new ones. For many pilots, this is one of the most important benefits of the process. The process has not been a smooth one, however, particularly in some two-tier areas where it placed existing relationships between the county and districts in particular under great strain.

Researchers thought that success means very different things in different pilots, and is often not what participants thought it would mean when they embarked on the process. For some, it has been a catalyst rather than a driver as many things were already happening. For some the benefits have come almost entirely from the stimulus the process has provided to partnership working. For others, the chance to rationalize funding streams will bring real benefits, although there is disappointment that so many strings have been attached. Other areas have not given up hope of a more radical transformation of relationships between centre and locality with a genuine devolution of strategy, prioritization and responsibility over resources to local level, and a more equal partnership between both levels of government. It is important not to underestimate the change to culture and assumptions about ways of working required at all levels to make this work. Many are waiting to see whether the potential will be realized, as evidenced by the number of comments to the effect that 'the jury is out'. Nevertheless others see it – in the words of one government office lead officer – as 'the most exciting government initiative in years'. There is a feeling that 'the genie is out of the bottle' and an unstoppable process has been put in train. There is a strong sense of achievement and at local level some important breakthroughs that will focus action and delivery on important social outcomes. The process has led to better dialogue and joint planning and hastened the development of holistic policies. While many of the other benefits are as yet unproven, the level of continuing enthusiasm and support demonstrates the opportunities that are there to be grasped.

3 'Efficiency – Transforming Local Services' from 'Strong and Prosperous Communities'

Everyone wants to see improvements to their local schools, hospitals, libraries and parks. They want, rightly, to be able to access the best possible services, shaped around their community's needs, at times that suit them. But they do not expect to have to finance that change through excessive tax increases. And nor should they. Our aim is that every local authority, working with its local partners, will be able to radically improve local services and drive forward efficiency.

By 1997, public services had suffered through under-investment and neglect. Many local services were not meeting the needs of local people and provided poor value for money for taxpayers. This was partly down to the bureaucratic and process-driven compulsory competitive tendering (CCT), which had stifled opportunities for innovation and limited procurement and performance management skills to those required for compliance with the regulations.[1]

We replaced CCT with a new performance framework, Best Value. This has required a rigorous approach to securing value for money across all services and achieving better outcomes, rather than complying with narrow processes. It provided a framework for making the right local choices on service delivery – requiring councils to challenge and review services and to choose the best option for delivery. Crucially, it put councils back in control of securing quality services.

In 2003, we jointly published with the Local Government Association the National Procurement Strategy (NPS).[2] This recognized that procurement was undervalued,[3] yet it was vital in securing better services and value for money.[4] The strategy set challenging milestones for councils in adopting better and more sustainable procurement practices. We also established nine Regional Centres of Excellence (RCEs). Owned and run by councils, they spread good practice, lead on sustainable procurement and are supporting over 300 local authority projects. In addition, 59 per cent of local councils are now involved in joint procurement, and 32 per cent of local councils are involved in creating a shared procurement function.

The Local e-Government Programme has also changed the local authority service delivery landscape in England, with over £1.1 billion of efficiency gains identified to date.

These developments have delivered big improvements. Current evidence suggests that councils are likely to meet the government's local authority 2007–8 efficiency target of £3.0 billion, a year ahead of schedule.[5] But people's expectations of public services are rising and the financial climate is changing, putting pressure on councils to deliver highly tailored services, without massive investment from central government, or excessive council tax increases.[6]

---

1   'Local authority experience of compulsory competitive tendering', *Local and Central Government Relations Research*, Joseph Rowntree Foundation, 1995.
2   National Procurement Strategy for Local Government in England (2003–2006), ODPM, 2003.
3   Local Authority Procurement: A Research Report, DETR, 2000.
4   Competitive Procurement, Audit Commission, 2002
5   Analysis of the annual efficiency statements for 2004–5, 2005–6 and 2006–7.
6   *All Our Futures: The Challenges for Local Governance in 2015*, ODPM, 2005.

In order to deliver the transformed services and value for money that communities want, councils will have to challenge traditional methods of delivery, rooting out waste, in order to drive efficiency.

The best local councils are already doing this. But we need to increase the pace of change. This will mean local councils and other public bodies working together to overcome administrative boundaries that sometimes act as a barrier to service transformation. It will mean sharing assets, systems, data, skills and knowledge more effectively, and keeping all council activity under review to drive out waste.

We see cross-sectoral working as a key element of delivering more efficient services. Chapter Five of this White Paper provides a focus for local councils acting as place-shaper and leaders of their communities and creates a framework for greater co-operation between local agencies through Local Area Agreements (LAAs). We expect local partners to consider as a priority how they can maximize the opportunities that LAAs provide in collectively driving efficiency and thus achieving better outcomes for citizens.

This chapter provides a framework to support local councils who are working hard to improve delivery and efficiency. It offers them new tools and increased flexibility to innovate. And it sets out effective challenges to those local councils who are underperforming. Proposals include:

- requiring ambitious efficiency gains to be achieved by local councils over the next few years as part of the 2007 Comprehensive Spending Review (CSR07), necessitating a more radical and ambitious value for money programme, with effective and direct challenge for poorly performing or coasting services;
- securing more collaboration between local councils and across all public bodies, where this improves effectiveness and efficiency, and ensuring that administrative boundaries do not act as a barrier to service transformation and efficiency;
- driving a more extensive use of business process improvement techniques, including new technology, to transform service delivery and focus services around the needs and preferences of users;
- ensuring greater contestability through the use of fair and open competition in local government services markets;
- providing a foundation of stable finance, which will enable councils to plan better, publish three-year council tax projections and provide more stable funding for partners in the third sector; and
- providing expert support to councils and their partners to meet their efficiency challenges, through a streamlined and co-ordinated approach to building capacity.

We expect all local councils to continue to drive down costs, but this is just part of the picture. Transformation and efficiency are just as much about delivering the right services to communities – services that meet their needs and which they will use and value.

We are already seeing progress in some areas. Customer service centres have transformed the way many local councils handle customer contact, while reducing costs. New technology is helping local councils to revolutionize service delivery. Some local councils are working more closely with local partners and central government to offer more effective and efficient services. But local people are hungry for more.

To meet this challenge, all local councils must adopt a strategic approach to service delivery. Our proposals in Chapter Five to strengthen the strategic commissioning role for councils will ensure that they start from an understanding of the needs and preferences of users, adopt best practice in service design, assess the full range of service delivery options, and implement optimal solutions that balance quality and value for money. Local councils must work closely with local partners, utilizing the capacity of the best service providers in the public, private and third sectors.

This change should also contribute to the creation of prosperous, cohesive communities, improving long-term outcomes for socially excluded groups and supporting a sustainable physical environment. For example, by developing a strategic vision for energy use, councils can deliver sustainable housing, ensure vulnerable people have warm homes, tackle road emissions and make use of renewable energy with major efficiency gains.

The Cabinet Office discussion paper *Transformational Local Government*, produced in collaboration with local government, set out a number of prerequisites for driving service transformation.[7] We will build on this, through a series of proposals set out in the rest of this chapter according to the following themes:

- business process improvement and flexible working
- collaboration between public bodies
- use of technology, including information sharing
- smarter procurement
- competition
- asset management
- stable finance
- challenge
- support.

BUSINESS PROCESS IMPROVEMENT AND FLEXIBLE WORKING

Significant improvement to services can be achieved by reviewing and reshaping the way public providers currently operate – techniques and methods typically given the umbrella term 'business process improvement' or 'BPI'.

Organizations employing these techniques routinely scrutinize delivery in order to drive out wasteful activity. The Department of Health's work with Regional Centres of Excellence and practitioners has identified changes to the referral, assessment and care management of patients that remove duplication, eliminate low value activity, free up frontline staff, improve information management and cut transaction costs.[8]

Local councils are securing quality and cost improvements of up to 20 per cent by adopting similar approaches:

- by better understanding what activities their staff performed in relation to their purchase-to-pay process, Basingstoke and Deane Borough Council was able to bring down the average overhead cost of purchases from over £92 per transaction to £11; and
- Peterborough City Council implemented a mobile system for housing repairs and maintenance using Personal Digital Assistants (PDAs), which communicate real-time information to back-office systems via Global Packet Radio Service (GPRS). This meant the authority could improve more homes with 50 fewer staff; an efficiency gain of £1.8 million a year.

---

7   Published 2006 the aim of the paper is to trigger a conversation across local government about what 'transformed local government', supported by modern technology, should look like.

8   Department of Health Care Services Efficiency Delivery Programme.

Building on work initiated in the North West e-government partnership with Blackburn with Darwen Borough Council, we will further support effective use of BPI techniques through a project we are carrying out in partnership with local government. We will ensure that the lessons learnt from this project are fully shared across local government, as part of an integrated package of improvement tools also covering technology and collaboration – a 'Business Improvement Package'.

COLLABORATION

There are significant opportunities to improve the quality and efficiency of services by joint working – either between some of the 388 councils in England, with other local public bodies, or at a regional or national level. We want all local councils to unlock these potential benefits by delivering more services in collaboration with each other, with other local public service providers and with the private or the third sector.

THE 'PUBLIC SERVICE VILLAGE PARTNERSHIP'

The Public Service Village Partnership in Suffolk brings together county and district councils, Suffolk Police, West Suffolk College, West Suffolk Primary Care Trust and Suffolk Magistrates Court. It seeks to unify the range of customer services across the organizations – improving customer access to services and creating a one-stop shop for all of the organizations. It achieves lower costs through rationalizing accommodation and administration and taking advantage of joint procurement power.

The potential benefits of collaboration for common transactional services have is involving RCEs, local councils and other partners in piloting recognized techniques to assess efficiency gains, enabling detailed guides to be established on how to achieve sustainable service improvement long been recognized, but frontline services can also benefit from partnership working and sharing.[9] The Innovation Forum's 'Joint Working in Waste' project highlighted the benefits of collaborative working, suggesting possible national efficiency gains of around £150 million. Case studies from waste partnerships in Shropshire, Norfolk, West Sussex, Halton, Warrington and Essex demonstrated substantial cost savings and environmental socio-economic benefits from integration and aggregation.

THE SHROPSHIRE WASTE PARTNERSHIP

The Shropshire Waste Partnership brings together the county council and four waste collection councils. Focusing on the procurement of an integrated contract for the collection and disposal of recycling and waste materials, the partnership aims to improve its recycling and compost 53 per cent of its municipal waste by 2010–11 and 60 per cent by 2020, while the joint procurement could deliver 11 per cent cost gains.

We are working with local councils and key stakeholders to gain a better understanding of the benefits of partnership models in relation to particular services. This will include consideration of the case for sharing back-office functions, transactional services and other key services, such as waste and social care functions.

We will work with public agencies to establish a number of pathfinder projects to spread and extend best practice. The aim will be to standardize business case information, develop benchmarking data, and test the scale and effectiveness of delivery models. The pathfinders

---

9   The National Process Improvement Project.

will also test opportunities in the new performance framework and strengthened LAAs to promote and deliver partnership working within and across local councils' boundaries.

Many efficiency improvements can be secured by joint planning, sharing resources and skills, aggregating demand and sharing services across a larger area. This can present a particular challenge to smaller district local councils, compounded in some two-tier areas by a sense that organizational boundaries can take priority over the most effective ways of delivering services. Many local councils are already breaking down these barriers and as a result are delivering improved services and greater efficiency. Where two-tier government remains we expect to see this 'virtual unitary' approach.

USE OF TECHNOLOGY

Technology is one of the most important tools for transformation. It can improve the life chances of socially excluded people by increasing opportunities to intervene and tackle emerging problems; help to deliver information and services in different ways; provide connections within organizations and partnerships; enable data sharing where appropriate and lawful between key organizations; gather and present information in ways which improve decisions and provide opportunities for staff to work in new ways.

The Local e-Government Programme has been a successful partnership between local and central government. Government investment of £675 million has put in place the technology infrastructure needed to transform the way local authority services are accessed and delivered, changing users' relationships with their local authority and councillors, while delivering substantial efficiency gains:

* a typical council has 98 per cent of its services e-enabled
* there has been a seven-fold increase in payments made via local authority websites in the last four years
* 113,000 electronic planning applications are expected via the Planning Portal this year.[10]

TECHNOLOGY ENABLING A SEAMLESS SERVICE

Citizens want right-first-time, seamless and accessible services. This is good for public agencies too, reducing the costs of rectifying mistakes and duplication. Services from a variety of public service providers can be brought together at the point of delivery – available in the customer's home via the internet or in contact centres or community one-stop shops.

DORSET FOR YOU

The Dorset for You partnership has developed and set up a web portal that will work in conjunction with individual partners' customer relationship management (CRM) solutions. The portal provides a comprehensive service including e-Pay online booking and transactional services, such as online job applications and planning. As a result, the partners have been able to shut down their individual websites.

A similar partnership approach within the Dorset for You programme unites the county, all districts councils, two unitary councils and Dorset Police in seeking inclusion for the second phase of the Home Office 101 initiative. Calls will be taken by both the county council and the police contact centres who will answer queries on behalf of all partners.

---

10   Communities and local government – annual IEG statements.

We will work with key technology partnerships, such as Government Connect,[11] the Digital Inclusion Team, the Digital Challenge Inclusion Network and other stakeholders to learn from good practice and incentivize joined-up access to services and their seamless delivery.[12]

We are currently reviewing the transformational government agenda and how channel delivery can be made more responsive to citizen and business need. Combined with proposals in this White Paper, the findings of Sir David Varney's review will seek to provide further opportunities for local and central government and other providers to work more closely together on customer centred services.

The ability of public providers to share information from citizens will be vital. It reduces duplication, enabling resources to be redeployed to value-adding activity. Government Connect will develop a system that enables citizens to authenticate themselves once, supporting the vision of the emerging management strategy led by the Identity and Passport Service. Citizens will be able to use this authentification to support further transactions with public organizations – removing the need to supply the same information to different providers. Common technology and clear protocols will create a secure and stable platform enabling a range of agencies to share information safely – nationally, locally and between tiers – whilst protecting individuals' rights.

CHANNEL MIGRATION

Few local councils understand the unit costs of delivering services by different delivery channels – or have a plan for moving customers to the most efficient ones.

TAMESIDE METROPOLITAN BOROUGH COUNCIL

Tameside Metropolitan Borough Council has measured unit 'costs to serve' for transactions over different types of access channel. In 2005–6, face-to-face contact cost £16.20, whereas a website transaction cost just 12 pence. They have set quality thresholds for each service and set about improving processes and encouraging customers to use appropriate channels. They have succeeded in managing their business more efficiently while providing the same or better service, during a time when the total number of customer contacts has risen.

We must accelerate the adoption of good practice, building on the national momentum created by the 'Take-up Campaign' to boost the number of citizens and local councils using the new channels for service delivery.[13] We have published a report looking at how to build on the examples of Tameside and others, showing how channel migration can be managed, while ensuring the customer has a strong voice in securing better delivery of their services.[14]

The results of our work on supporting customer-focused services, migration of customers to cheaper delivery channels and understanding unit costs will all be published as part of the Business Improvement Package in early 2007.

---

11   The Government Connect programme is looking to provide a secure bridge between local councils and central government that will allow any sensitive information to be transferred online, quickly, easily and accurately.
12   www.digitalchallenge.gov.uk.
13   See www.communities.gov.uk/takeup.
14   www.nwegg.org.uk/interface/view_document.asp?id=1418.

SMARTER PROCUREMENT

Sir Ian Byatt's Review of Local Government Procurement in England highlighted the key role of procurement in providing high quality services and its potential to extend choice.[15] It led to a framework through the NPS for taking forward improvement and change. Five local councils were awarded Beacon status in 2006 to further support the delivery of the targets laid down in that framework.

LEEDS AND PLYMOUTH CITY COUNCILS

Leeds and Plymouth city councils, through two Supporting People Value Improvement Projects, have collaborated on the development of a step-by-step guide to the procurement of services for vulnerable people. This has involved applying a range of mainstream procurement tools and techniques to housing-related support and social care services for the first time. The results have been compelling: significant improvements in the quality and availability of those services and substantial improvements in value for money. We plan to launch the Procurement Pack, in conjunction with the Care Services Improvement Partnership.

Three critical aspects of effective procurement are addressed in the next section:

- the use of e-procurement
- understanding spend
- aggregating procurement demand.

E-PROCUREMENT

A relatively straightforward way of delivering e-procurement efficiencies is through the use of procurement cards. Around 20 million invoices are processed manually by councils every year, at an average cost of £10 per transaction. It is estimated that 20 per cent of these could be migrated to procurement cards, generating efficiency gains of £40 million.

KENT COUNTY COUNCIL AND E-AUCTIONS

Kent County Council has changed the way in which it pays suppliers of care management services. Using purchase card technology through the Royal Bank of Scotland's transaction data matching system, the local authority is paying an estimated £50 million per year through 12 payments to RBS, instead of processing 30,000 transactions manually, achieving £700,000 of efficiency gains in the administration of social care.

The first wave of national e-auctions has generated efficiency gains of almost £13 million, worth an average saving of 27 per cent on each contract. With an investment of only £137,000, this represents a return of £94 for every pound of investment. Management of the e-auctions was made possible by government funding through the RCEs.

The effective use of e-marketplaces can also help local councils dramatically improve their procurement processes. It imposes an organizational structure and approval process for all purchases which leads to: reduction in 'maverick' spend; improved contractual arrangements with more competitive prices; an improved audit trail; improved control over spending; better procurement intelligence with real-time management information and new opportunities for collaborative procurement.

---

15   *Delivering Better Services for Citizens*, DTLR, 2001.

E-MARKETPLACE

Essex County Council expects to save £4.8 million in three years through its use of IDeA: marketplace where the council transacts £10 million of business each month (equivalent to 20 per cent of its non-school and staff spending).

UNDERSTANDING PROCUREMENT SPEND

Understanding local councils procurement spend – what they procure, who they procure from, the total value of all their contracts – is critical to identifying the opportunities for greater efficiency. It is also key to understanding the potential environmental, social and economic benefits which could arise from sustainable procurement.

SOUTH WEST REGIONAL CENTRE OF EXCELLENCE

The South West Regional Centre of Excellence estimates that local councils can save £3 million of transaction costs annually. Critical to this is a better understanding of the region's spending profile. An analysis by the South West RCE, covering 35 councils and over 95 per cent of the region's spending, highlighted many new facts such as 22 large suppliers attract 10 per cent of the region's spending and up to 2 per cent (£2.5 million) of gains could be achieved through collaborative relationship management. The region will use this information to develop procurement strategies which are appropriate and targeted to the needs of councils.

AGGREGATING DEMAND

Joint procurement can help secure efficiencies by aggregating demand. These arrangements have been used for some time by local councils as a way to increase efficiency. Local councils can use their purchasing power to support national and local priorities in areas such as climate change, waste prevention and the third sector. But reaping the opportunities of joint procurement requires local councils to have a good understanding of procurement spending and the operation of local markets.

The Office of Government Commerce (OGC) and RCEs have worked closely together and are committed to implementing a national procurement programme for commodities, goods and services. The project will provide reliable benchmarks for every local authority. In addition, the north-west RCE is developing a contracts register which local councils can use to share or compare common contracts. The south-east RCE has carried out an analysis of the prices offered by 13 consortia for 3,000 items as well as an analysis of prices paid from over 200 sources in the public and private sector.

SUPPORTING FURTHER IMPROVEMENT IN PROCUREMENT

Building on this experience and the ideas featured in the recently published Sustainable Procurement Taskforce report, we will provide further advice to support effective procurement.[16] The aims will be to: utilize technology; develop a more consistent approach to data gathering; increase the use of regional or sub-regional procurement consortia to aggregate purchasing power to secure better deals for local councils; develop RCEs as a pool of procurement experts who local councils can turn to for support in driving procurement changes and efficiencies;

---

16   www.sustainable-development.gov.uk/government/taskforces/procurement/index.htm.

and work with sector organizations, such as the RCEs, the Local Government Taskforce and the OGC, to increase access to good value framework contracts.[17]

COMPETITION

The introduction of greater competition and the availability of a diverse and innovative supply base supports the delivery of better services. By improving commissioning and procurement processes, local councils can encourage more providers to enter the market and to compete for contracts.

Best Value will continue to underpin the use of competition in local authority services. The Best Value councils are required to secure continuous improvement in the way in which functions are exercised. We will issue one piece of revised guidance which will strengthen the key principles of Best Value. This will cover the commissioning role of councils, community participation and provide that local councils should regularly test the competitiveness of their performance in comparison with others. When services are found to be underperforming, where practical, they should introduce fair and open competition.

Decisions about how a local authority secures services should be based on objective assessment and accurate information. Those making decisions should represent the interests of service users and take any steps necessary to avoid real or apparent conflicts of interest, where their own organization is competing to deliver the service. Working with local government, inspectorates and the private and third sectors we will build a consensus through a code of practice on competition on the core practices expected in all local councils and suppliers.

We will work with the Audit Commission to clarify the current role of the appointed auditor to investigate complaints relevant to their work with local councils and how this will relate to the other redress mechanisms, such as Community Calls for Action. Where appropriate we will strengthen the auditor's ability to respond to complaints from service providers about unfair and unlawful procurement.

MARKET DEVELOPMENT

We have already undertaken research on the relationship between positive attitudes towards competition and improved service performance[18] and will shortly publish a report on developing the local government services market.[19] Working with local government, commissioners and providers, we will explore opportunities to develop and shape the local government services market, to encourage a diversity of suppliers across the public, private and the third sectors. This will include considering ways to:

- stimulate new markets in order to secure alternative provision and enable both commissioner and user choice in areas of local government which are currently uncontested or not fully contested; and
- increase the capacity and competitiveness in existing supply markets, including streamlining procurement processes and cutting red-tape.

This will be complemented by sector-specific activities, led by the relevant central government department, working with communities and local government, local government

---

17   Set up in response to Sir John Egan's 1998 Rethinking Construction report.
18   Long-term evaluation of the Best Value regime: Summary Report, Communities and Local Government, 2006.
19   Developing the local government services market to support a long-term strategy for local government, Communities and Local Government, 2006.

and the private and third sectors. This will build upon the work already undertaken by government on markets such as children's services, social care and waste infrastructure, and the work of the RCEs.

The third sector – voluntary, community and social enterprises – will be a key part of this mixed market, bringing with it a wealth of expertise and experience with user groups, as well as innovative and cost-effective approaches to delivery. The government recently announced a framework to strengthen the role of the third sector in the delivery of local public services, and place them on a level playing field.[20]

ASSET MANAGEMENT

Managing assets effectively is vital to achieving cost savings for local councils and helping them to deliver better outcomes for citizens: disposing of, or improving, underperforming assets, and modernizing assets that can be expensive to maintain is key to this. For example, the efficient management of roads is critical to the delivery of other services.

Asset management was one of the themes of Round Six of the Improvement and Development Agency's (IDeA) Beacon councils scheme. Five asset management Beacon councils – Cambridgeshire, Leeds, Ashford, Rotherham and Hertfordshire – have been working with the IDeA to offer a range of tailored support – such as mentoring and visits – to help other local councils drive improvement in managing their assets.

The Beacons identified six main elements as crucial to effective asset management:

* the need to integrate asset planning with corporate planning and the local authority's strategic vision for the area
* key elected members and officers being engaged in decision-making
* forecasting and meeting future asset requirements being done jointly with key partners and in discussion with the local community
* a structured approach to challenging whether assets are needed and are fit for purpose
* effective data and information management to enable decision-making
* effective project management of major capital schemes.

Progress has been made. However, there is still some way to go to realize the potential gains of raising performance to that of the best practitioners. We will consider asset management as part of CSR07.

Better asset management will assist in improving service outcomes. It should also encourage the disposal of underperforming assets, enabling local government to contribute towards the objective set in the 2004 Spending Review for disposals of £30 billion of public assets by 2010–11. In particular, we should look at the benefits and disadvantages of encouraging more transfer of assets to community management or ownership, where this will lead to best value in service delivery and social benefit.

STABLE FINANCE

The government will ensure that local government is supported by a fair and sustainable finance system. Within that context, it remains absolutely essential that local councils – in line with the rest of the public sector – are rigorous in managing expenditure pressures. This

---

20   A framework for strengthening the third sector's role in local public service delivery, a speech by Phil Woolas MP, Minister for Local Government, to the Three Sector Summit, 2006.

will require not only achievement of demanding efficiency gains, but also tough decisions on priorities. Government will not allow excessive council tax increases.

The annual cycle of grant allocations has made it more difficult for local government to budget and manage expenditure. We have already begun the move to three-year formula grant settlements. These will provide local government with the opportunity – which we would expect it to take – of publishing three-year council tax figures. The first full three-year formula grant settlement will cover 2008–2011.

Greater stability of funding for local government provides an opportunity for a step-change in the funding and procurement relationship between local government and the third sector. This is essential if we are to see a strong and vibrant third sector working with local government to achieve many of the aims set out in this White Paper. The general starting point will be three-year grant funding, except where this does not represent best value in individual cases, and in terms of overall affordability. This will be supported by key Compact funding and procurement principles and best practice guidance for local government on third sector funding. This will also build on existing Treasury guidance, developed in partnership with the LGA, the Audit Commission and Chartered Institute for Public Finance and Accountancy (CIPFA).[21]

CHALLENGE

Councils should be able to demonstrate that they are delivering high-quality services by the most cost-effective method. This section sets out proposals to strengthen the challenge to current standards of provision.

INTEGRATING EFFICIENCY WITHIN THE PERFORMANCE FRAMEWORK

The targets set for efficiency across the public sector in 2004 have provided a sharper focus to an activity that has always been core to all good organizations. In addition, the framework for reporting efficiency gains has identified a range of innovation and good practice in the sector. And the discipline of reporting gains has acted as a spur to develop reliable measurement systems – key to effective performance management.

The CSR07 will reflect an ongoing challenge on efficiency across the public sector, as well as what is achievable within local councils, which will be at least as ambitious as the current spending review period. We will embed efficiency as part of the new performance framework and we will explore ways of using the framework to monitor local councils' performance in this area and challenge poor performance. One option would be for local partners to come together to agree an efficiency target as part of their LAA which they would then work jointly to achieve.

To tackle difficult cross-cutting issues and maximize the value for money of public resources, services should be designed around the needs of the citizen and the community, not around the processes and structures of individual agencies. Collaboration is, therefore, essential if we are to really transform our services. LAAs provide a focus for harnessing the energy of local partners, and we will work to align efficiency into the broader LAA framework.

We will also work with the Audit Commission to explore how the annual scored 'Use of Resources' assessment could be developed, without expanding its cost and burden, to provide

---

21   Improving Financial Relationships with the Third Sector, Guidance to Funders and Purchasers, HM Treasury, 2006.

robust assurance about organizational effectiveness and councils' performance in delivering increased efficiency.

The new performance framework will reveal where local councils, and taxpayers are not getting value for money – where performance is weak, costs are high and efficiency poor. We expect local councils to challenge their own performance and to respond positively and quickly to evidence of underperformance, drawing from expertise in the sector, including peer support and review. However, where underperformance is not addressed and effectively dealt with, the performance framework sets out clear steps for tailored support and intervention.

UNDERSTANDING AND COMPARING COSTS

The Audit Commission is further developing its tool for measuring value for money, using data which is already available. This tool allows local councils, auditors and others to compare the relationship between spending and performance in different local councils. Users can create customized charts to compare service performance within groups of local councils in an area or with similar characteristics. We strongly support the development of this type of information. We expect local councils to use it in challenging their own performance. Auditors, inspectorates and government will also draw from it in identifying unacceptable levels of performance and deciding on appropriate responses.

Increasing efficiency is not about organizations making service delivery choices to secure their own benefits simply by passing costs onto others. We also want to ensure efficient and effective service delivery choices that benefit citizens. This is a complex area – understanding and addressing these flows will not be easily or quickly solved.

We will work with local councils to understand how these flows across local agencies can be identified, measured, discussed and agreed in localities. We will also explore how to incentivize co-operation between local agencies to secure effective business improvement and the best efficiencies for citizens, even where a particular individual organization may not gain. This work needs to be taken forward carefully on a sector-by-sector basis. Our research, which we will test with local councils, will initially examine key interfaces, such as local councils' adult social care interactions with Primary Care Trusts (PCTs). Government departments will aim to agree and publish guidance and toolkits as part of CSR07.

SUPPORT

Local councils are best placed to identify their own developmental needs and how to address them, either through building up in-house capacity, or by supplementing in-house skills with those from external specialist sources. With our support, the sector has put in place structures, organizations and peer review initiatives to support and drive sustainable business improvement through shared learning and the development and dissemination of best practice.

Effective support from RCEs has supported local councils in meeting their current efficiency target. A range of other national and regional organizations also aim to provide the appropriate mix of skills and tools to support local delivery. These include Regional Improvement Partnerships and other local, regional and national arrangements including the IDeA, 4Ps, and Local Government Employers.

The landscape overall can, however, be confusing. We are working with partners to review the current arrangements with the aim of creating clear strategic direction, improving co-ordination and streamlining available resources. This will establish a new programme of integrated and joined-up regional capacity building, led by the sector itself, in touch with the sector's changing needs. It will also develop mechanisms for sharing key information, particularly benchmarking information, and continue to support key projects.

CONCLUSION

It is a primary role for all public service providers to deliver the best possible services in the most cost-efficient way. It is up to local councils to decide how best to achieve this, but there is a changing financial climate and they must think fundamentally about how they can achieve improved efficiency, service performance and outcomes.

This White Paper gives local councils the tools, flexibility and support they need to truly transform local services around the needs and wants of their community.

Further Reading

Audit Commission (2002) *Competitive Procurement*. London: Audit Commission.

Audit Commission (2002a) *Delivering Comprehensive Performance Assessment – Consultation Draft*. London: Audit Commission.

Audit Commission (2005) *CPA – The Harder Test: The New Framework for Comprehensive Performance Assessment of Single Tier and County Councils from 2005 to 2008*. London: Audit Commission.

Audit Commission (2005a) *The Efficiency Challenge: The Administration Costs of Revenues and Benefits*. London: Audit Commission.

Audit Commission (2005b) *Supporting People Programme – Wiltshire County Council*. Inspection report. 8 March. London: Audit Commission.

Bangemann, T.O. (2005) *Shared Services in Finance and Accounting*. Aldershot: Gower.

Bovaird, A.G. and Martin, S.J. (2003) 'Evaluating public management reforms: Designing a "joined up" approach to researching the Local Government Modernization Agenda.' *Local Government Studies* 29 (4): 17–30.

Boyne, G.A. (2003) 'Sources of public service improvement: a critical review and research agenda.' *Journal of Public Administration, Research and Theory* 13 (3): 367–94.

Boyne, G. (2003a) 'What is public service improvement?' *Public Administration* 81 (2).

Brand, A. (2006) *The Politics of Shared Services*. London: New Local Government Network.

Byatt, I. (2001) *Delivering Better Services for Citizens*. London: DTLR.

Cabinet Office e-Government Unit (2005) *Transformational Government, Enabled by Technology*. London: Cabinet Office.

Cabinet Office Strategy Unit (2002) *Creating Public Value*. London: Cabinet Office.

CIPFA CJC (2001) *Competitiveness and Competition*. London: Chartered Institute of Public Finance and Accountancy – Competitiveness Joint Committee.

Competitiveness Joint Committee (2003) *The CJC Guide to Choosing Partnerships Vehicles*. London: Chartered Institute of Public Finance and Accountancy – Competitiveness Joint Committee.

Cowell, R., Downe, J., Leach, S. and Bovaird, A.G. (2005) *Meta-evaluation of the Local Government Modernization Agenda: Progress Report on the Public Confidence in Local Government*. London: ODPM.

Davis, H., Downe, J. and Martin, S.J. (2004) *The Changing Role of Audit Commission Inspection of Local Government*. London: Audit Commission.

Department of Communities and Local Government (2006) *Stronger and Prosperous Communities – The Local Government White Paper*. London: Department of Communities and Local Government

Gershon, Sir P. (2004) *Releasing Resources to the Frontline: Independent Review of Public Sector Efficiency*. London: HM Treasury. (The Gershon Report.)

HM Treasury (2005) *The Lyons Inquiry into Local Government: Consultation Paper and Interim Report*. London: HMSO.

Hodges et al. (1996) 'Corporate governance in the public services: issues and concepts.' *Public Money and Management* 16 (2): 7.

Hughes, M. (1999) *How to Choose the Best Value Service Option*. London: Inter-Councils Group.

Hughes, M. and McLaughlin, K. (2002) *Best Value – Making Choices*. Edinburgh: Scottish Executive.

Huxham, C. (1996) 'Advantage or inertia? Making collaboration work.' In R. Paton et al. (1996) (eds) *The New Management Reader*. London: Routledge.

Huxham, C. and Vangen, S. (2000) 'What makes partnerships work?' In P. Osborne (2000) (ed.) *Public–Private Partnerships: Theory and Practice in International Perspective*. London: Routledge.

Martin, S.J. and Bovaird, A.G. (2005) *Meta-evaluation of the Local Government Modernization Agenda: Progress Report on Service Improvement in Local Government*. London: Office of the Deputy Prime Minister.

Martin, S.J., Enticott, G., Entwistle, T., Chen, A., Ashworth, R. and Boyne, G.A. (2004) Evaluation of the long-term impact of the Best Value regime: Second draft interim report. Unpublished report to the Office of the Deputy Prime Minister, London.

Office of the Deputy Prime Minister (2002) *Structures for Partnerships*. London: Office of the Deputy Prime Minister, Strategic Partnering Taskforce.

Office of the Deputy Prime Minister (2002a) *VFM and Strategic Partnerships – Technical Advisory Note*. London: Office of the Deputy Prime Minister, Strategic Partnering Taskforce.

Office of the Deputy Prime Minister (2003) *Local Government Act 1999: Part 1. Best Value and Performance Improvement*. Circular 03/2003 London: Office of the Deputy Prime Minister.

Office of the Deputy Prime Minister (2003a) *Rethinking Service Delivery Vol. 1: An Introduction to Strategic Service Delivery Partnerships*. London: Office of the Deputy Prime Minister, Strategic Partnering Taskforce.

Office of the Deputy Prime Minister (2003b) *National Procurement Strategy for Local Government*. London: Office of the Deputy Prime Minister.

Office of the Deputy Prime Minister (2003c) *From Vision to Outline Business Case – Rethinking Service Delivery Vol. 2*. London: Office of the Deputy Prime Minister, Strategic Partnering Taskforce.

Office of the Deputy Prime Minister (2003d) *Government Engagement with Poorly Performing Councils*. London: Office of the Deputy Prime Minister.

Office of the Deputy Prime Minister (2004a) *Strategic Partnering Taskforce – Final Report*. London: Office of the Deputy Prime Minister, Strategic Partnering Task Force.

Office of the Deputy Prime Minister (2004b) *Balance of Funding Report*. London: Office of the Deputy Prime Minister.

Office of the Deputy Prime Minister (2004c) *Making the Partnership a Success – Rethinking Service Delivery Vol. 5*. London: Office of the Deputy Prime Minister, Strategic Partnering Task Force.

Unison (2004) *Strategic Service Delivery Partnerships*. London: Unison.

Walker, R.M., Ashworth, R., Boyne, G.A., Dowson, L., Enticott, G., Entwistle, T., Law, J. and Martin, S.J. (2004) *Evaluation of the Long-term Impact of the Best Value Regime: First Interim Report*. London: Office of the Deputy Prime Minister.

Index

Figures are indicated by bold page numbers. Roman numeral page numbers indicate glossary entries.